african BIOGRAPHY

Volume 2
K^{ru}-M^{us}

Virginia Curtin Knight, Editor

U·X·L®
AN IMPRINT OF GALE

DETROIT · NEW YORK · LONDON

African Biography

Virginia Curtin Knight, Editor

Staff

Sonia Benson, *U•X•L Senior Editor*
Carol DeKane Nagel, *U•X•L Managing Editor*
Thomas L. Romig, *U•X•L Publisher*

Mary Beth Trimper, *Production Director*
Evi Seoud, *Assistant Production Manager*
Deborah Milliken, *Production Assistant*

Cynthia Baldwin, *Product Design Manager*
Barbara Yarrow, *Graphic Services Director*
Pamela A. E. Galbreath, *Senior Art Director*
Shalice Shah-Caldwell, *Permissions Associate*
LM Design, *Typesetter*

Library of Congress Cataloging-in-Publication Data

African Biography / Virginia Curtin Knight, editor

p. cm.
Includes bibliographic references and index.

Summary: Presents biographical entries on seventy-five noteworthy Africans, historical and contemporary, in a variety of fields, from a wide range of sub-Saharan countries.

ISBN 0-7876-2823-9
(set : alk. paper)

ISBN 0-7876-2824-7 (volume 1)
ISBN 0-7876-2825-5 (volume 2)
ISBN 0-7876-2826-3 (volume 3)

1. Africa, Sub-Saharan—Biography—Juvenile literature. [1. Africa, Sub-Saharan—Biography. 2. Blacks—Africa, Sub-Saharan—Biography.]. I. Knight, Virginia Curtin.

CT1920.A39 1998
920.067—dc21

98-14069
CIP

Contents

Nelson Mandela

Volume 1

Volume 2

Volume 3

Entries by Nationality

Bold numerals indicate volume numbers.

Moshoeshoe

Entries by Field of Endeavor

Bold numerals indicate volume numbers.

Fela Kuti

Heads of Government: prime ministers, presidents, dictators

Heads of International Organization

Labor Leaders

Medicine

Military Leaders

Musicians

Nobel Prize Winners (peace)

Nobel Prize Winners (literature)

Political Activists

Publishers (book)

Publishers (newspaper)

Religious Leaders

Rulers: kings, queens, chiefs, and emperors

Slave Traders

Translators

Writers

Reader's Guide

For students and interested browsers who want to learn more about the world, *African Biography* presents biographical entries on some of its most remarkable people. Spanning most of the recorded history of Africa, this three-volume reference resource includes people living from the year 1182 to modern times from areas that now comprise 23 nations of sub-Saharan Africa. Through reading about the lives of its noteworthy people, the reader will confront many of Africa's important historical and social issues, such as the ancient kingdoms, the early Muslim and Christian influences, Europeans and the devastating slave trade, the colonial governments, African nationalism, and the triumphs and struggles of the newly formed independent nations. The people profiled are the kings, presidents, and dictators, religious and military leaders, musicians, activists, traders, environmentalists, and writers who have helped to shape the continent's history.

In *African Biography* readers will find:

- 75 alphabetically arranged biographical entries, each focusing on the childhood and formative experiences of the subject as well as his or her career; the background and traditions held by

Miriam Makeba

the subject; and the overall historical or political situation in the nation or area upon which the subject made an impact.

- Sidebars that provide information on people, events, historical background, and other fascinating facts related to the entry.

- Sources for further reading and a full bibliography that inform students where to delve even deeper.

- More than 150 portraits, illustrations, and maps.

- Locator maps in most entries that identify the nations within the continent.

Each volume of *African Biography* begins with a listing of biographical entries by nationality and by field of endeavor; an introduction to, and timeline of, important events in African history; and a glossary of terms used in the text. Volumes conclude with a subject index so students can easily find the people, places, movements, and events discussed throughout the set.

Acknowledgments

The editor would like to thank the U•X•L staff, particularly the photo research department, for all their hard work behind the scenes. Special thanks to U•X•L senior editor Sonia Benson for her enthusiastic support for this project. Thanks are due also to Remer Tyson who worked on the biographies and enjoyed the research as much as I did.

Special thanks are due for the valuable comments and suggestions of U•X•L adviser Ann Marie Laprise, Detroit Public Library, Elmwood Park Branch, Detroit, Michigan.

Comments and Suggestions

We welcome your comments on *African Biography* as well as your suggestions for topics to be featured in future editions. Please write: Editors, *African Biography,* U•X•L, 27500 Drake Rd., Farmington Hills, Michigan 48331-3535; call toll-free: 1-800-877-4253; or fax (248) 699-8066.

Preface: An Overview of Africa's History

The inscription welcoming researchers to the building housing Zimbabwe's historical records says: "There is a history in all men's lives." Just as each person's life holds a history, each life also reveals part of the history of a specific time and place. In these biographies of 75 African men and women, the history of the continent emerges.

The Africans included in these volumes are people living south of the Sahara Desert. For centuries the desert has divided the peoples of the continent. Those living along the Mediterranean and north Atlantic Ocean coasts have a history different from those living to the south. The people in the North were part of the history of Egypt and the early Roman empire while the South remained largely untouched by the experiences of the North.

Historians such as Herodotus (c. 425-484 B.C.) made occasional isolated tours into Africa as early as the fifth century B.C. But historians began to collect comprehensive knowledge of Africans living in the vast regions south of the Sahara with the beginning of Portuguese exploration in the 1400s. From the records and diaries kept by the sailors, priests, and representatives of the kings, the lives of prominent African men and women come alive. Their history and those of future generations reveal a pattern of resistance, perhaps because of the nature of their relationship with the Europeans. In the earlier period, Africans clashed with outsiders who were seeking to exploit the continent's mineral wealth and later to expand the horrendous trade in slaves. Later, resistance took the form of nationalism and demands for independence from European rule. Today, Africans are demanding an end to the corrupt and tyrannical African governments that have cheated them of their share of their countries' resources.

Majesty and wealth

For the early historical period of the great empires in West Africa the documented history is scant. Along the reaches of the Niger and Senegal rivers in West Africa, Africans developed large powerful kingdoms based on trade and warfare. These early empires of the 400s to 1500s—Ghana, Mali, and Songhai—stretched from the Atlantic Ocean as far as the northwest of modern Nigeria. So fabulously wealthy were these kingdoms that Arab traders from the north crossed the Sahara Desert with their huge camel caravans to trading centers like Timbuktu and Gao along the Niger River. There they traded their salt and textiles for the gold of the western African kingdoms. In southern Africa, from the Zambezi River to the Indian Ocean, the rulers of Great Zimbabwe (1000-1400s) controlled the trade in gold and ivory. African traders brought their goods to the Indian Ocean Coast where they traded with Arab merchants from Kilwa and Mombasa along the Kenyan coast.

Along the Red Sea, the Christian kingdom of Aksum reached its height in the 1100s. **Lalibela** (1182-1255), the Emperor of Aksum (Ethiopia), is the first person about whom we have enough information to form a biography. Lalibela was responsible for the construction of 11 Christian churches, still standing today, built into the sides of stone cliffs in northern Ethiopia. In this earlier period **Mansa Musa** (1312-1337), the enormously wealthy ruler of the kingdom of Mali, gained a place in history when he made a pilgrimage, or *haj,* from his capital at Timbuktu to the Muslim holy city of Mecca, in today's Saudi Arabia. The trip took him two years. On his return, he established in Timbuktu one of the leading Islamic intellectual centers in the world.

European interests

In the 1400s the Portuguese sailed around the West African Coast and in their wake European slave traders followed. This trade distorted the normal development of African communities for nearly 500 years. Faced with expanding penetration by Portuguese traders in the East and Arab traders along the Indian Ocean coasts, African communities reacted in several different ways. Some adapted themselves to the trade and grew wealthy from the capture of slaves and the trade in guns. Others resisted.

Sent out by Portuguese Prince Henry the Navigator to make their way around the continent, the Portuguese set up trading posts along the coast. Stimulating the early explorers was the myth of the fabulously wealthy realm of an African Christian king named Prester John. Islam, the faith founded by the prophet Muhammad, had rapidly spread from Saudi Arabia into Africa and Asia from the 600s onward. The Christian church in Europe wanted to believe that Christian kingdoms existed beyond the reach of Islam, and the myth of Prester John suited their purpose. To avoid the Muslim-controlled Sahara Desert, Prince Henry planned to sail along the Atlantic Coast, and then follow the large rivers inland until he found Prester John.

As they explored along the coast, the Portuguese established settlements. Following their discovery of Brazil in the 1500s and the development of plantations there, they began taking slaves from Africa to work these plantations. They sailed around the Cape of Good Hope and along the Indian Ocean Coast. There they explored the inland river systems and wrote descriptions of **Mwene Mutapa Negomo Mupunzagutu,** the ruler of the Mutapa dynasty along the Zambezi River in the 1550s. As in other earlier African kingdoms, the Portuguese were welcomed and provided with accommodation. Often, their Christian priests converted the African rulers and their courts to Christianity. In many instances this caused dissent within the ruler's court between the traditional authorities and priests and those who adopted the new ways. Struggles for power within the kingdom were fueled by the outsiders who supported one side against the another.

Later, other European explorers kept diaries of their contact with African rulers and their societies: among these were the Dutch in the 1600s and the French, British, and Germans in the 1700s and 1800s. On the heels of the explorers came the missionaries, adventurers, and traders. Confronted by European expansion, African societies were forced to turn outward to respond to the pressures. There were some fascinating exceptions, like **Afonso I** of the Kongo in the 1480s, but most ultimately resisted the European presence. Sometimes resistance followed accommodation. The West African kings of Dahomey, for instance, initially profited from the slave trade with the Europeans and strengthened their kingdom. Later, however, French colonial forces defeated the Dahomeans and exiled their king. From the East Coast of Africa, the Arabs and later the Portuguese followed the rivers inland to open up the continent to Europeans from the Indian Ocean Coast.

Anna Nzinga, the queen of the Ndongo in the 1600s in present-day Angola, was a good strategist and formed alliances with the Dutch to try to keep the Portuguese from destroying her kingdom. Ultimately, however, the wealth derived from the trade in slaves won the day. The slavers destroyed African societies, corrupted their leaders, and sent thousands of people into slavery in the Americas. Some men, such as **Olaudah Equiano** and **Samuel Ajayi Crowther,** who were taken as slaves, gained their freedom and wrote descriptions of their experiences. Crowther returned to his native Nigeria and became the first black bishop in the Anglican Church of England. Others became wealthy from trading in slaves. **Tippu Tib** from Zanzibar was one of the greatest African slavers in the interior.

In southern Africa resistance took other forms. Internal conflicts in the region had much more impact on the societies than slavery did. In the early 1800s, **Shaka,** the Zulu king, displaced tens of thousands of people as he sought to increase his powerful kingdom. Later, as the whites from the Cape Colony began moving northward, the conflicts centered on white encroachment and African resistance. The intensity of resistance escalated toward the end of the 1800s as the governments of Europe vied with one another for control of Africa. The British faced armed resistance in southern Africa from the Afrikaners under **Paul Kruger,** from the Zulus under **Cetshwayo**, and from the Matabele under **Lobengula.** In South West Africa (Namibia), **Samuel Maherero,** leader of the Herero, put up stiff resistance to German occupation. Elsewhere in Africa, in the Belgian Congo **Simon Kimbangu** began a religious movement that opposed the repressive, cruel treatment meted out to Africans by the agents of Belgian King Leopold II. In Madagascar, Queen **Ranavalona I** used her authority to keep all

Christian missionaries out of her country for nearly 40 years, thus allowing the traditional culture to flourish unimpeded by European culture. In Ethiopia, **Menelik II** took up arms to defend his country against the Italian invasion. His troops defeated the Italians at the battle of Adowa in 1896, one of the greatest defeats of a European power in Africa.

Demands for independence

During the Second World War, Africans fought in the armies of the colonial powers. When they returned home from the war, they began demanding the same rights for themselves that they had fought for in Europe and Asia. They formed political parties and nationalist movements to rid their countries of European rule. Over a period of 30 years, some by arms and others through negotiation, the African leaders achieved independence for their countries. **Kwame Nkrumah** was the first president of Ghana, the first sub-Saharan African country to win its independence. Nkrumah was a formidable intellectual presence who promoted the idea of Pan-Africanism, a united Africa. During the 1960s, the flood gates opened and in 10 years' time nearly 30 African countries won their independence from their colonial rulers. Some countries under leaders such as **Félix Houphouët-Boigny** in Côte d'Ivoire and **Léopold Sédar Senghor** in Senegal experienced a smooth transition to independence and kept close ties with the French, their former colonial power. Other countries under nationalist leaders like **Patrice Lumumba** in the former Belgian Congo (Zaire and now the Democratic Republic of the Congo) experienced turmoil and bloodshed at independence.

Nationalists and independence leaders

Once African countries had become independent, many leaders experienced difficulties administering their nations and reconciling the conflicting interests of regional and cultural groups. Some leaders like Nigeria's **Abubakar Tafawa Balewa** fell under the gun of military rule. Other rulers ignored constitutional limits and declared themselves presidents for life. Men such as **Hastings Banda** of Malawi, **Kenneth Kaunda** of Zambia, and **Julius Nyerere** of Tanzania all ruled over governments that recognized only one political party—theirs.

In the aftermath of World War II, rivalry grew up between China, the Soviet Union and the Communist bloc countries, and the West. The period of Great Power rivalry is known as the Cold War. It lasted until 1989 when the Communist governments of Eastern Europe fell. During this time, the East and West provided their supporters with arms and ammunition. Africans fought major wars in Angola, Mozambique, Somalia, Ethiopia, and Eritrea. To prevent the East from influencing other governments, the West supported friendly dictators such as **Mobutu Sese Seko** of Zaire to keep them in power. The West wanted to prevent Communist countries from coming in and exploiting the continent's mineral resources and from gaining strategic bases in Africa.

African writers used their powers to criticize and interpret the changes taking place in their societies. Among the most prominent of the writers in the post-World War II period were Nigerians, **Chinua Achebe** and **Wole Soyinka. Alan Paton** used the power of his novel *Cry the Beloved Country* to personalize the plight of Africans in his home country of South Africa. Resistance to the racist policies of the South African government of **Hendrik Verwoerd** continued under such people as Chief **Albert Lutuli, Miriam Makeba, Steve Biko, Winnie Madikizela-Mandela, Nelson Mandela,** and former Archbishop **Desmond Tutu.**

With the collapse of Communism in eastern European and the Soviet Union, the African nations were left alone and some were able to bring stability to their countries. The major benefactors of the end of the Cold War were black South Africans and South Africa's neighbors, Namibia, Mozambique, and Angola. In the absence of the Communist threat, South African National Party leader **Frederick Willem de Klerk** could justify to his followers the advantages of releasing **Nelson Mandela** from nearly 30 years in prison. Mandela's release opened the way to a multiparty system in South Africa and the normalizing of relations with African countries in the southern region.

Today, the leaders of African countries are being evaluated for their competence rather than their loyalties. In many cases they do not stand the test of providing a leadership for the benefit of their people. Many have performed miserably; some have stayed in power for many years and enriched themselves and their families while impoverishing their countries. With the broader vision of democracy and sound economic policies, African societies are beginning to demand a fairer deal from their leaders. In Uganda,

Yoweri Museveni has ended the terrible ethnic fighting and brought stability to his country, although he too refuses to allow competing political parties. In South Africa, **Nelson Mandela** turned over the presidency of his political party to a younger generation, and he has promised to leave office by 1999—setting a precedent that an African leader can serve his or her people by leaving office at the peak of power.

A note about this collection

In these volumes the numbers of prominent political South African activists are greater than in any other single country. Various circumstances account for this. The struggle for freedom and majority rule lasted longer in South Africa than in other countries, and the struggle gave rise to activists, black and white. Of the sub-Saharan African countries, South Africa also has the most developed economy and infrastructure, giving greater opportunities and outlets for activism.

African women are noticeably underrepresented in these biographies. Many African cultures are dominated by men, and they have assigned women to inferior positions. That some women have emerged as powerful leaders is all the more tribute to their strengths and perseverance. In modern Africa, women such as Kenyan environmentalist **Wangari Maathai** are in the forefront of women who have succeeded despite the prejudices of their families, husbands, peers, and governments. Women in many contemporary cultures are challenging the traditional ways that have kept them in subservient positions.

Finally, one of the most difficult aspects of compiling this collection of biographies was to limit the number of entries to 75. Many interesting and noteworthy people were necessarily omitted in an effort to achieve a wide representation of people by region, race, sex, and field of endeavor.

Virginia Curtin Knight
Harare, Zimbabwe
January 1998

Desmond Tutu

Words to Know

A

Abolitionist: someone who is in favor of, or works for, the elimination of slavery.

Advocate: to support or speak in favor of; or someone who speaks in favor of.

African nationalism: a strong loyalty to the traditions and political and economic interests of Africa and its people. The term generally refers to Africans who tried to free Africa from colonial governments and worked for self-rule.

Afrikaans: a language derived from the Dutch language of the seventeenth century, spoken by the Afrikaners or Boers and one of the official languages of the Republic of South Africa.

Afrikaner: an Afrikaans-speaking South African native of European descent, usually Dutch, German, or French. Afrikaners started arriving in South Africa in the middle of the seventeenth century, where the majority became farmers.

African National Congress (ANC): the oldest black political organization in South Africa, founded in 1912 by a group of black lawyers for the purpose of promoting the interests of blacks in the newly created Union of South Africa. After 1948 the organization led the opposition to apartheid, and it was outlawed in the 1960s. In the 1990s the ban on the ANC ended; in 1994 the party won in the first elections open to all races in South Africa.

Afro-Beat: a modern musical style that fuses jazz with the sounds of traditional African music with lyrics in both a native African language and in pidgin English.

Agnostic: someone who believes that human beings cannot know if God or any supreme being exists, or understand what the nature of the supreme being is.

Amnesty: the granting of pardon—forgiveness without punishment—to a group of people by the authorities involved (as a government).

Anarchy: lawlessness or disorder due to the absence of government or authority.

Ancestral lands: lands passed down within a group or family from one generation to the next.

Anthropology: the study of the way humans have lived and developed over the ages.

Apartheid: the policy of segregating and practicing economic and political discrimination against non-European groups; *apartheid* policies were in effect in South Africa from 1948 until the early 1990s.

Archaeology: the study of past human life by digging up and examining the material remains, such as fossils and artifacts.

Asceticism: the practice of strict self-denial for the purpose of gaining spiritual discipline.

Assimilation: the absorbing of an individual or a group into the cultural mainstream.

Atrocities: appalling and brutal acts.

Authoritarianism: placing a nation's power in a leader or group of leaders who are not accountable to the people for their actions.

Autocracy: a government in which one ruler has unlimited power.

Autonomy: self-governing.

Axiom: an established principle or rule.

B

Banning order: legal restrictions imposed by the National party government of South Africa upon an individual that prohibited travel from a set area, speaking in public, appearing in certain public places, and restricted who, or how many people, could visit at one's home, and placed other limitations on the individual's freedoms of movement and speech.

Baptism: a Christian ritual in which a person is purified by means of water and then accepted into the Christian community.

Boer: a South African of the Afrikaans-speaking community.

Boycott: a united effort of refusing to deal with an organization, such as a company, or its products, in order to express disapproval.

Bureaucracy: a system of administration, generally known for its inefficiency, in which decisions and tasks must be filtered through many different specialized officials and conform to many rules in order for an action to be taken.

C

Cabinet: a body of advisers to a ruler.

Caliph: a ruler in an Islamic state who is considered a successor of Muhammad and rules politically as well as spiritually.

Calvinism: a Christian sect developed by John Calvin (1509-1564) that emphasizes the idea of predestination, the belief that some people are fated for salvation and are guided by God.

Capitalism: an economic system in which property and businesses are owned by individuals and corporations (rather than being owned by the government or by the society as a whole). Profits in a capitalistic system are based on competition and enrich the individual owner or the investors in a corporation.

Caravan: a group of people who travel together through deserts or hostile territories.

Censorship: the system of examining public statements or the arts, written or spoken, for ideas or material that is objectionable to the interests of a governing body, and not allowing these statements to be expressed in a public forum.

Centralization: the placement of the majority of power in one concentrated office, as in a strong central government as opposed to a federation of individually governed states.

Civil rights: the nonpolitical rights of a citizen, as in the rights of personal liberty guaranteed to U.S. citizens: equal treatment and equal access to housing, free speech, employment, and education.

Civil disobedience: the refusal to go along with government orders, as in purposely disobeying a discriminatory law or ordinance. Usually *civil disobedience* is carried out by a group in order to protest something or to get concessions from the government.

Civilian government: a government that is not led by the military or police forces.

Coalition government: a temporary joining together of two parties or interest groups within the government for a common goal.

Cold War: a term used to describe the tensions between the West and the Communist bloc countries of Eastern Europe and the former Soviet Union that arose after World War II (1939-45) and ended when the Berlin Wall fell and the Soviet Union dissolved at the end of the 1980s.

Collaboration: cooperation between two individuals or groups that are not normally connected.

Collective farm: a farm formed from many small farms, run jointly by the group of owners and usually supervised by the government.

Colony: a territory in which settlers from another country come to live while maintaining their ties to their home country, often setting up a government that may rule over the original inhabitants of the territory as well.

Colonialism: control by one nation or state over a dependent territory and its people and resources.

Communism: an economic theory in which there is no private property—all goods are owned in common; also the doctrine of the former Soviet Union, in which a single authoritarian governing body controls all means of production.

Confederation: to be united in a league or alliance for mutual support or common goals, as in the union of the 11 states that seceded from the United States in 1860 as the Confederate States of America.

Consensus: an agreement by most or all concerned with an issue.

Conservation: protection and preservation of something (often the environment); a carefully planned management system to prevent exploitation, destruction, or overuse.

Conservative: wishing to preserve what is already established, such as traditions or political or economic structures.

Consolidate: to join different elements or groups together to form one solid unit.

Constitution: a written document that sets forth the basic principles and laws of a nation, establishing the powers and duties of a government and the basic rights of its citizens.

Consul: an official appointed by one nation to live in a foreign country and to represent the business interests of his or her home nation in the foreign country.

Convoy: a protective escort.

Coptic church: a Christian sect that differed from the Western church in the belief that Jesus had only one nature, a divine one; orthodox creed holds that Jesus had both a divine and a human nature.

Corruption: the state of being outside of moral, legal, and proper behavior; acting in ways that benefit oneself or one's connections but hurt the society, such as offering or accepting bribery.

Coup: (from the French *coup d'etat,* "stroke of state") the violent overthrow of a government by a small group.

Cultural integration: to bring many cultures together into a whole as equals within a society, but not necessarily as distinct entities with separate beliefs and traditions.

Culture: the set of beliefs, social habits, and ways of surviving in the environment that are held by a particular social group. *Culture* is also a word for a group that shares these traits.

D

Delegation: a group of people chosen to represent a larger group, such as an organization, a political party, or a nation.

Democracy: a government in which the people hold the power and exercise it either directly or through elected representatives.

Denounce: to publicly criticize, accuse, or pronounce someone or something evil.

Depose: to remove a monarch from the throne or a leader from power.

Dictator: a ruler who has absolute authority and is often oppressive in his use of it.

Diplomacy: the art of handling affairs and conducting negotiations, especially between nations or states, without creating tensions.

Disfranchise: to deprive of the right to vote.

Diviner: someone who practices the arts involved in foreseeing the future or finding hidden knowledge.

Dominate: to exert mastery and control over another.

Dynasty: a powerful family that stays in power over many generations.

E

Elite: a group considered to be socially superior; or a powerful minority group.

Emirate: a state under the control of an *emir,* a ruler in an Islamic country.

Entourage: a group of attendants; the people who surround an important or famous person.

Environmentalist: someone who supports the preservation and improvement of the natural environment.

Ethnic group: a group of people that shares customs, language, beliefs, and a common history and origins.

Evacuate: to leave, or be removed from, a place in an organized way, often for protection from danger.

Évolué: a Western-educated African.

Evolution: in the struggle for survival, the process by which successive generations of a species pass on to their offspring the characteristics that enable the species to survive.

Excavation: to dig up or uncover in order to expose to view, as in digging up ancient fossils.

Exile: removal from one's native country, often forced but sometimes voluntary.

Expatriate: someone who lives in a foreign country.

Expedition: a journey taken for a specific reason.

Expropriate: to take property and put it in one's own name; to take away someone's property rights.

F

Famine: an extreme shortage of food causing starvation within a certain area.

Fascism: a political system headed by a dictator in which the nation is exalted above its individual citizens, all opposition to the government is prohibited, and powerful police and military forces use strong-arm tactics to ensure obedience and conformity to strict government regulation.

Fetish: an object that is believed to have magical powers that will protect its owner.

G

Garrison: a military station.

Genocide: the deliberate killing of everyone belonging to a particular ethnic group.

Grass roots: at the local community level, often referring to rural society away from the political centers.

Guerrilla: someone who fights, generally with a small group of rebels, using nonmilitary methods, such as sabotage and harassment.

H

Harlem Renaissance: a highly creative period among artists and writers in the community of Harlem in New York City that started in the early 1920s and lasted until the Great Depression in 1929.

Hereditary rulers: leaders who inherit the right to rule by reason of being born into a particular station within the ruling family.

Heretic: someone who will not conform to the established beliefs or doctrines of the prevailing religion.

I

Impeach: to accuse a public official or ruler of a crime against his or her office.

Indentured servant: someone who enters into a binding contract to work for someone else for a set period of time and in return usually receives travel and living expenses.

Indigenous: being native to a particular place or having one's origins there.

Inflation: a growing rise in the prices of goods due to an economy in which more money and credit are available than goods.

Infrastructure: the basic structure underlying a system; in a nation, the *infrastructure* includes government and public works, roads and other transportation systems, and communication networks.

Insurrection: rebellion against a government or other authority.

Integration: incorporation of different groups of people into a society as equals.

Isolationism: the chosen condition within a nation or territory of keeping apart from other nations, abstaining from alliances, trade, or intermingling of populations.

J

Judicial system: the system within a state or nation that administers justice, generally through a network of courts and judges.

K

Koran: the holy book of Muslim people, containing sacred writings that are revelations given to the prophet Muhammad by the Muslim god Allah.

L

Labor union: a group of workers organized to bargain together as a strong unit with employers for better wages, benefits, and working conditions.

Legislative body: the group within a government that is in charge of making laws and collecting taxes.

Liberal: broad-minded and open to the reform of established rules, authorities, traditions, and social structures.

Lobby: to attempt to persuade public officials to take action or vote a particular way on an issue.

M

Martial law: the law administered by a country's military forces during a declared emergency situation, when the normal security forces are not sufficient to maintain public safety and order. *Martial law* often involves a temporary suspension of certain individual civil and legal rights.

Mercenary: a soldier who is hired to fight with an army for pay, often coming from a foreign land and serving for profit, without any patriotic motivations.

Migrant worker: a person who moves from place to place to find temporary work.

Migration: the movement of a group of people from a home territory to another region.

Military rule: a government run by the armed forces, as opposed to a civilian government.

Missionary: a person belonging to an organized effort by a religious group to spread its beliefs in other parts of the world.

Monopoly: the exclusive control, ownership, or rights to something, like a product or a particular business.

Mosque: a building where Muslims practice public worship.

Multiparty politics: a political system in which parties representing different interests run against each other in elections, giving individual voters a variety of options and allowing for opposition to be expressed.

Muslim: a follower of the Islam religion, who worships the god Allah as revealed to the prophet Muhammad through the Koran, the holy book of Islam.

Mutiny: resistance to authority; particularly, revolt against a superior officer, as in the crew of a ship against the commander.

Mysticism: the belief that one can obtain a direct knowledge of God or spiritual truth through inner, or subjective, experience.

N

Nationalism: pride and loyalty toward one's nation, usually to the extent of exalting that nation above all others.

Nationalization: investing control and ownership, usually of a business or property, to the national government.

Nation-state: a political unit in which a particular group sharing the same beliefs, customs, history, and political interests comprises its own state and is self-ruled.

Negritude: the state of being pridefully aware of the culture and history of the African people.

Nomad: a member of a group of people who do not live in one set place, but move around as necessary, usually in pursuit of a food supply.

O

Opposition: the position of believing and expressing something contrary to another; in politics, the *opposition* party is one that disagrees with and is ready to replace the party in power.

Organization of African Unity (OAU): An organization founded in 1963, currently with more than 50 member nations, to promote unity among African states, to eliminate colonialism, to develop sound health and economic policies, and to maintain defense of the African nations.

Overlord: a supreme ruler, who rules over other less powerful rulers within his or her realm.

P

Pagan: a word used by Christians and westerners to identify people who believe either in many gods or in no gods.

Pan-Africanism: a movement for greater cooperation and unity among the different regions or nations of the African continent.

Parliament: the highest legislative body of a nation, which meets regularly and is the forum for gathering and discussion among different assemblies.

Pass laws: laws under which blacks in South Africa had to carry documents that identified them and certified that they had authorized jobs in white areas.

Passive resistance: nonviolent defiance of a government or power usually exerted through noncooperation (as in not following commands).

Patronage system: a method of distributing jobs, often used in appointing government jobs, in which jobs are granted as a reward for increasing the political or financial standing of the person or group making the appointments.

Peasant farmers: members of a social class of either small landowners or laborers who work the land, who are generally quite poor and often uneducated and lacking in political influence.

Philanthropist: one who works to promote the welfare of others or the society.

Pidgin English: a simple form of English-based speech used for communication between someone who speaks English and someone who speaks a different language; or, a mixture of English and another language.

Pilgrimage: a journey to a sacred place.

Plantation: a large farming establishment in which the labor is usually provided by workers who live on the premises.

Plateau: a region of high, flat land that is raised sharply above land next to it on at least one side.

Police state: a nation or other political unit under the power of a repressive government that uses a powerful and often secret police force to administer the areas of government usually left to civilians, such as judicial and social matters.

Political prisoner: someone who is jailed because of beliefs or actions that are perceived to be contrary or in opposition to the government.

Polygamy: the practice of having more than one spouse at a time, applicable to either sex.

Polygyny: the practice of a male having more than one wife at a time.

Premier: the prime minister, or the leader who is first in rank as head of the cabinet or ministry of a nation or state.

Prime minister: the leader who heads the cabinet or ministry of a nation or state.

Protectorate: the relationship that occurs when a state assumes the authority position over another state.

Province: a regional division of a nation, like a state, with a regional government of its own, but ruled in federal matters by the national government.

Puppet government: a political body that is controlled by an outside authority, usually referring to a leader who appears to rule but is in fact carrying out the demands of a more powerful and less apparent entity.

Purge: literally, to rid (the nation) of something that is undesirable; *purges* have taken place in many areas in which one ethnic group attempts to destroy another.

R

Recession: a time of decreased economic activity.

Refugee: someone who flees from his or her own country, often to another country, to escape persecution.

Regent: someone who governs a kingdom standing in for the sovereign ruler, generally because the sovereign is under the legal age, absent, or disabled.

Regime: a government in power.

Reparations: payments made after a war by the defeated nation for damages another nation or group of people suffered as a result of the war.

Resistance: the act of opposing the dominant authority; *resistance* can also refer to a political organization that fights an occupying power within its nation, using underground methods such as guerrilla warfare and sabotage.

S

Sabotage: a deliberate act of destruction or obstruction, designed to damage an enemy's ability to carry out its functions.

Sanctuary: a place of protection from persecutors or immunity from the law.

Secession: a formal withdrawal from an organization or a political unit.

Secretary-general: the main administrative officer of an organization.

Socialism: an economic and political system in which the government owns businesses and distributes goods to the people.

Solitary confinement: a punishment used in prisons that involves being placed in a cell by oneself and not allowed to see or speak with others for a set amount of time.

Sovereignty: freedom from controls from outside; self-government.

Statesman: someone who is wise in the arts of leadership and can govern fairly, without becoming involved in factions and partisanship.

Strategic: necessary in the conduct of war and not available in the warring nation's own country; of great importance.

Strike: a stoppage of work by an organized group of workers in order to make an employer respond to demands about wages, job security, or work conditions.

Sub-Saharan Africa: part of Africa south of the Sahara desert (see map, inside front or back cover).

Subsidize: to grant money to a business or another nation in order to provide assistance or to obtain favors.

Subsistence farming: a system of farming in which a family farms a small amount of land to grow just the things they need to live, without significant extra harvest to be sold.

T

Terrorism: using threats and violent acts to inspire extreme fear in an enemy in order to force the enemy to agree to demands.

Textiles: cloth.

Totalitarian: describing a dictatorial state in which one powerful person or group rules with near total control and the state is exalted above the individual.

Tradition: a custom or institution from among the beliefs, social habits, methods, systems, arts, etc., of a people that is handed down from generation to generation, such as a ritual, a story, or a courtship practice.

Treason: the offense of trying to overthrow a government or kill its ruler.

Tribute: a payment made from one nation or group to another, usually when the paying group has been conquerred by the group they are paying. *Tribute* is either payable to the dominant party as a kind of tax, or it is paid in exchange for protection.

Tyranny: excessive and repressive power exerted by the government.

U

Unify: to bring together different elements and make them into a coherent whole.

Unitary state: an undivided state or nation: one with only one political party and a strong central government.

United Nations: an international organization established after World War II for the purpose of maintaining international peace, developing good relations among nations, and finding solutions to economic, social, and humanitarian problems throughout the world.

V

Vanguard: those who lead a movement or action, or the forefront of a movement.

W

West: a term referring to the countries of western Europe and the United States, usually those countries that have not been under Communist regimes in the twentieth century and have some similarities in customs, political and economic philosophy, and ethnicity.

Westernization: the adoption of, or conversion to, traditions and qualities of the West.

White supremacy: a belief in the superiority of the white race over the black race and the consequent need to maintain whites in powerful positions over blacks.

White-minority government: a government led and administered by white people in a population that is comprised of a majority of non-whites who are excluded from the political process.

World Bank: The International Bank for Reconstruction and Development, an agency of the United Nations that loans money to member nations for the purpose of developing economic growth.

Picture Credits

The photographs and illustrations appearing in *African Biography* were received from the following sources:

On the cover: Haile Selassie I, Miriam Makeba, and Nelson Mandela: **AP/Wide World Photos. Reproduced by permission.**

Photograph by J. P. Laffont. United Nations: xlix; **Photograph by Jerry Bauer. Reproduced by permission:** p. 1; **AP/Wide World Photos. Reproduced by permission:** v, xv, xxiii, lv, lviii, lix, 18, 23, 39, 44, 50, 55, 59, 64, 93, 138,143, 147, 157, 162, 166, 173,175, 177, 181, 183, 229, 232, 235, 261, 269, 283, 306, 309, 315, 328, 346, 359, 379, 396, 400, 418, 433, 437, 441, 448, 454, 466, 471, 498, 502, 504, 510, 525, 530, 534, 543, 554, 562; **Photograph by Reuters/Jeff Christensen. Archive Photos. Reproduced by permission:** p. 28; **Photograph by Rick Wilking. Archive Photos. Reproduced by permission:** 32; **Library of Congress:** 34, 119, 292, 350; **Archive Photos. Reproduced by permission:** lvii, 47, 187, 192, 238, 241, 254, 263, 341, 362, 364, 365, 427, 521, 571, 587, 589, 596; **United Nations:** 62, 578; **Corbis-Bettmann. Reproduced by permission:** lii (top and bottom), 73, 201, 285; **The Granger Collection, New York.**

Nadine Gordimer

Reproduced by permission: 79, 220, 388; Photograph by Howard Burditt. Archive Photos. Reproduced by permission: 86, 385; Photograph by Van Lierop. United Nations: 90; Illustration by Donna V. Benson, Gale Research: 95, 195, 294, 459, 478; Reuters Corbis-Bettman. Reproduced by permission: lxi, 112, 116, 319; Photograph by Wyatt Counts. AP/Wide World Photos. Reproduced by permission: 125; Photograph by Juda Ngwenya. Archive Photos. Reproduced by permission: 130, 282; Reproduced with the kind permission of the Estate of Bessie Head: 149; Zimbabwe National Archives. Reproduced by permission: 246, 248, 249, 515; Tony Stone Images. Reproduced by permission: 206; Photograph by Tom Costello. AP/Wide World Photos. Reproduced by permission: 212; Photograph by Robert Caputo. Time Magazine. Reproduced by permission: 216; Corbis Images. Reproduced by permission: 223; Adrian Arbib/Corbis Images. Reproduced by permission: 271; Photograph by Hos Maina. Archive Photos. Reproduced by permission: 275; Photograph by Peter Andrews. Archive Photos. Reproduced by permission: lx, 277; Photograph by Chester Higgins Jr. Photo Researchers, Inc. Reproduced by permission: xxi, 304; Kenya Information Services. 321; Corbis Corporation. Reproduced by permission: 330; Express Newspapers/L932/Archive Photos. Reproduced by permission: 353; Photograph by Reinhard W. Sander. Reproduced by permission: 443; The Kobal Collection. Reproduced by permission: 476; Mansell Collection/Time Inc/The New York Times Magazine. Reproduced by permission: li (bottom), 485, 489; Photograph by Caton Woodville. Mansell Collection/Time Inc/New York Times Magazine. Reproduced by permission: li (top), 518; Archive Photos/Trappe. Reproduced by permission: 536; Photograph by Y. Nagata. United Nations: 561; Photograph by Peter Van Niekerk. Reproduced by permission: xxxi, 580.

A Timeline of Important Events in African History

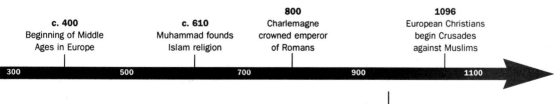

Angolan children celebrate their nation's independence.

300 Aksum, the first recorded kingdom of Ethiopia (founded by Arab traders in the first century A.D.), adopts Coptic Christianity.

700 Mombasa (Kenya) develops as a center for Arab trade in slaves and ivory.

1000-1400 Great Zimbabwe, the largest and strongest city of its time in central and southern Africa, controls the gold trade in southern Africa. Lying in the high plateau area of present-day Zimbabwe, the population of Great Zimbabwe reached about 18,000 and its rulers controlled an area of about 60,000 square miles.

1182 Lalibela becomes emperor of Ethiopia.

c. 400
Beginning of Middle
Ages in Europe

c. 610
Muhammad founds
Islam religion

800
Charlemagne
crowned emperor
of Romans

1096
European Christians
begin Crusades
against Muslims

| 300 | 500 | 700 | 900 | 1100 |

1324-27 Ruler of Mali Kingdom **Mansa Musa** makes pilgrimage to Mecca, the holy city of Islam, and returns to rebuild the capital city of Timbuktu into an urban center of commerce and learning.

1400-96 Sunni Ali, the great leader of the Songhai Empire in Mali, takes Timbuktu; his empire becomes the largest in ancient Western Africa.

1482 Afonso I of the Kongo welcomes Portuguese explorers into his kingdom and establishes relations with Portugal; in addition to bringing Christianity and Western education, the Europeans establish an enormous slave trade in the Kongo kingdom.

1482 The Portuguese establish a trading post at Elmina, Gold Coast.

1505 Portuguese burn Kilwa (in Kenya) and continue penetration along the Indian Ocean Coast and inland.

1550 Mwene Mutapa Negomo Mupunzagutu rules the Mutapa Dynasty in current-day Zimbabwe.

1591 Moroccans invade Songhai, defeat its army, and occupy Timbuktu (in Mali).

1591 The Portuguese invade Angolan kingdoms and increase the slave trade to Brazil.

c. 1600 African trading states develop along the Atlantic Coast as partners of Europeans in slave trade.

1622 Anna Nzinga represents the Ndongo (Angola) in negotiations with the Portuguese.

1652 Dutch East India Company establishes a settlement at the Cape of Good Hope in southern Africa.

1673 Dahomey (Benin) becomes a powerful slave trading kingdom.

1789 Former Nigerian slave **Olaudah Equiano** publishes his memoirs.

Slavers moving captives.

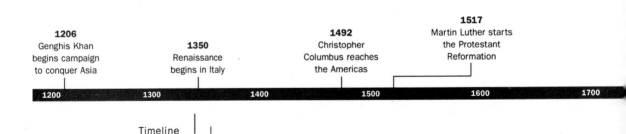

1206
Genghis Khan
begins campaign
to conquer Asia

1350
Renaissance
begins in Italy

1492
Christopher
Columbus reaches
the Americas

1517
Martin Luther starts
the Protestant
Reformation

1200　　1300　　1400　　1500　　1600　　1700

1804 Usuman dan Fodio declares a holy war in northern Nigeria and founds the Islamic Sokoto Empire.

1807 British parliament passes the Slave Trade Abolition Act outlawing maritime (at sea) slave trade.

1815 The British take Cape Colony in southern Africa from the Dutch.

1818 Zulu chief **Shaka** begins 10 years of expansion in southern Africa. His warriors raid villages, causing chaos and forcing millions of people to flee. People displaced by Shaka in turn displace or absorb other peoples, changing forever the mixture of people, language, and culture throughout southern Africa and parts of central Africa. This period in African history is referred to as the *mfecane* or the "crushing."

Shaka meets Lieutenant Farewell.

1818-58 King **Guezo** of a newly strong and independent Dahomey directs his army to move eastward in a relentless pursuit of slaves.

1833 Slavery is outlawed in the British Empire.

1835-43 Afrikaners begin Great Trek northward from Cape Colony in southern Africa to get beyond the influence of the British colonial government.

1835 Queen **Ranavalona I** of Madagascar forbids all religious teaching in the country in an attempt to eliminate foreign influence and preserve the traditional culture of her people.

Ranavalona I.

1843 Gambia and Natal (in southern Africa) become British colonies.

1847 Liberia becomes a republic. American blacks had begun settling there in 1821, and by 1867 approximately 20,000 people had settled in Liberia, mostly on land that had been purchased from local tribes.

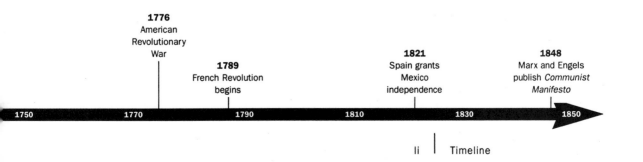

1776
American
Revolutionary
War

1789
French Revolution
begins

1821
Spain grants
Mexico
independence

1848
Marx and Engels
publish *Communist
Manifesto*

1750　　1770　　1790　　1810　　1830　　1850

Slaves leaving ship.

1860 M'Siri becomes leader of the Katanga Kingdom in Congo. M'Siri expands his territory methodically, taking captives and trading them for more guns and powder, which he uses to take more slaves. At the height of his reign M'Siri controls a territory larger than the state of California.

1861 British establish colonial presence in modern-day Nigeria.

1862 Mutesa I is the first Bugandan king to receive Europeans in his kingdom.

1867 Tippu Tib establishes himself as one of the greatest traders in ivory and slaves in eastern and central Africa. He amasses such a great fortune that he is recognized as the overlord of a vast area.

1868 Moshoeshoe, the chief of a small Sotho clan, arranges for Basutoland to become a British protectorate after Afrikaners move North and settle on land claimed by Moshoeshoe. His diplomacy laid the foundation for the current-day nation-state of Lesotho.

1871 Gold is discovered in the Transvaal (southern Africa).

1873-74 Kumasi (Ghana) is burned in the Ashanti-British War.

1874 The Gold Coast becomes a British colony.

1879 Zulu leader **Cetshwayo**'s army, with weaponry consisting mostly of *assegais* (short stabbing spears) and some firearms, defeats the British army at Isandhlwana (South Africa).

1883 Paul Kruger is elected the first president of the Transvaal Republic (South Africa) after successfully leading his people against the British army in 1880 to restore independence to the Transvaal.

1884-85 At a conference in Berlin, European nations carve out their spheres of influence in Africa.

Cetshwayo.

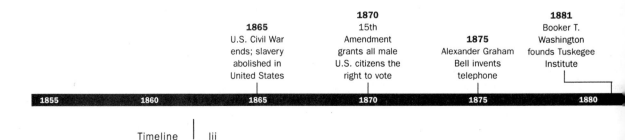

1865
U.S. Civil War ends; slavery abolished in United States

1870
15th Amendment grants all male U.S. citizens the right to vote

1875
Alexander Graham Bell invents telephone

1881
Booker T. Washington founds Tuskegee Institute

1855   1860   1865   1870   1875   1880

1885 The Mahdi, a Muslim visionary who declared himself the successor to the prophet Muhammad, defeats British general Charles Gordon at Khartoum (Sudan) in an uprising against the territory's Egyptian overlords and their British administrators.

1885 King Leopold II of Belgium creates the Belgian Congo as his personal kingdom.

1889 Menelik II becomes emperor of Ethiopia. He is the only African leader to keep control of his country as European powers carve up the continent into colonies.

1889 Great Britain grants the British South Africa Company a royal charter for Rhodesia (Zimbabwe). A large, permanent white settlement is established at Fort Salisbury the next year.

1893-94 Matabele chief **Lobengula** is defeated by British South Africa Company in Rhodesia. With Lobengula's death in 1894, the line of inherited leadership of the Ndebele ends.

1894 Samuel Crowther is consecrated bishop of Nigeria and becomes the first black bishop in the Anglican Church.

1895-96 Ethiopians defeat Italian invaders at the battle of Adowa.

1896 Ashanti king **Prempeh I** negotiates with the British in order to save his 200-year-old kingdom.

1896-97 Ndebele and Shona revolt against the British (in Zimbabwe).

1899-1902 The Boer War is fought between Afrikaners in the Transvaal and Orange Free State against the British. Although the Boers win early victories, the British win the war and the Afrikaners accept British rule.

1900 The first Pan African Congress is held in London. Early Pan-Africanism advocates the merging of smaller African states into one huge African nation.

The Mahdi.

Samuel Crowther.

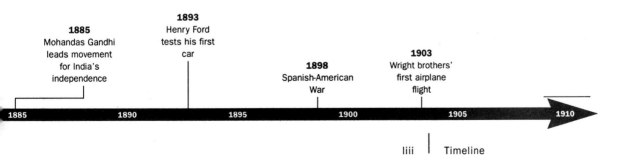

1885
Mohandas Gandhi leads movement for India's independence

1893
Henry Ford tests his first car

1898
Spanish-American War

1903
Wright brothers' first airplane flight

| 1885 | 1890 | 1895 | 1900 | 1905 | 1910 |

Boer soldiers.

Adelaide Smith Casely Hayford and pupils.

1900 Queen mother of the Ashanti **Yaa Asantewa** leads Ashanti army in war against the British in a heroic but futile battle against the colonizers.

1908 German troops defeat the Herero army at Waterberg (Namibia). **Samuel Maherero,** supreme chief of the Herero nation, makes a brave but ultimately hopeless attempt to get the land back from the Germans. When the Herero revolt begins, the population stands at about 80,000, but within one year more than 65,000 Herero are dead.

1915 Malawi nationalist **John Chilembwe** leads uprising against British colonists. Chilembwe, an African Christian leader in Nyasaland (present-day Malawi) whose "Rising" failed miserably, became a folk hero to the people of Nyasaland, a symbol of resistance to white rule.

1919 Adelaide Smith Casely Hayford establishes her Girls' Vocational and Industrial School in Freetown, Sierra Leone.

1921 Congolese religious leader **Simon Kimbangu** establishes a following after starting one of the most important independent Christian religious movements in central Africa.

1921 Sobhuza II is installed as "Lion" or king of the Swazi. Sobhuza will become the world's longest-reigning monarch, ruling for 60 years.

1930 Haile Selassie I becomes emperor of Ethiopia. During his rule, he abolishes slavery, institutes tax reform, promotes education, creates a constitution, and plays a dominant role in the formation of the Organization of African Unity (OAU).

1935 Italy invades Ethiopia under the orders of Italian dictator Benito Mussolini. **Haile Selassie** appeals to the League of

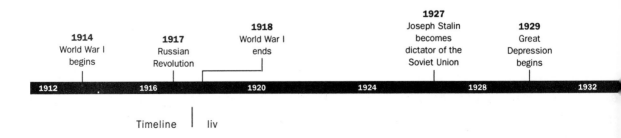

1914 World War I begins

1917 Russian Revolution

1918 World War I ends

1927 Joseph Stalin becomes dictator of the Soviet Union

1929 Great Depression begins

| 1912 | 1916 | 1920 | 1924 | 1928 | 1932 |

Nations for help to stop the Italian invaders, but England and France refused to cooperate. The next year, Italy occupies Ethiopia and Haile Selassie goes into exile.

1941 Italy is evicted from Ethopia; **Haile Selassie** is restored to the throne.

1944 William V. S. Tubman is named president of Liberia.

1946 General rise of African nationalism throughout colonial Africa at end of World War II.

1948 Kenyan anthropologist **Mary Leakey** discovers fossilized bones of *Proconsul africanus,* an apelike creature between 25 and 40 million years old. This is the first significant find to suggest that humans may have originated in East Africa

1948 Olufunmilayo Ransome-Kuti organizes Nigerian market women. The Abeokuta women's campaign protest abuses of British rule.

1948 The National party, comprised mainly of conservative Afrikaners, wins elections in South Africa and establishes a society based on racial separateness and discrimination, or apartheid.

1948 South African writer **Alan Paton**'s novel *Cry, the Beloved Country* is published, bringing South Africa's racial policies worldwide attention.

1952 The Mau Mau uprising in Kenya begins, a violent rebellion by Kikuyu terrorists who fight against the seizing of Kikuyu land by the British. In the next few years, nearly 3,000 Kikuyu die, many at the hands of the Mau Mau rebels, who terrorize blacks suspected of supporting the white regime. By the end of 1955 the revolt is put down.

Haile Selassie I.

Louis S. B. Leakey.

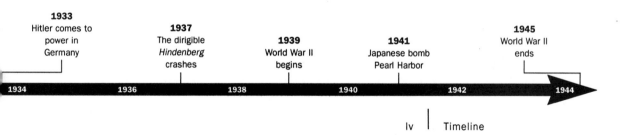

1933
Hitler comes to power in Germany

1937
The dirigible *Hindenberg* crashes

1939
World War II begins

1941
Japanese bomb Pearl Harbor

1945
World War II ends

1934   1936   1938   1940   1942   1944

1953 Federation of Northern and Southern Rhodesia and Nyasaland is formed. Following pressure from the white settler groups in Southern Rhodesia, Northern Rhodesia (now Zambia), and Nyasaland (now Malawi), Great Britain allows the three territories to unite as the self-governing Federation of Rhodesia and Nyasaland. Black Africans strongly oppose the formation of the white-run federation, which lasts until 1963.

1955 Alice Lenshina forms the Lumpa Church, which will become the largest and most powerful peasant movement in Zambian history. The expanding Lumpa Church challenges the state, the established churches, and the traditional leaders.

1957 Kwame Nkrumah becomes prime minister of independent Ghana, the first British colony in Africa to achieve independence after World War II.

1958 Sékou Touré becomes president of Guinea as it achieves independence from France.

1958 Hendrik Verwoerd takes over as prime minister of South Africa and reinforces Bantustan policies that were initiated in South Africa in 1951. Under these policies, citizenship and voting rights for blacks is restricted to nine districts or Bantus. The land reserved for blacks is of poor quality and equals about 14 percent of South Africa's total land, whereas blacks make up about 85 percent of the population.

1958 Nigerian writer **Chinua Achebe**'s *Things Fall Apart* is published.

1960 Joshua Nkomo is elected president of the National Democratic Party, the forerunner to the Zimbabwe African People's Union, one of the main groups that successfully fought for the independence of Rhodesia.

Sékou Touré, Kwame Nkrumah, and William V. S. Tubman

1946 Cold War begins

1949 Mao Zedong creates People's Republic of China

1950 Korean War begins

1953 Korean War ends; Korea splits into two governments

1955 Polio vaccine created

1956 Nasser establishes a republic in Egypt

1946　1948　1950　1952　1954　1956

1960 South African singer and political activist **Miriam Makeba** begins exile from South Africa that will last 30 years. Singing throughout the world, she uses music as her forum in the fight against apartheid and racial discrimination.

1960 At a mass demonstration pushing for an end to pass laws for blacks in Sharpeville, South Africa, policemen fire into a crowd of 5,000 unarmed demonstrators, killing 69 and wounding 300.

1960 **Patrice Lumumba** of the Congo Republic, **Félix Houphouet-Boigny** of Côte d'Ivoire, **Léopold Sédar Senghor** of Senegal, and **Julius Nyerere** of Kenya are sworn in as heads of their newly independent nations.

1960 South African chief and African National Congress (ANC) president **Albert John Lutuli** wins the Nobel Peace Prize.

1960 **Moïse Tshombe** declares Katanga independent from Congo and becomes the president of the secessionist state.

1961 Tanganyika, Rwanda, and Sierra Leone become independent.

1962 Uganda and Burundi achieve independence.

1963 Organization of African Unity is founded to promote unity among African states.

1963 **Nnamdi Azikiwe** becomes president of the Republic of Nigeria.

1964 **Kenneth Kaunda** becomes president of Zambia.

1964 **Jomo Kenyatta** is inaugurated president of Kenya.

1965 Prime Minister **Ian Douglas Smith** declares Rhodesia's independence from Great Britain to avoid an independence granted by the British that would be based on majority rule.

Julius Nyerere

Jomo Kenyatta and Tom Mboya

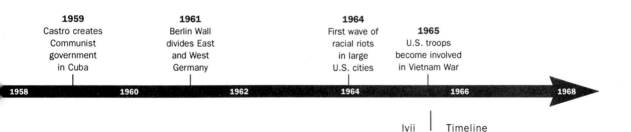

1959
Castro creates Communist government in Cuba

1961
Berlin Wall divides East and West Germany

1964
First wave of racial riots in large U.S. cities

1965
U.S. troops become involved in Vietnam War

| 1958 | 1960 | 1962 | 1964 | 1966 | 1968 |

1966 Nigerian writer **Flora Nwapa** publishes her first novel, *Efuru.*

1966 In a military coup in Nigeria, Prime Minister **Abubakar Tafawa Balewa** is assassinated. Another military coup occurs this year in Ghana.

1966 Hastings Banda becomes president of Malawi.

1966 Sir Seretse Khama becomes president of independent Botswana.

1966 Basutoland becomes independent Lesotho.

1967-70 Civil war erupts in Nigeria. In the second military coup since independence, military officers from the Muslim North overthrow the existing government. A Muslim-dominated government takes over, and tens of thousands of Ibos who live in the North are killed. The federal government announces plans to split the Eastern Region, the home of the Ibo, into three separate states. In response, the Eastern Region secedes and proclaims itself the independent Republic of Biafra. Nigerian troops go into Biafra to put down the rebellion. A two-and-a-half year bloody conflict follows before Biafra falls to federal forces. An estimated one million Biafrans die of starvation because of the food shortages caused by the war.

1967-97 Mobutu Sese Seko establishes himself as president of Congo (Zaire).

1968 Swaziland and Mauritius become independent.

1969 Mozambique nationalist **Eduardo Mondlane** is assassinated.

1969 Kenyan trade unionist **Tom Mboya** is assassinated.

1969 Exiled South African writer **Bessie Head** publishes *When Rain Clouds Gather.*

1971 Idi Amin takes power in Uganda.

Mobutu Sese Seko and troops.

Idi Amin being sworn in.

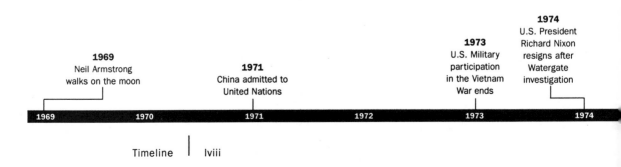

1969
Neil Armstrong walks on the moon

1971
China admitted to United Nations

1973
U.S. Military participation in the Vietnam War ends

1974
U.S. President Richard Nixon resigns after Watergate investigation

1969 1970 1971 1972 1973 1974

1974 A military coup in Portugal ends the fight in Mozambique for independence from Portugal. The Portuguese army—tired of the endless wars they were sent to fight in Africa and desiring a democratic system at home—overthrow the government of Marcello Caetano. The new government in Portugal hold a series of meetings with Mozambique's nationalist leaders and works out a plan for independence.

1974 Ethiopian emperor **Haile Selaisse I** is assassinated.

1975 Mozambique becomes independent.

1976 Soweto, South Africa, erupts in violence as school children demonstrate against the school authorities' decision to use Afrikaans as the language for teaching.

1977 South African authorities banish activist **Winnie Madikizela-Mandela** to Orange Free State for eight years.

1977 South African activist **Steve Biko** dies in police custody.

1977 Kenyan environmentalist **Wangari Maathai** establishes the Green Belt Movement; in years to follow 50,000 people involved in the effort will plant an estimated 10,000,000 trees.

1978 Daniel arap Moi becomes president of Kenya after **Jomo Kenyatta**'s death.

1980 Robert Mugabe becomes prime minister of Zimbabwe, the last of the British colonies in Africa to become independent.

1981 Jerry Rawlings overthrows the elected Ghanaian government in his second coup as Ghana's economy nears collapse.

1984 South African Anglican archbishop **Desmond Tutu** wins Nobel Peace Prize.

1986 Nigerian writer **Wole Soyinka** wins Nobel Prize for literature.

Winnie Madikizela-Mandela.

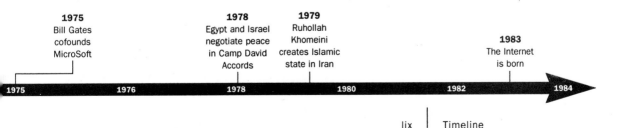

1975
Bill Gates
cofounds
MicroSoft

1978
Egypt and Israel
negotiate peace
in Camp David
Accords

1979
Ruhollah
Khomeini
creates Islamic
state in Iran

1983
The Internet
is born

1975   1976   1978   1980   1982   1984

1986 Joaquim Chissano is named president of Mozambique.

1986 Yoweri Museveni takes over as the head of government in Uganda.

1990 Nelson Mandela is released from prison after 27 years.

1990 The first president of Namibia, **Sam Nujoma,** is sworn in.

1991 Nigerian writer **Ben Okri** wins the Booker Prize.

1991 South African fiction writer **Nadine Gordimer** wins the Nobel Prize for literature.

1992 President **Joaquim Chissano** helps to end the 16-year-long civil war in Mozambique and brings the rebel group headed by Afonso Dhlakama into the government through the country's first multiparty elections.

1993 South Africans **Nelson Mandela** and **Frederick Willem de Klerk** are jointly awarded the Nobel Peace Prize for their efforts to form a democratic, representative government in South Africa.

1994 Nelson Mandela is inaugurated as the first black president of South Africa. His political party, the African National Congress, is elected as the majority in South Africa's parliament.

1996 Ghanaian diplomat **Kofi Annan** is named Secretary General of the United Nations.

1997 Nigerian Afro-Beat singer **Fela Kuti** dies of AIDS.

1998 U.S. embassies in Nairobi, Kenya, and Dar es Salaam, Tanzania, are bombed.

Nelson Mandela and Frederick Willem de Klerk.

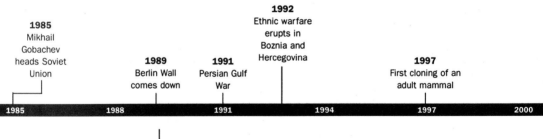

1985
Mikhail Gobachev heads Soviet Union

1989
Berlin Wall comes down

1991
Persian Gulf War

1992
Ethnic warfare erupts in Boznia and Hercegovina

1997
First cloning of an adult mammal

1985   1988   1991   1994   1997   2000

african BIOGRAPHY

Paul Kruger

Born 1825
Bulhoek, Cape Colony (South Africa)
Died 1904
Switzerland

*Military leader and president
of the Republic of the Transvaal*

tephanus Johannes Paulus (Paul) Kruger, a hot-tempered old Boer farmer of few words and odd habits, successfully led his people against the British army in 1880 to restore independence to the Transvaal. (The Boers, or Afrikaners, were Afrikaans-speaking white farmers born in the Dutch colony at Africa's Cape.) Affectionately known as Oom Paul (Uncle Paul), Kruger won election as president of the Transvaal (a former province located in the northeastern section of present-day Republic of South Africa) for four consecutive terms (1883-1900).

In his lifetime Kruger participated in the critical events of his people's history. His family was one of the early Trekboers—people who embarked on what is called the "Great Trek" from the Cape Colony (in what is now South Africa), venturing to the interior in search of land and freedom. Kruger fought the Zulus at Blood River in 1838, triumphed over the British at Majuba in the

"Flinch not and fall not into disbelief . . . for the time is at hand for God's people to be tried in the fire."

—Paul Kruger, in a farewell address to the people of Transvaal

first Boer War (1880-1881), and led his people against the British in the second Boer War (1899-1902). The wars were fought by the British and the Boers for control of the gold-rich Boer republics of the Transvaal and the agricultural Orange River Colony, known today as the Orange Free State. The second Boer War ushered in a new era of brutal fighting tactics. These included a British "scorched-earth" policy (the wholesale destruction of farms, crops and animals). The British also set up concentration camps in which thousands of Boer women and children perished. Boer fighters perfected guerrilla warfare (behind the lines military tactics carried out by volunteers against a regular army) against the invading British army. The war also ended forever the independence of the two Boer republics, the Transvaal and the Orange River Colony. The fight for independence had been Paul Kruger's consuming lifelong interest.

Kruger was born in 1825 to a family of fiercely independent Cape Dutch farmers. His father, Casper Jan Hendrik Kruger, and his mother, Elsie Steyn, had both come from Germany to the Cape in the 1700s. Paul Kruger was one of four children, living with his parents on a remote farm in the Cape Colony. They lived far away from all schools, so Kruger had little formal education. His mother, the better educated of his parents, died when he was only eight. Nevertheless, like most Calvinist (adherents of a religion started by sixteenth-century Protestant reformer John Calvin) Boers of his generation, he was extremely well read in the Bible and frequently compared his life and experiences with those of the Israelites in the Old Testament. (Like the Children of Israel, the Boers believed that they enjoyed God's special favor.)

Family moves north

When Kruger was 10, his father and several other families decided to join one of the great Boer treks into the interior of southern Africa. Their motive was to get beyond the influence of the British colonial government at Cape Town. The English-speakers in the Cape were in the minority, yet they had political power over the majority of Afrikaans-speakers. Under the leadership of Hendrik Potgieter, the group of Boers moved north, across the Orange River, into an area that later became the Orange River Colony and then the Orange Free State. At Vechtkop on August 15, 1836, the tiny group of Boers confronted a hostile army of 6,000

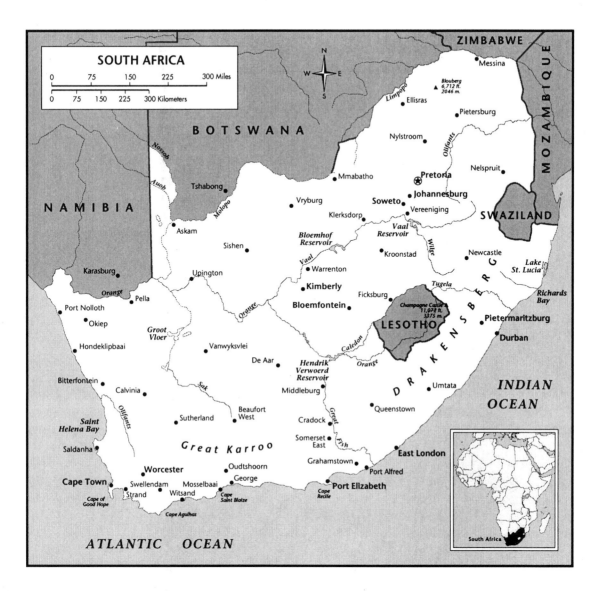

of Ndebele king Mzilikazi's tribesmen and had to fight. Since the Boer group had only 40 adult men, the help of children like Paul Kruger in loading guns was essential. Two Boer men were killed and 14 were wounded in the battle; the Ndebele died by the hundreds and were at last forced to retreat. The Boers interpreted this victory, like the more famous one against Dingane's Zulus at Blood River in 1838, as further signs of God's providence (divine care). The young Kruger stayed on with Potgieter as a cavalry (on horseback) fighter and survived several more desperate encounters against heavy odds.

Eventually Kruger settled at Potchefstroom on the Mooi River. He married Maria du Plessis when he was 17 years old, and they quickly prospered, building up a large herd of cattle. After his first wife died, he married her cousin, Gezina du Plessis. In all Kruger had 16 children—nine boys and seven girls.

Kruger loved to hunt and undertook many daring expeditions. The cranky farmer was undeniably tough. According to biographer John Fisher:

> He escaped being gored by a buffalo by holding its head under water in a swamp, and went on the same day to shoot two others. Once he was pinned to the ground by a white rhinoceros and shot the beast from below. During another rhino-hunt Kruger's gun burst and blew off most of his left thumb. Jumping on his horse, he galloped for his life, pursued by the enraged beast. Later, using turpentine as an antiseptic, he took a knife and cut off the stump of his thumb himself.

Commando campaigns against Africans

Kruger also led Boer commandos when they needed him. Commandos were military units in the Boer's army—the people's army. Each commando had between 500 and 2,000 men and elected its own civilian (nonmilitary) leader. They did not train to fight; rather, they fought as they knew how—on horseback and according to their own instincts. The commandant-general of the regular army supplied them with guns and ammunition and helped to coordinate strategy. Kruger showed himself a cool and capable fighter in the continuing wars against the native Africans, who resisted fiercely the takeover of their land by the Boers. He distinguished himself in an 1854 commando campaign against Langa chief Mankopane, risking enemy rifle fire to get the body of his slain general and prevent it from being mutilated. Kruger's people regarded themselves as the racial superiors of the Africans they were displacing. These nineteenth-century Boer sentiments laid the foundations for the apartheid system of segregation that would later polarize race relations in South Africa for 40 years.

The Transvaal gained its independence from Great Britain in 1852 and called itself the South African Republic; the Orange River Colony was declared independent two years later. At the time the Boers had not developed a sense of Boer or Afrikaner nationalism (devotion to their republics). Most Boer farmers hated interference from any authority, and, without the unity of a central authority, rival political factions (groups with opposing interests) soon developed among them. A shooting war between two rival groups nearly broke out in 1857 when M. W. Pretorius claimed authority over all the land between the Orange and Vaal rivers. Kruger stepped in and prevented an armed clash between Pretorius and his rival, Stephanus Schoeman. To prevent further conflicts over authority, the Boers wrote down rules in a constitution in 1859. W. A. DeKlerk, writing in *The Puritans in Africa,* describes the government in the Transvaal as "an amateur road show, meeting here and there, with not much to do, because there was no money."

British declare Transvaal a colony

Warfare between African tribes and the Boers continued throughout the 1850s and 1860s. The 1870 British annexation (adding on to its empire) of diamond-rich Griqualand West (later the site of the Kimberley diamond mines) confirmed that Britain was still a key player in the race to dominate the area. Britain's colonial secretary Lord Carnarvon was eager to unite the Boer republics with the British colonies of Natal and Cape Colony. He anticipated further diamond finds and wanted to establish Britain's claim to the wealth. Carnarvon sent his agent, Theophilus Shepstone, to propose a union with the Transvaal in 1874. Most of the Boers are said to have treated Shepstone with the suspicion they usually turned on outsiders. In 1877, though, Shepstone claimed that the majority of the people favored an alliance with Queen Victoria and sought British protection. He raised the British flag and declared the Transvaal a British colony, without a fight from Transvaal president T. F. Burgers.

In response to the annexation, Kruger, who had become vice president of the Transvaal, led a protest deputation (a group of representatives) to London, but the British government would not take him seriously. The class-conscious, traditional-minded British press ridiculed him as a primitive country bumpkin and made fun of his rustic ways. Returning to the Transvaal, Kruger led a Boer meeting at Wonderfontein in 1879 at which the opponents of annexation swore to regain their freedom. In light of these events, the late 1870s saw the dawning of a new Afrikaner nationalism. Cape Colony minister Stephanus Jacobus du Toit founded the Fellowship of True Afrikaners in 1875 and an Afrikaans-

Armed Boers in South Africa.

language newspaper—the first of its kind—the following year. Du Toit also established the Afrikaner Bond, a region-wide political party favoring confederation of the four provinces (Cape, Natal, Orange Free State, and Transvaal), but only if complete independence from Britain accompanied it.

The British were preoccupied with a war against the Zulus in 1879 and underestimated Kruger's steadfast determination. In 1880, following the Wonderfontein meeting, the Transvaal Boers declared the Transvaal independent and created a three-person provisional government consisting of Kruger, Piet Joubert, and Pretorius. Despite a shortage of ammunition, they made good on their declaration of independence by defeating a British army column at the battle of Bronkhorstspruit. A second line of British soldiers—overconfident and poorly led—also failed to defeat the Boers at Majuba Hill in early 1881. They lost 300 men in a humiliating defeat. Kruger triumphed: the Transvaal regained its independence, at least for the time being, and London recognized its independence in an 1881 treaty. This marked the end of the first Boer War. When the Majuba campaign was over, Kruger was elected president for the first of four consecutive terms (in 1883, 1888, 1893, and 1898).

Diamonds and gold

As long as the interior of South Africa offered only the prospect for farming and herding, the British were willing to leave it and its Boer inhabitants alone. But the discovery of diamonds on the Vaal River and gold at Johannesburg changed the situation, making the Orange Free State and the Transvaal highly desirable territories. (Johannesburg is the largest, most industrialized city in the present-day Republic of South Africa. Located in the country's northeastern section, Johannesburg was founded in 1886 after gold was discovered there.) The British knew that their imperial rivals, France and Germany, also had their eyes on these prizes. The late 1880s and early 1890s witnessed a huge surge of miners to the Witwatersrand (White Water Range) of the Transvaal, comparable to the California gold rush of 1849. Although the mining community came from all over the world, Britons and Americans were the most numerous participants.

The miners' relationship with the Calvinist Boer farmers was uneasy from the start. The Boers called the miners *uitlanders* ("outsiders") and took advantage of their lucrative business to tax them heavily without offering any corresponding political benefits.

The dominant figure in the development of the diamond and gold mines was British industrialist Cecil Rhodes. Rhodes made his fortune in diamonds and used his money to buy up gold fields. Entering politics, Rhodes was elected prime minister of the British Cape Colony in 1890. He and Kruger—Rhodes representing imperial interests (the interests of Britain) and Kruger representing the interests of his people—came up against each other in the 1890s. Kruger was determined to avoid a second annexation by Britain and equally determined to prevent the contamination of his Bible-fearing fundamentalist republic by Rhodes's uitlanders. (Calvinists stressed a strict adherence to the writings in the Bible and believed in predestination, the concept that a person's fate—either eternal damnation in hell or salvation in heaven—is willed by God and sealed at birth.) The Transvaal parliament passed legislation that deprived nearly all the uitlanders of a political voice. Parliamentary members also granted monopoly (exclusive) rights to their own relatives and neighbors for the sale of alcohol, dynamite, mining supplies, and even water. The monopolists charged the miners unfair prices, thus interfering with the development of their mines and communications network.

Kruger's Boer friends welcomed these actions. They did nothing to dim his mystique, which had already reached almost legendary proportions. As president, he lived in a simple house in Pretoria with a corrugated iron roof. He spent part of every day sitting on his porch on a rocking chair, smoking his enormous pipe, and inviting anyone with news, business—or just an eagerness to talk—to sit with him. He wore baggy black suits, readily displayed a dry, understated sense of humor, and had the habit of emphasizing what he said by spitting on the ground when he had finished speaking. His wife milked the cows herself, the family attended church every Sunday, and Kruger often preached the sermon. On the Sabbath Kruger never discussed political business, and nearly every day he was in bed by eight o'clock in the evening.

The mining companies strongly objected to Kruger's taxes and revived their hopes of relief through a British takeover. In an effort to prevent the Transvaal from expanding further, the British government and Rhodes's company annexed its neighboring territories (now Botswana and Zimbabwe) and Zululand in 1887. Kruger responded by building a railway east into Portuguese Mozambique to reach the Indian Ocean at Lourenço Marques (Maputo). He also offered enticing deals to traders along this route. The rail link was completed in the mid-1890s.

At this point Transvaal was nearly encircled by British territory and becoming more and more isolated. Kruger then sought to create an alliance with Germany. Chancellor Otto von Bismarck (chancellor 1871-90) had recently unified Germany, which was the most rapidly rising power in Europe. When a Conservative party (a party whose members favor tradition over change) government came to power in Britain in 1895, its colonial office conspired with Cecil Rhodes to overthrow Kruger. The plan failed, causing Britain intense diplomatic embarrassment and Rhodes's resignation as premier of the Cape.

The second Boer War begins

Still, the British government remained eager to gain full control in the Transvaal. Sir Alfred Milner, the new high commis-

Cecil John Rhodes was a British business magnate, imperialist, and politician who made a vast impact in the southern regions of Africa as he grew wealthy on its resources. The son of a clergyman, Rhodes first went to South Africa at the age of seventeen to join his brother there. The next year, in 1871, the two brothers staked a claim in the Kimberley diamond fields, which had just been opened. Rhodes would make most of his vast fortune in these diamond mines. By 1880, he had formed the De Beers Mining Company, the second largest company of its type in the industry, and by 1888, through skillful mergers, he had secured a monopoly over the Kimberley diamond production.

For many years Rhodes traveled back and forth from England to Africa. By 1875 he had developed a vision of British rule over all of southern Africa, and later he would advocate British rule of the whole continent. With this political outlook, in 1881 he entered the parliament of Cape Colony; he would become prime minister in 1890. In this role he persuaded the British government to establish a protectorate over Bechuanaland and, after tricking Matabele King Lobengula (see entry) into granting him mining rights, organized the British South Africa Company, which established control over the area now known as Zimbabwe.

Rhodes sympathized with the English uitlanders in the Transvaal and sought to overthrow Paul Kruger's government there. He was involved in the Jameson Raid against the Afrikaners in 1895, and because of this, the British government forced him to resign as prime minister of Cape Colony. After that, he focused on Zimbabwe, or Rhodesia as it was then called in his honor. When he died in South Africa, Rhodes left most of his huge fortune to public causes. He is probably best known today for the Rhodes Scholarships to Oxford, which provide 170 scholarships for students from former British colonies, the United States, and Germany.

sioner for South Africa, was even more determined than Rhodes had been to curb Kruger's independence. He did all he could to energize the mining community against the Boer government. Kruger reacted quickly, imposing censorship (restrictions) on the English language press, expelling some aliens (citizens of foreign countries) without trial, and preventing some categories of uitlanders from entering Johannesburg at all.

In May 1899 Milner and Kruger held a dramatic conference in Bloemfontein, the capital of the Orange Free State, but each made demands that the other found impossible to accept. Recognizing that these tensions could lead to war, Milner urged the colonial office to reinforce the British military post in South Africa. Before extra troops arrived, however, Kruger (age 74 at the time) and his allies in the Orange Free State attacked the isolated British settlements in Natal and Cape Colony. In this way, in October 1899, the second Boer War began.

Many of Kruger's rivals and opponents had underestimated his political and military know-how. In fact, he had outwitted all of them. His mobile farmer-troops, the commandos, were some of the most gifted cavalry in the history of warfare. They continued to block the efforts of the British forces for almost three years. The Boer armies, however, were not well coordinated. Soldiers came and went from their units at pleasure rather than following orders from a centralized headquarters.

Forced into exile

The war was fought in three phases. At first the Boers had the upper hand. They occupied the northern districts of Natal and surrounded Ladysmith. As they invaded the Cape midlands, sympathetic Boers joined their ranks. In the West they surrounded British military posts at Mafeking and Kimberley, but by May 1900 British forces led by Lord Roberts had sprung into action, freeing the besieged cities. The British then counterattacked by invading the Transvaal and Orange Free State and taking control of the entire railway system. Supporters urged the aging and sick Kruger to escape rather than be captured. He fled through Mozambique and went to the Netherlands. In a farewell address Kruger urged that his people "flinch not and fall not into disbelief . . . for the time is at hand for God's people to be tried in the fire."

Despite these British victories, the war did not end. The desperate Boer commandos continued to fight an unconventional guerrilla war. A series of unexpected commando attacks on the British forces' line of communication throughout 1900 and 1901 enraged the new British commander, Lord Kitchener. He decided to attack the Boers' resources as well as their forces by burning crops and houses and rounding up Boer families into concentration camps. The entire population was persecuted in the pursuit of Kitchener's objectives. Conditions in the concentration camps were horrible—28,000 Boers, most of them under the age of 16, died of diseases and malnutrition there.

In March 1902, the Treaty of Vereeniging finally brought the war to an end, though Kruger was not there to witness it. Many modern-day British historians see it as one of the most disgraceful episodes in Britain's imperial history, but at the time it provided a welcome peace. Only a few British, such as future Liberal prime minister David Lloyd George, spoke out against the war in general and the concentration camp policy in particular. South Africa became a key part of the British empire, the mines resumed their operation under more favorable terms, and all but a minority of Boers came to terms with the new political situation.

Kruger spent his last years in Holland and Switzerland. His second wife died in Pretoria in his absence, and he died in 1904—by this time a very disillusioned man. Authorities shipped his body back to South Africa and buried him in Pretoria. His funeral procession symbolized the Afrikaners' determination to maintain their culture, their unity, and their determination, even if they had lost their political independence.

Further Reading

Davenport, T. R. H. *South Africa: A Modern History.* Toronto, Ontario, Canada: University of Toronto Press, 1987.

DeKlerk, W. A. *The Puritans in Africa.* Rex Collings, 1975.

Fisher, John. *The Afrikaners.* Cassell, 1969.

Fisher, John. "Paul Kruger." In *Historic World Leaders.* Edited by Anne Commire. Volume 1. Detroit: Gale, 1994.

Meintjes, Johannes. *President Paul Kruger.* Cassell, 1974.

Pakenham, Thomas. *The Boer War.* Macdonald, 1982.

Thompson, Leonard. *History of South Africa.* New Haven, CT: Yale University Press, 1990.

Wilson, Monica, and Leonard Thompson, eds. *The Oxford History of South Africa.* New York: Clarendon Press, 1971.

Fela Kuti

Born October 15, 1938
Abeokuta, Nigeria
Died August 2, 1997
Lagos, Nigeria

Musician, activist, and rebel

"America needs to hear some good sounds from Africa, man. . . . The sanity of the world is going to be generated from Africa through art. Art itself is knowledge of the spiritual world. Art is information from higher sources."

—Fela Kuti, quoted during a tour of the United States

n innovative musician and renowned rebel, Fela Kuti created a new musical style celebrated throughout the world as Afro-Beat. He also battled Nigeria's military dictators, toppled social conventions, and strutted as his country's most outrageous showman. His passing in 1997 carried special significance, since Kuti was the first Nigerian publicly acknowledged to have died of AIDS (acquired immunodeficiency syndrome). Prior to his death, Nigerian officials covered up the nation's high number of HIV-positive cases (people whose blood tests positive for antibodies to the human immunodeficiency virus [HIV], which often leads to AIDS), ignoring the need to educate the country's 100 million people about the deadly disease and its principal methods of transmission. (AIDS is transmitted primarily through unsafe sex with an infected person and through intravenous drug use with contaminated—usually shared—needles. As of 1998 neither a cure for AIDS nor a vaccine against HIV had yet been developed.) Shortly after Kuti's death, health officials admitted that 2.25 million Nigerians were HIV-infected and that the disease was spreading at "an alarming rate" in Africa's most populous country.

Mixture of Jazz and African music

Kuti's chief musical legacy lies in the creation of Afro-Beat, a fusion of jazz and African rhythmic influences. Afro-Beat is marked by pulsating horns and a mingling of lyrics in both the native Yoruba language and so-called "pidgin" English, a combination of English and indigenous (native to the land) languages spoken by many Nigerians. Kuti's lyrics talked of the problems of African men ("Why Black Man Dey Suffer"), greedy politicians ("zombies" in his lyrics), and corrupt dictatorship ("Government of Crooks"). Sometimes his songs lasted more than an hour.

Although Kuti's exact output is still unknown, music experts estimate that he produced about 77 albums with 133 songs. At his death, his family held eight unreleased Kuti compositions. Some musicians take several years to put out a single album. Kuti claimed he could finish three albums in two weeks. "I'm playing deep African music," he told one interviewer. "The rhythm, the sounds, the tonality, the chord sequences, the individual effect of each instrument and each section of the band—I'm talking about a whole continent in my music."

London journalist Robin Denselow knew Kuti well and attended his performances in the Lagos, Nigeria, suburb of Ikeja. He described the environment:

> The best place to hear Kuti's blend of firebrand politics and musical invention was his own, much raided-club, The Shrine. . . . By the time he arrived—often around two or three in the morning—the crowds were already crammed around the stage, packed between the corrugated iron walls, the wooden cages holding Kuti's scantily clad dancers. . . . The air was heavy with marijuana when Kuti finally appeared, invariably puffing a joint as he launched into his angry attacks on the military or corruption in Nigerian society; on problems of Lagos traffic; on the economic systems that lead to African poverty. His songs mixed thunderous percussion, lengthy improvised solos from Kuti himself on keyboards and saxophone, and passages of call-and-response vocals in which he was answered back by his well-choreographed female chorus of 20 or more.

The Ransome-Kuti family

Fela Ransome-Kuti was born October 15, 1938, at Abeokuta, a town about 30 miles northwest of Lagos. The famous Ransome-Kuti family was Yoruba, Anglican, well educated, independent minded, business oriented, and musically talented. Fela Kuti's grandfather, the Reverend Canon J. J. Ransome-Kuti, was known as the "Singing Minister." Fela's mother, Chief Olufunmilayo Ransome-Kuti (1900-1978; see entry), studied music at Wincham Hall College in Manchester, England, and was an aggressive advocate of women's rights and socialism. (Socialism is a political and economic system based on government control of property and jobs.) The Reverend Israel Oludotun Ransome-Kuti, Fela's father, was a prominent church leader and educator in Nigeria. Fela's brothers, Beko and Olikoye, are both medical doctors and human rights activists seeking to end military dictatorship in their homeland.

In 1951 Kuti completed his secondary education at Abeokuta Grammar School, an institution owned and operated by his parents. He took a colonial government job in Lagos until 1958. His parents wanted him to become a physician like his brothers. In 1959 he set off for London with a grant to study medicine, but he ended up entering Trinity Music College instead and studying trumpet, piano, and voice. While in London, Kuti played in jazz bands and met prominent local musicians. He started his own band, Koola Lobitos, his very first year abroad. And in 1961 he married Remi Taylor. They had three sons and three daughters.

Music changed, ideas changed

Graduating from Trinity in 1962, Kuti returned home two years after Nigeria gained independence from Britain. He began a series of musical experiments, mixing jazz, African Highlife, and traditional music forms until his distinctive Afro-Beat emerged. In 1969 Kuti took his band on tour to the United States. The tour flopped, but it changed his life. He met members of the Black Panther party and was exposed to the ideas of other black power advocates and civil rights leaders in the States. He was especially influenced by the writings of African American activist Malcolm X. When Kuti returned to Nigeria, he was a staunch Pan-Africanist, meaning he supported the idea of a united Africa. To demonstrate his newly acquired philosophy, he changed the name of his band from Nigeria 70 to Africa 70; then, in 1982 he switched the band's name once more—this time to Egypt 80, explaining in a WUSB-radio interview: "It's just to make my people, the Africans, realize that the Egyptian civilization belongs to the African man."

As Kuti's new musical style and radical political ideas took shape in the 1960s and 1970s, Nigeria saw the assassination of its first head of state, fought the Biafran civil war (1967-70) that killed a million Nigerians, and existed under a series of military dictatorships. From the time of independence, Nigeria's political leaders were interested in nurturing and centralizing their own national power; in other words, they were decidedly opposed to the Pan-Africanism espoused by Kuti.

High priest of The Shrine

Kuti set up a communal night club, first known as Africa Spot and later as The Shrine, where hordes of fellow musicians, friends,

hangers-on, and dancers and singers lived a wild life of music, drugs, and sex. Anointing himself chief priest and proprietor and often parading around The Shrine in his underwear, Kuti developed into a singer-composer, a trumpet, saxophone, and keyboard player, a bandleader, and a politician—the virtual head of his own independent country. "It got to be heavy-o," he said, as quoted by *Revolutionary Worker Online.* "I was making eight albums a year.

I was getting very powerful. Very listened to. Very liked. But for the authorities, very daaaaaangerous."

By 1974 Kuti's notorious behavior and his blistering attacks on the "zombie" dictators had drawn the attention of Nigeria's head of state, General Yakubu Gowon, and other military rulers. Authorities raided his club looking for drugs. Police jailed Kuti for the first of several times. He was acquitted of charges of possessing marijuana and abducting young girls. After his release, Kuti installed an electric fence around his club and compound, declaring the territory the independent Kalakuta Republic. He changed his surname from Ransome-Kuti to Anikulapo-Kuti, the new name meaning "he who emanates greatness, who has control over death and who cannot be killed by man."

But Kuti governed his commune in anything but democratic (by the people) fashion. According to John Darnton in the *New York Times:*

> [Fela] ruled over the Kalakuta Republic with an iron hand, settling disputes by holding court and meting out sentences—cane lashings for men and tin shed 'jail' for women in the backyard. . . .To some degree, these trappings of power account for his popularity among authority-conscious Nigerians. . . . Stories abound of his setting fire to hotel rooms, . . . firing penniless band members on overseas gigs, making interviewers cool their heels for days and then receiving them in his underwear.

His republic burned

On February 18, 1977, soldiers of General Olusegun Obasanjo, then the latest in a series of Nigerian military rulers, destroyed the Kalakuta Republic. The attackers threw Olufunmilayo Ransome-Kuti, Kuti's 78-year-old mother, out a second-floor window, causing injuries that resulted in her death several months later. The soldiers beat Kuti and others in the compound and sent them to jail or to the hospital. Kuti contended that his singers and dancers had been raped. He sued for damages, only to be charged himself with damaging an army motorcycle.

Kuti went into self-imposed exile in neighboring Ghana, where he soon encountered trouble with authorities for supporting students rebelling against dictator Ignatius Acheampong. So Kuti returned to Nigeria in 1978 and kicked up his showmanship a few notches. He married all 27 women dancers and singers in his troupe as a bold protest against the Westernization of African culture. ("The West" refers broadly to the United States and Europe, where, unlike most of Africa, polygamy, or having more than one spouse, is illegal.)

In 1979, when General Obasanjo turned military rule over to civilian (nonmilitary) authorities in anticipation of national elections, Kuti presented the outgoing military regime with a replica of his mother's coffin. He also formed the Movement of the People and announced his candidacy for the presidency of Nigeria. His party failed to win recognition, however, thus dooming his presidential bid.

Legal troubles

Kuti had established himself as an international star by 1984, when he was embarking on a major U.S. tour. But that tour was canceled after the Nigerian government arrested Kuti on charges of changing money illegally. He was once again facing a military-run government that had been reestablished in Nigeria in 1983. Kuti was convicted by a military tribunal (court) and sentenced to 10 years in prison. He spent 20 months in jail, asserting that he knew full well his country's latest regime "didn't want us to go to the U.S. to play," but maintaining that he "never expected them to do anything as low as this." The London-based human rights organization Amnesty International then declared Kuti a "political prisoner."

When another general, Ibrahim Babangida, took control of Nigeria in 1985, he released Kuti from prison. The judge who had sentenced Kuti later claimed he had done so under pressure from the previous regime (government). Kuti celebrated his release by performing at an Amnesty International fund-raising show in New Jersey in 1986. Upon his release, he also admitted that his marriage to the 27 women was a bad idea. (He ended up divorcing them.)

In 1991 Kuti returned to the United States to perform at New York City's Apollo Theater accompanied by 30 support players. "America needs to hear some good sounds from Africa, man," he once said. "The sanity of the world is going to be generated from Africa through art. Art itself is knowledge of the spiritual world. Art is information from higher sources."

Spirits take over

Despite his growing international audience, Kuti continued to encounter trouble with Nigerian authorities. He was jailed on a murder charge in 1993 after an electrician died at The Shrine. The charge was eventually dropped. Three years later he was jailed again on drug charges. The Nigerian Drug Law Enforcement Agency closed The Shrine in 1997.

"He remained a rebel and a maverick right to the end, but in recent years there were signs that he tired of battling with military authorities," recalled Denselow in a Guardian News Service report. "When I visited his hippy commune of a home in Ikeja in late 1994 he told me he was more interested in religion than politics. He refused to sign a new recording deal with Motown's Tabu label, saying he had been 'told by the spirits' that the time was not right. And when he was found unconscious in July of this year [1997] he refused to eat, or even [to] let a doctor examine him . . . 'for religious reasons.'"

Fela Kuti died on August 2, 1997. His oldest son, Femi, a part of The Shrine band for many years, is expected to preserve and continue his father's musical history. Two days after Kuti died, USAfrica publisher Chido Nwangwu gave the elder Kuti a parting salute:

> His courage to speak the truth, his strong, unvarnished views to the face of power and 'all dem oppressors' will be missed by millions of other Africans and people of the world. He remained a tower of guts, even while his pants were barely on!

Further Reading

Contemporary Musicians. Volume 7. Detroit: Gale, 1992.

Makers of Modern Africa: Profiles in History. 3rd. ed. Africa Books, 1996.

New York Times, *July 24, 1977; November 7, 1986.*

Nwangwu, Chido. "USAfrica: The Newspaper." USAfrica ONLINE. www.usafricaonline.com, August 4, 1997.

"Revolutionary Worker Online." www.msc.net.rwor, #920, August 17, 1997.

Additional information for this entry was taken from a Guardian News Service report by Robin Denselow dated August 5, 1997, and from a WUSB 90.1 FM (Stony Brook, NY) radio broadcast featuring Lister Hewan-Lowe, June 21, 1986.

Lalibela

Born sometime after 1150
Roha, Wollo province, Ethiopia
Died c. 1225
Ethiopia

Emperor of Ethiopia

alibela was the mastermind behind Ethiopia's most enduring architectural legacy—11 magnificent churches cut from volcanic rock in mountains 8,000 feet high. The rock churches, built more than eight centuries ago in the northern Wollo province, stand today as some of the world's outstanding religious monuments. As emperor from 1182 to 1225, Lalibela kept Ethiopia a Christian territory even as the Islamic crusade swept across Arabia and the Horn of Africa, the northeast region west of the Red Sea. He became a saint in the Ethiopian Coptic church.

Records of Lalibela's ancestors are incomplete and unreliable. He may have been the son of Emperor Zan Seyum, thus a member of the Zagwe dynasty (succession of rulers) that ruled Ethiopia in the twelfth and thirteenth centuries. Born at the town of Roha in Wollo province, his mother named him Lalibela, which means "Bees have acknowledged his supremacy." The name commemorates his survival when at birth a swarm of bees landed on him. As a boy Lalibela claimed he had a vision and heard God's voice telling him to build at Roha (now called Lalibela) the most majestic churches in all of Ethiopia. In order to carry out these instructions, he had to become emperor of the land.

At the time, however, Lalibela's half-brother, Harba, ruled as emperor. Viewing Lalibela as a serious threat to his hold on the Ethiopian throne, Harba did everything he could to make his rival's life miserable. In early manhood Lalibela fled to the mountains in Ethiopia's northern Tigre province to escape persecution by Harba. There Lalibela met Masqal Kebra, described as a devout and gentle woman, and married her.

The Pope's interest in Prester John

Christian rulers in twelfth-century Europe believed in the existence of the legendary Prester John, a powerful Christian king who presided over a vast, rich kingdom located south of the Islamic belt in black Africa. The hunt for Ethiopia's Prester John contributed to the discovery of America and the sea route around southern Africa to the Orient.

Around 1180 Lalibela made a pilgrimage (a religious journey), probably traveling through Egypt, to Jerusalem, which was still in the hands of the Christian Crusaders from Europe. (The Crusades, or Holy Wars, were undertaken by European Christians between the eleventh and thirteenth centuries to reclaim the Holy Land from the Muslims.) Earlier, Pope Alexander III (1159-1181) sent his personal physician, Master Philip, to seek Prester John. The pope hoped the mythical priest-king could be persuaded to come to the aid of European Christians whose shaky hold on the Holy Land was being threatened by Islamic armies. No one knew exactly where the physician went, since no one knew where to find Prester John. Master Philip disappeared, never to be seen again.

If Philip had traveled to Ethiopia in search of Prester John, it would not be surprising that he did not return. Ethiopians, fearing foreigners would try to take over their country, welcomed them with lavish hospitality—a mansion, servants, and a harem. But foreigners were never allowed to leave Ethiopia for fear they would return with troops and seek to conquer the land.

Around the time of Lalibela's pilgrimage, Emperor Harba is believed to have begun talks with the Christian church based in Rome. According to Ethiopian tradition, Harba sent two missions to papal headquarters to propose an alliance between Ethiopia and Rome. Such a proposal would have surely caused a rebellion among leaders of the Ethiopian church: the Coptics had split from the European churches in A.D. 451 in a dispute over the nature of Christ. Churches in Rome and Constantinople (now Turkey) believed Jesus Christ to be both divine (meaning he had come forth directly from God) and human (meaning he had been born of a woman). Christians in Alexandria, Egypt, then the cultural center of the world, disagreed. They thought Jesus Christ was the reincarnation of God and, therefore, in no way human. Out of the dispute rose the Coptic church of Alexandria.

Ethiopia is more than 1,500 miles from Alexandria, but the seeds of Christianity had been planted there long before the debate over Christ's nature arose. Tradition holds that a young Syrian Christian named Frumentius brought Christianity to Ethiopia in the fourth century, when he was shipwrecked off the coast of Africa. Ezana, then ruler of an Ethiopian state, took the stranded Christian in and was eventually converted to the Alexandrian version of Christianity. Ezana is thought to have become emperor of Ethiopia sometime between A.D. 320 and 325. Within 20 years of his conversion, Emperor Ezana was appointed the church's first bishop of Ethiopia by Saint Athanasius of Alexandria (c. 293-373).

God wills him to the throne

When the dispute over Christ's nature erupted in A.D. 451, the Ethiopian Christians—along with Armenians and Syrians, among others—sided with the Alexandria church (which held that Jesus was in no manner human). It is likely, therefore, that Ethiopian church officials were alarmed by Emperor Harba's twelfth-century negotiations toward an alliance with the Christian church in Rome (which held that Jesus was both divine and human). When Lalibela returned from his pilgrimage to the Holy Land in 1180, the region was in turmoil and the future of the kingdom was uncertain. Lalibela saw his chance at the throne. Two years later his half-brother reportedly abdicated (or gave up the throne) in favor of Lalibela, saying it was God's will.

As emperor, Lalibela was called "Gabra Masqal," meaning "Servant of the Cross." The emperor tried to put into practice his

Christian beliefs of voluntary poverty and charity toward all people—except when he had to fight off invaders at his borders or put down upstarts within his kingdom. To insure their support, he endowed church officials with special privileges. His kingdom also may have been protected by an event that took place about six centuries prior to his reign. History tells us that Armah, king of the Aksumite in Abyssinia (as Ethiopia was then known in Arabia), granted asylum (protection) to 100 followers of the prophet Muhammad (c. 570-632) in his early struggles to establish Islam. (Ethiopia's hospitality to strangers remains famous today.) Among those protected by the Ethiopians were two of Muhammad's future wives. The founder of Islam is said to have shown his gratitude by commanding future Islamic warriors "to leave the Abyssinians in peace."

More than 200 years after Lalibela's reign, European fascination with the elusive Prester John remained high. When Portugal's Henry the Navigator (1394-1460) set up a school for geographers and navigators in 1416, his top priority for explorers was to find the Christian king who would aid him in the fight against the Moors, Muslims from northern Africa. (The Moors occupied parts of Portugal and Spain for 800 years, beginning in A.D. 700.) Henry's school set in motion a series of oceanic explorations in the late fifteenth century. These ventures led to Christopher Columbus's expedition across the Atlantic to America in 1492 and Vasco da Gama's 1497 discovery of the route to India around Africa's southern cape.

Architectural vision made in heaven

Lalibela remains best known for the role he played in the construction of Ethiopia's famous rock churches. He claimed that the breathtaking designs were revealed to him in a heavenly vision, and he personally supervised the building process to ensure that the churches were constructed according to plan. Representative of the highest Ethiopian architectural accomplishments, the Lalibela monuments include intricate, honeycombed underground corridors, trenches, stairways, and inner courts—all complete with a water system. More than 1,000 priests work to maintain the churches, which are now threatened by decay because of high tourist traffic. Over five centuries after their completion the structures remain a place of pilgrimage. Lalibela's tomb lies in one of his splendid churches, Biet Golgotha.

Further Reading

Dictionary of African Biography. Volume 1. Algonac, MI: Reference Publications, 1977.

Forbath, Peter. *The River Congo.* New York: Harper, 1977.

Forster, E. M. *Alexandria: A History and a Guide.* Bath Press, 1922.

Gossler, Horst. *Portfolio Lalibela.* Africa Environment and Wildlife, 1996.

The Leakey Family

Louis S. B. Leakey

Born August 7, 1903: Kabete, Kenya
Died October 12, 1951: London, England

Mary Leakey

Born February 6, 1913: London, England
Died December 9, 1996: Nairobi, Kenya

Richard Leakey

Born December 19, 1944: Nairobi, Kenya

*Family of world-renowned archaeologists
working in central Africa*

he Leakey family is in great part responsible for the increased anthropology activity during the late twentieth century. (Anthropology is the study of the way humans have lived and developed over the ages.) Louis and Mary Leakey completed important early excavations—or archaeological "digs," in which they unearthed and studied ancient material remains of past civilizations—at the Olduvai Gorge in the east African country of Tanzania. In the 1970s their middle son, Richard, made equally significant discoveries at Lake Turkana (also known as Lake Rudolf) along the border between Kenya and Ethiopia. The work of this pioneering family of scientists has expanded knowledge of the stages of human evolution and the conditions under which they occurred. As a result of the Leakeys' dedication and perseverance over more than 60 years, the story of the pre-history of human

As a result of the Leakeys' dedication and perseverance over more than 60 years, the story of the pre-history of human beings has revealed itself to be far more ancient and complex than ever before imagined.

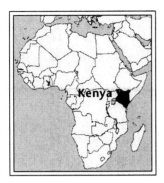

beings has revealed itself to be far more ancient and complex than ever before imagined.

As a result of Louis and Mary Leakey's work, anthropological research shifted from Asia to Africa, and experts came to accept that humanity's evolutionary descent (the development and change of the species through succeeding generations) took much longer than anyone had ever dreamed. Even though their 1959 discovery of *Zinjanthropus,* a humanlike skull some 1.75 million years old, led Louis to draw some conclusions that were later proven incorrect, the discovery is still considered the event that launched the modern scientific study of human origins. Richard Leakey provided the first solid evidence to support his and his father's contention that evolution did not progress in a straight line. Instead they showed it was an overlapping process during which several types of humans and near-humans lived side by side. For these reasons, the Leakey name has become virtually synonymous with (means the same as) the search for, and discovery of, the fossilized remains of the earliest human ancestors.

Louis Leakey uncovers the origins of humans

Louis Seymour Bazett Leakey was the oldest of four children born to Anglican church missionaries Harry and Mary Bazett Leakey on August 7, 1903, in Kabete, a village outside Nairobi, Kenya. He spent his entire childhood and adolescence among members of the Kikuyu people and absorbed their traditions and language to the point that the tribal chief once described him as "the black man with a white face." His early interest in bird-watching gave way to a fascination with archaeology after he came across some stone arrowheads and tools during one of his explorations in the wild.

Leakey later studied archaeology and anthropology at Cambridge University in England. When he was 21 he accompanied a British Museum archaeological expedition to the eastern African region of Tanganyika (now Tanzania). That experience convinced him there was much more to be uncovered in east Africa about the origins of humans. His professors tried to discourage him; at that time, Asia—not Africa—was widely accepted as the birthplace of the human race. But throughout the late 1920s and early 1930s Leakey alternated work on his doctorate at Cambridge with additional field research in east Africa, primarily Kenya.

In 1929 Leakey accidentally stumbled across a 200,000-year-old hand ax that convinced him he was indeed on the right track. A 1931 expedition led him to the remote Olduvai Gorge, an 800-foot-deep, 20-mile-long dry canyon that slices through what was once a shallow lake in northern Tanzania. On Leakey's first day there, he uncovered some prehistoric stone tools and a few fossilized human remains. It was merely a hint of what he might encounter with more serious study. Thus Olduvai Gorge, which would turn out to be one of the richest troves of fossilized human and animal bones in the world, became the center of Leakey's existence for virtually the rest of his life.

Mary Leakey begins archaeological career

During one of his stays in England in 1933, Leakey met a young archaeologist and illustrator named Mary Douglas Nicol. Born in London, England, on February 6, 1913, she was the only child of Cecilia Marion Frere Nicol and Edward Nicol, an artist. Her father'sprofession kept him on the road a great deal, and as a result Mary had a rather unconventional childhood. For example, she did not attend a regular school until she was a teenager. Her father taught her to read, and he also instilled in her a love of ancient relics and monuments. On several occasions while the family was living in southwestern France, she was able to visit various prehistoric caves and excavation sites and view magnificent cave paintings. She even received permission from French archaeologists to sort through objects they had unearthed. It was all Mary needed to persuade her to pursue a career in archaeology.

The collaboration begins

From 1930 until 1934 Mary Nicol served as an assistant to archaeologist Dorothy Liddell at a major Neolithic (a period of history from 8000 to 3500 B.C.E.) site in southern Britain. She typically spent summers in the field and winters attending lectures in geology (the scientific study of the history of the earth as it is recorded in rocks) and archaeology at the University of London and the London Museum. Having inherited a considerable amount of artistic talent from her father, she also began to do some drawings of the stone tools uncovered at the excavation. When the drawings appeared in several scientific publications, they caught the eye of another archaeologist, Gertrude Caton-Thompson, who asked the budding artist to illustrate a book she was writing on Egyptian stone tools. Caton-Thompson subsequently introduced Mary Nicol to Louis Leakey, who also asked for her help with some illustrations for his 1934 book *Adam's Ancestors*.

Despite a 10-year age difference (as well as the fact that Louis was already married to Henrietta Wilfrida Avern [Frida] and the

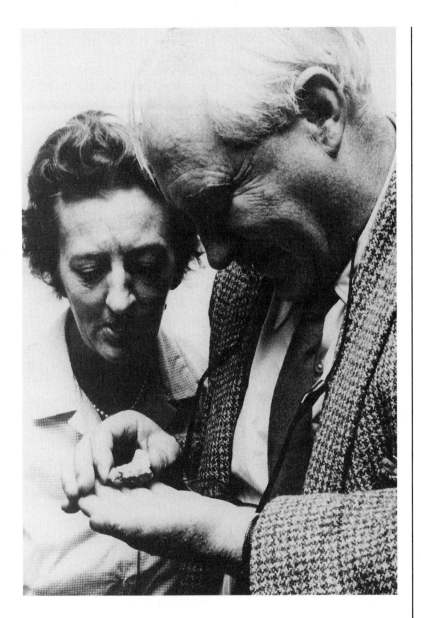

Louis and Mary Leakey examine a piece of bone from a 14-million-year-old creature, 1962.

father of two children), Mary and Louis soon became constant companions. They made their first journey together to Olduvai in April 1935, and in December 1936, after Louis obtained a divorce from Frida, they married and left again for Africa.

The Leakeys conducted excavations at various east African sites until World War II (1939-45) erupted in 1939; Louis Leakey then suspended his fieldwork to serve with the British military intelligence in Nairobi until 1945. Mary continued the excavations on her own throughout the war years. During this time she gave birth to their sons Jonathan and Richard, and to a daughter, Deborah, who died in infancy. (A third son, Philip, was born in 1949.) Mary uncovered thousands of stone tools from various periods, including some that were the oldest known at the time. She also found samples of Iron Age (beginning sometime before 1000 B.C.E.) pottery and the bones of numerous, unusual extinct animals, but she unearthed no human remains.

Makes revolutionary find

After the war Louis Leakey was named full-time director of the Coryndon Museum in Nairobi, leaving him with only a few weeks each year to devote to excavating Olduvai. Funds were a problem, too, since research grants for such work were scarce. Then, in 1948, while digging at a site on the island of Rusing in Lake Victoria, Mary discovered a fossilized skull and other bones that turned out to be those of an apelike creature between 25 and 40 million years old. Called *Proconsul africanus,* it had humanlike jaws and teeth and walked on its hind legs. The first significant find to suggest that humans may have originated in east Africa, this discovery focused world attention on the Leakeys and encouraged them to begin digging in earnest at Olduvai around 1952.

Seven years later, on July 17, 1959 (a day when Louis was ill and resting in his tent), Mary spotted some fossilized molars or back teeth protruding from a small slope. Days of painstaking excavation with dental picks and brushes followed, uncovering a complete, humanlike skull some 1.75 million years old—nearly twice as old as scientists had estimated the human species' age to be. Because Louis initially believed the remains to be a distinct, new form of hominid (upright walking human ancestors), he gave it the name *Zinjanthropus,* or "East Africa man." He also proclaimed that he and his wife had found the long-sought missing link between the more apelike *Australopithecus* (discovered some years before in South Africa) and modern human beings. This was later shown to be incorrect—*Zinjanthropus* is now regarded as another form of *Australopithecus* and has been renamed accordingly. Because of its age, however, the *Zinjanthropus* remains a revolutionary find.

Another revolutionary find

The publicity resulting from the *Zinjanthropus* discovery brought the Leakeys worldwide acclaim as well as much-needed funding from the National Geographic Society, which allowed them to live and work at Olduvai on a year-round basis. In 1960 and 1962 they unearthed fossil fragments, a skull, and some tools of a new species they named *Homo habilis,* or "handy man," in recognition of the fact that he made tools. More humanlike than *Zinjanthropus* but of roughly the same age, *Homo habilis* was at that time considered the earliest known ancestor of the genus (or biological classification) *Homo. Homo* includes the later *Homo erectus* and modern *Homo sapiens,* our own species. Also in 1962, at an excavation site 40 miles east of Lake Victoria, Louis discovered a 14-million-year-old fragment of jaw and teeth belonging to an apelike creature similar to Mary's *Proconsul* find. He called it *Kenyapithecus* (also known as *Ramapithecus*).

By the mid-1960s the Leakeys felt they had assembled enough evidence to prove that early humans had existed in Africa at least 2 million years ago—and perhaps as many as 14 million years ago. Louis Leakey created a controversy in the archaeological world by stating that, contrary to the scientific opinion of the day, different strains of *Homo sapiens* and near-human species had existed side by side in the same time frame. Throughout the remainder of the 1960s, Leakey spent more and more of his time away from Olduvai on lecture tours, driving himself at such a furious pace that it affected his health. In 1964 he organized a team in the United States to excavate near the Calico Mountains in southern California. He and his team discovered evidence that humans lived in America more than 50,000 years ago.

He also began making some unproven claims that Mary, who was always the more conservative scientist of the pair, found difficult to support. And he was growing estranged from his middle son, Richard, the only child who showed any interest in carrying on the family's research. No longer physically able to work in the field after surgery for an arthritic hip in 1968, Louis remained active on the lecture circuit. While in London for a speaking engagement in 1972, he suffered a fatal heart attack.

Richard Leakey joins in the field

While Mary carried on the research at Olduvai, Richard Erskine Frere Leakey was starting to generate some headlines of his own. Born in Nairobi on December 19, 1944, he had since infancy accompanied his parents on various excavations. As a youngster he was able to identify fossils and rattle off appropriate anthropological jargon at will. While the subject fascinated Richard, he had no interest in trying to make a name for himself in the same field as his strong-willed father. Nor did he have any desire to go to college and study something else. So he dropped out of high school and found work as a safari guide. (He already had years of experience escorting scientific visitors around Olduvai.)

Within just a few years Richard was making an excellent living but was thoroughly bored with the work. After quitting the safari business around 1963, he started doing some excavation in northeastern Tanzania and unearthed the lower jaw of an *Australopithecus*. Realizing that if he truly wanted to pursue anthropology he needed to broaden his background, Richard went to London to complete two years of high school in seven months. He then passed his university entrance exams but ran out of money before he could start classes. So he returned to Kenya and concentrated on gaining his education in the field.

Carrying on the family tradition

In 1967 Richard joined an expedition his father had organized in southern Ethiopia, not far from the border of Kenya. While piloting his plane around the area, he spotted a desolate stretch of land along the shores of Lake Turkana in northern Kenya. He thought the spot looked like a promising place for some research. Accompanying his father to a business meeting with the National Geographic Society in 1968, the brash 23-year-old asked for funds so he could investigate the site. The committee agreed, and before the end of the year Richard was established at Turkana in a camp named Koobi Fora, which has turned out to be what one newspaper reporter called "an anthropological mother lode," even richer than Olduvai.

Almost immediately the young and ambitious Leakey found a wealth of fossil evidence suggesting life had thrived in the Turkana area at least 4 million years ago. At first he and his team uncovered only animal bones, but then they located *Australopithecus* jaw fragments and a skull. Finally they found some crude tools about 2.6 million years old that had not been made by the vegetarian *Australopithecus* but by a more humanlike hunting hominid alive in the same area at the same time. In 1971 Richard discovered the remains of *Homo habilis,* which supported the theory that this humanlike creature existed alongside the apelike *Australopithecus*. More proof of the theory surfaced in 1972 with the discovery of a *Homo habilis* skull called "1470" (after its registration number). It was eventually determined to be 1.9 million years old. Richard's find was the oldest *Homo habilis* specimen at that time, making it a revolutionary discovery that rivaled his mother's *Zinjanthropus* in importance. Based on what he had uncovered at Turkana, Richard concluded that at least three kinds of early humanlike species coexisted in east Africa approximately 2 to 3 million years ago: *Homo habilis* and two varieties of *Australopithecus*.

Recognition and resentment

Richard Leakey's discoveries brought him instant acclaim and placed him in the company of the leading researchers of the origins of humans. His success led to resentment on the part of some academically trained anthropologists, who looked on him as an untrained upstart. Richard's fame also strained relations with his father, who had dominated African anthropology for so many years. Their feud ended just a few days before Louis Leakey's death in 1972, after he paid a visit to Turkana and expressed genuine excitement and pride at Richard's 1470 find and predicted even greater achievements for him in the future.

Since his big discovery, Richard Leakey has uncovered more evidence at Turkana that several varieties of early humans coexisted there. In 1975, for example, in a layer of deposits that had already given up some *Australopithecus* remains, he found a *Homo erectus* skull approximately 1.5 million years old. Richard's hope is that anthropologists will one day be able to demonstrate a common origin for humans and thus put superficial differences between people, such as skin color, into proper perspective.

Mary Leakey continues her work

Throughout the 1970s and into the early 1980s, Mary Leakey continued her work at Olduvai and gradually emerged from behind her husband's shadow to become a popular speaker and fund-raiser in her own right. She also made another exciting and significant discovery in 1978 when she came upon a beautifully preserved stretch of hominid footprints—apparently of two adults and a child—at Laetoli on the Serengeti Plain in Tanzania, about

Mary Leakey presents a skull to Tanzanian President Julius Nyerere (see entry) in 1965.

30 miles south of Olduvai. Nearby excavations at the same level as the footprints unearthed human fossils dating back some 3.5 million years and similar to the well-known "Lucy" skeleton (properly known as *Australopithecus afarensis*). Also about 3.5 million years old, Lucy was discovered in Ethiopia in 1974 by Donald Johanson. Anthropologists are still arguing over whether the bones at each site represent one or two species.

Richard Leakey heads wildlife agency

In 1982 Mary Leakey lost the vision in one of her eyes, prompting her to cut back on research in the field. She eventually turned over the Olduvai Gorge camp to the Tanzanian Department of Antiquities and moved to Nairobi, where she died on December 9, 1996. Richard, meanwhile, gave over much of the research at Turkana to his wife, Maeve Epps, and focused his efforts on another Leakey tradition: conservation work. Not long after his 21-year tenure (term of office) as director of the National Museums of Kenya ended in 1989, the lifelong environmental activist was named head of the Kenya Department of Wildlife Services. He cracked down on corruption in the agency that allowed poaching (killing or taking wild animals illegally) to flourish, taking a major step toward preserving the endangered elephant population. He also sought to revitalize the country's wildlife parks and do a better job of attracting and spending tourist dollars.

Leakeys divided by political conflict

In 1994 Richard lost both of his legs in an airplane crash and now walks on artificial limbs. This was not his first brush with death. During the late 1970s, when Richard was near death from kidney disease, his brother Philip (who had not spoken to Richard for nearly 10 years) gave him a lifesaving kidney. Richard's tenure as director of the Kenya Department of Wildlife Services ended with his resignation in 1994, after five years of conflict with the Kenyan government (which he accused of being corrupt).

Richard Leakey has since become involved in a democratic movement in Kenya—the newly formed Safina party (Safina is the Swahili term for Noah's Ark)—placing himself in yet another dangerous situation in a highly volatile political climate. As an environmentalist, he made political enemies among both black and white members of the ruling party led by Kenyan president Daniel arap Moi (see entry). While Richard's campaign for democratic reforms is supported by some black and some white Kenyans, his movements are closely monitored by government security forces. And his activities have once again put him at odds with Philip, who was the first white member of the Kenyan parliament and one of Richard's most vocal opponents. A few weeks before the December 1997 presidential and parliamentary elections, the government gave Safina permission to run candidates. Safina won four seats out of 222. Although Richard Leakey did not win in his district, the party appointed him to a seat and he took up his new role as a member of the Kenyan parliament.

The search continues

Anthropologists continue to search for the true origins of the human species. In January 1991, for example, scientists working in Ethiopia reported finding an older version of a "Lucy" who walked upright, dating back 4 million years. Thus, known human origins were pushed back at least another 500,000 years. In February 1992 another group of scientists succeeded in dating a *Homo habilis* skull fragment originally discovered in 1965 in Kenya. Only recently subjected to modern dating techniques, it proved to be 2.4 million years old. The fragment is therefore half a million years older than 1470, the skull Richard Leakey found in Turkana, which was the previous record-holder for *Homo habilis*. And in March 1992 theories about east Africa being the center of evolution were turned upside downwhen anthropologists announced the unearthing of a 13-million-year-old jawbone belonging to an ape-like creature in Namibia in southwestern Africa. This astonishing and unprecedented find suggests evolution in apes and humans actually has occurred over a much broader geographic area than previously believed.

Further Reading

"Can He Save the Elephants?" In *New York Times Magazine,* January 7, 1990.

"An Interview with Kenya's Zookeeper." In *Audubon,* September 1990.

Leakey, Louis. *White African: An Early Autobiography.* Originally published in 1937. Reprinted. New York: Ballantine Books, 1973.

Leakey, Louis. *By the Evidence: Memoirs, 1932-1951.* Orlando, FL: Harcourt, 1974.

Leakey, Mary. *Disclosing the Past.* New York: Doubleday, 1984.

Leakey, Richard. *One Life: An Autobiography.* Salem House, 1984.

Morell, Virginia. *Ancestral Passions: The Leakey Family and the Quest for Humankind's Beginnings.* New York: Simon & Schuster, 1995.

"The Most Dangerous Game." In *New York Times Magazine,* January 7, 1996.

Scientists: The Lives and Works of 150 Scientists. Volume 2. Detroit: U•X•L, 1996.

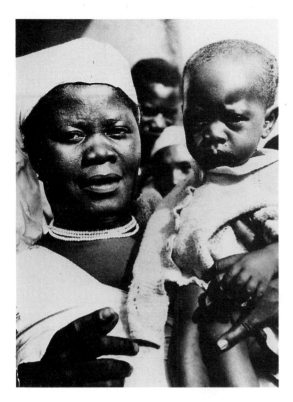

Alice Lenshina

Born c. 1924
Chinsali district, Northern Rhodesia (Zambia)
Died December 1978
Lusaka, Zambia

*Zambian religious leader and founder
of the Lumpa church*

*Lenshina took her large
following and formed
what she called the
Lumpa church, which in
Bemba means "excelling
all others." Within a
few years she had
organized a group of
about 65,000 people.*

Alice Lenshina founded and led the largest and most powerful peasant movement in Zambian history. Her movement grew out of a religious experience. Over time, though, her church expanded and began challenging the rules of the state, the norms of the established churches, and the powers of traditional leaders. The Lumpa church angered these institutions to such an extent that by 1964 Lenshina's followers found themselves at war with the newly elected black government in Zambia.

In January 1964 elected political leader Kenneth Kaunda (1924– ; see entry) formed a new government in the British protectorate of Northern Rhodesia as it prepared for independence. The territory achieved full independence as the Republic of Zambia on October 24, with Kaunda as president. On the eve of independence, the country's first African government declared a state of emergency and took military action against its own African citizens. One of the targets was the Lumpa church. When the fighting between the police and church members finally ended, about 1,500 Lumpa followers had been killed, tens of thousands were driven into exile (forced absence from one's home country), all the church property was destroyed, and Lenshina was jailed. The confrontation between Lenshina's followers and the new government proved a severe embarrassment to black nationalists (Africans who sought independence from the rule of foreign nations.)

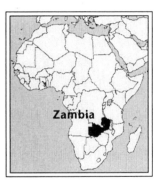

Alice Lenshina was born around 1924 in a small village near Lubwa Mission in Kasomo. Her father, Lubusha, had fought with British forces against the Germans near the Tanzanian border in World War I (1914-18). After the war he became a messenger for the British in Northern Rhodesia, as Zambia was then called.

Lenshina had her first vision in 1953. She believed she had died and met Jesus Christ, the Christian savior, who told her about the power of songs or hymns. She claimed he had given her a new Christian text intended for Africans and told her to return to earth to carry out God's works. She continued to have these experiences and two days after her fourth vision she went to the the Church of Scotland's Lubwa Mission and relayed her story to the Reverend Fergus Macpherson.

Lenshina's rising

When this semiliterate (barely able to read or write) young Bemba woman approached Macpherson claiming that she had died four times and each time had risen again, he believed her story. Under his instruction, Lenshina learned about the Bible and in 1953 became a baptized Christian, taking the name Alice. The missionaries at the Lubwa Mission encouraged Lenshina to give testimonials (public statements describing the benefits) about her experience to other congregations. The mission even provided a truck to transport her to smaller rural churches. Word of her unusual story spread quickly, and she attracted a large following.

During Macpherson's leave, Lenshina began baptizing people and calling on them to give up their magic charms used in witchcraft. She refused to hand over to the mission the money collected at church services. The mission would not tolerate her behavior. In 1955 she was declared a heretic (someone who expresses disagreement with church doctrine) and forced out of the church.

Lenshina then took her large following and formed what she called the Lumpa church, which in Bemba means "excelling all others." She probably took the name Lenshina at this time, which is the Bemba pronunciation of Regina ("queen"). Within a few years she had organized a group of about 65,000 people, many of whom were from the Lubwa Mission and from the neighboring Roman Catholic Mission of the White Fathers.

Attracts a following

In the mid-1950s in Northern Rhodesia, the political culture was in a state of transition. Without consulting the Africans of Northern Rhodesia (now Zambia), Southern Rhodesia (now Zimbabwe), and Nyasaland (now Malawi), in 1953 the colonial governments (governments that put themselves in power to rule over territories other than their home country) of the three British territories formed a federation (an alliance or union) designed to uphold colonial rule.

Under colonial rule, many peasant or small-scale farmers had been forced off their land and into the labor market. Thrown into an entirely new way of life—an urban life of mixed cultures and new prospects—the blacks of Northern Rhodesia faced an uncertain future. Feelings of jealousy and insecurity—feelings that were thought to have stemmed from sorcery or witchcraft—grew among the people. Lenshina attracted traditional-minded peasant farmers and migrant workers precisely because she denounced sorcery as a social evil and demanded that sorcerers give up these practices. She cleverly blended African and European belief sys-

tems, reducing the power of outside forces and promising salvation to believers.

By setting down strict rules of behavior, Lenshina created a sense of security for her followers. She prohibited polygamy (having more than one spouse), adultery, divorce, dancing, drinking, and smoking. Gradually, however, she and her followers began to see themselves as being above the law, as a society outside the control of civil and traditional authorities. Those who did not join the church were often treated as outcasts by the community and even risked being branded as sorcerers or witches.

Lenshina's following swelled, with many of her members coming from the established Christian churches. She set up headquarters in her home village of Kasomo, which she renamed Sioni or Zion. By 1955 more than 65,000 pilgrims had come to visit her church. Meanwhile, the congregation at the Lubwa Mission fell from 3,000 to 400. The White Fathers' Catholic Mission, operating since 1899, suffered a similar drop in membership. By 1956 most people in the Chinsali district belonged to Lenshina's church. The church had about 148 congregations and an estimated membership of between 50,000 and 100,000 people. In 1958 the church completed construction of a large cathedral in Kasomo. Members of the church—all volunteers—built the church out of burnt bricks.

As the Lumpa church grew in size, its wealth also increased. With funds accumulated from donations and contributions, Lenshina's husband bought two five-ton trucks that were used to transport choirs to rural churches. The church also created a chain of rural stores and used the trucks to stock them with supplies.

Lenshina gained even more exposure by traveling to the cities to preach to the migrant workers. According to Andrew Roberts, Europeans who saw her at the peak of her power described her as a "quiet motherly woman, usually to be seen with a baby in her arms," or as a "healthy, rather plump and happily relaxed village matron."

Too much power

Lenshina established a hierarchical structure for the church, placing herself at the top and appointing people to positions below her. Although she was the absolute authority and the only one allowed to perform baptisms, she did allow deacons to preach. Problems with traditional chiefs in the Chinsali district began when many of her followers decided to settle at Kasomo without the chiefs' permission. In traditional society, the land is said to belong to the community. One of the main responsibilities of the chief is the allocation (dividing up) of land. By ignoring the role of the traditional leaders, the Lumpa church offended and antagonized a potentially powerful group. The church also angered the newly formed United National Independence Party (UNIP) by refusing to allow church members to join political parties.

Tensions increase

As the clash grew between the church members and the established authorities—the chiefs of the area, Northern Rhodesia's political leaders, and local missions—the church began losing its rural members. Several events increased the friction between these groups, eventually to the point of armed warfare. In 1956 an African Catholic priest visited a Lumpa village. One of the villagers called him a sorcerer. Accusing someone of witchcraft was an offense under the Witchcraft Ordinance, so the priest lodged a complaint with the local civil authority. When the authorities captured the offender and took him to district headquarters, a large crowd of Lumpa members gathered to protest his detention. The crowd was led by Petros Chitankwa Mulenga, Lenshina's husband. Disorder followed as the villagers became unmanageable. Authorities then arrested Mulenga and sentenced him to two years of hard labor.

In 1959 the Lumpa church ignored the chiefs when it attempted to set up its own settlements at Kasomo. When the church tried to purchase the land, the chiefs refused. This confrontation heightened tension with the newly formed United National Independence Party (UNIP)—the party to which the chiefs generally belonged. Faced with this hostility from several quarters, the Lumpa members withdrew into other villages.

The conflict with UNIP intensified in the early 1960s. Lenshina had been away from her Sioni headquarters visiting churches in the copper mining areas for quite some time. When she returned, she found the church rural membership had dropped considerably, from 70 percent to 10 percent of the local population. UNIP, which replaced the outlawed nationalist party known as the Zambia African National Congress, had been recruiting supporters in the rural areas and had organized the peasants. Many leaders of the Lumpa church had also been members of the Zambia African National Congress, so their political views were similar to those of the UNIP.

For several years the nationalists and the church functioned harmoniously. As Lenshina tightened her control over the church and its members even more, however, the nationalists broke away from her. Finally, Lenshina ordered all Lumpa church members to burn their UNIP membership cards; in their place she issued church cards. Violent clashes between Lumpa and UNIP members became fairly commonplace. UNIP destroyed Lumpa members' homes, their pole and mud churches, and their granaries. In retaliation, Lumpa church members murdered seven UNIP members and assaulted others.

Closing in on themselves

The Lumpa members withdrew into their villages, fortifying them with barricades (barriers). They began making simple weapons and preparing magic protective potions in preparation for Judgment Day (or the end of the world). In their isolation, they became more and more intolerant of the rest of Zambian society. When Lenshina forbade all Lumpa children from attending government schools, the newly elected government led by UNIP decided to challenge her. The government ordered Lenshina and her followers to withdraw from the villages, which it claimed they occupied illegally. The Lumpa members refused. As the police and the army troops began to remove the villagers from their homes, the church members offered fierce resistance. After a final battle on October 10, 1964, the Lumpa admitted defeat and Lenshina surrendered to the police. She, her husband, and their children were put into rehabilitation camps. An estimated 1,500 people had been killed in the conflict.

In 1968 the Zambian authorities declared an amnesty (or pardon) for the regular members of the church, meaning they would not face any punishment. But the 1964 ban outlawing the church remained in place. Following the amnesty, an estimated 20,000 followers left Zambia and went into exile in neighboring Congo (called Zaire, 1971-97, then renamed Democratic Republic of the Congo). Lenshina was not released until 1975; thereafter she was restricted to the Lusaka area. She died in 1978.

Further Reading

Binsbergen, W. M. J. van. "Religious Innovation and Political Conflict in Zambia: A Contribution to the Interpretation of the Lumpa Rising." In *African Perspectives: Religious Innovation in Modern African Society.* Volume 2. Leiden: Afrika-Studiecentrum, 1976.

Bond, George C. "A Prophecy That Failed: The Lumpa Church of Uyombe, Zambia." In *African Christianity: Patterns of Religious Continuity.* Academic Press, 1979.

Greschat, Hans-Jurgen. "Legends? Frauds? Reality? Alice Lenshina's Prophetic Experience." In *Africana Marburgensia.* Edited by Hans-Jurgen Greschat and Hermann Jungraithmayr. Volume 1. 1968.

Roberts, Andrew. "The Lumpa Church of Alice Lenshina." In *Protest and Power in Black Africa.* Edited by Robert Rotberg and Ali Mazrui. New York/UK: Oxford UniversityPress, 1970.

Lobengula

Born 1836
Marico Valley, South Africa
Died 1894
Bulawayo, Matabeleland (former province of
Rhodesia; now part of Zimbabwe)

Last king of the Ndebele people

*"White men, I am
conquered. Take this
and go back."*

—Lobengula, offering 1,000 gold
coins and a note of surrender to
white forces at Bulawayo

obengula (*low-BEN-gyoo-leh*) and his father, Mzilikazi (*um-zee-lee-KAH-zee*), were kings of the Ndebele nation. For 50 years they prevented the British, Afrikaners, and Portuguese from expanding into southern Africa. The Ndebele had little contact with the outside world until white missionaries and speculators arrived on the scene. Lobengula was the second and last king of the Ndebele. Although he was a competent and intelligent leader, he was powerless in the face of European technological advances and the explosion of knowledge that occurred in the nineteenth century.

Lobengula was born in the Marico Valley, near Pretoria, South Africa, in 1836. Shortly after Lobengula's birth, his father, Mzilikazi, abandoned the settlement and led his people northward across the Limpopo River into what is now southern Zimbabwe. Mzilikazi died in 1868, leaving no designated successor. While his sons' families—Mzilikazi had several wives—argued for two years over who would succeed him, the kingship remained vacant. Finally an elderly official presented Lobengula, a son by one of the king's lesser wives, to be king. He was accepted and installed in January 1870.

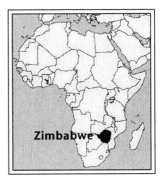

Zimbabwe

A place of killing

Upon becoming king, Lobengula had to settle several challenges to his authority. The most threatening was an uprising by an army regiment (military unit) that supported one of his elder brothers. Lobengula ruthlessly crushed the rebellion, killing everyone involved in it. As a reminder of his victory over the commanders who rebelled against him, he named his capital "GuBulawayo" (now Bulawayo), which means "the place of the killing."

Like the Zulus, the Ndebele king depended on his military. The Ndebeles based their system on regiments, consisting of unmarried young men who lived together in units throughout the kingdom, separate from all others. The young men, trained and loyal to the king, gradually became part of the communities through marriage.

At its peak the Ndebele army had between 15,000 and 20,000 men. The Ndebele had no cavalry (soldiers on horseback); they fought close up using long shields and short stabbing spears called *assegais,* first used so effectively by Zulu chief Shaka (see entry). When the soldiers were not defending the king or enforcing the tributary system (smaller states paying money to a conquering force) with outlying clans, they watched over the national herd of cattle.

The king ruled over the entire nation; he was the military head, the political leader, and the spiritual leader. Once a year the entire nation came together at a ceremony, where the king's subjects showed their loyalty to him and honored the royal spirits. At the ceremony, performances by military units reinforced the sense of Ndebele national power and pride.

The Europeans get involved

Lobengula became king at an important time in the history of the region. The year before Mzilikazi's death, Europeans discovered

Mzilikazi

Mzilikazi was the founder and first king of the Ndebele nation. (The term "Ndebele" means "people of the long shields.") In the early 1800s the Zulu nation, led by famed chief Shaka (see entry), was very powerful in eastern South Africa. Between 1818 and 1828 Shaka's highly disciplined warriors raided villages and robbed them of their crops and their cattle, forcing millions to flee. The Ndebeles fled Shaka's Zulu warriors in the 1820s, eventually settling in what is now Zimbabwe. On the trek northward, Mzilikazi gathered up other refugees—mainly people of weaker tribes—and before long created an army of 5,000, which he modeled on the Zulu military system.

By 1825 the Ndebele had established their capital near modern-day Pretoria, South Africa. But the Zulus threatened them again and in 1832 they moved farther west to the Marico Valley. White Dutch farmers moving out of the Cape Colony to escape British rule reached the plateau in 1837. Overwhelmed by the whites' superior firepower, Mzilikazi fled across the Limpopo River to southern Zimbabwe.

Mzilikazi eventually established a capital called Matlokotloke in the Bulawayo-Inyati area. His disciplined and well-trained warriors conquered the local peoples and incorporated them into the Ndebele state. Mzilikazi died in 1868 at the age of 74.

gold in southern Zimbabwe along the Umfuli River, 70 miles south of Bulawayo. The discovery of mineral resources in Matabeleland threatened the Ndebele because it drew white prospectors, traders, and adventurers to the kingdom. The resources themselves did not interest the Ndebele—cattle were the measure of wealth in their value system.

Lobengula wanted to avoid conflict between his people and the whites, but his relationship with the Europeans was uneasy at best. He sought to limit the number of whites in his kingdom, but he realized that the new settlers possessed the knowledge and skills that would help him cope with the growing technology of the nineteenth century. Lobengula became dependent on whites for a variety of things ranging from wagon repair to writing up and interpreting contracts to modern health care. Diets rich in beef—washed down with a cloudy beer made from corn meal and millet—caused health problems for both Mzilikazi and Lobengula. Leander Starr Jameson, Lobengula's doctor, wrote that Lobengula

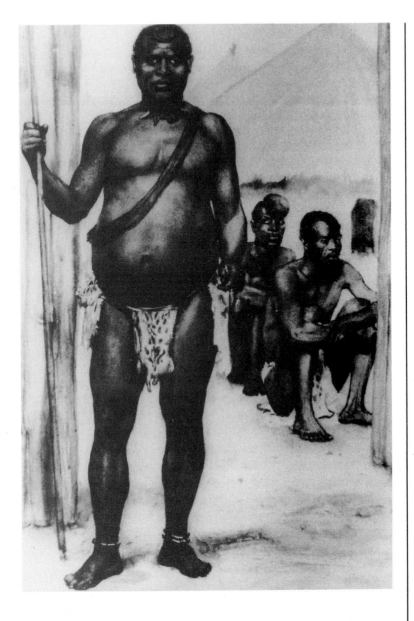

had many symptoms of an alcoholic and that he also suffered from gout, a painful swelling around the joints cause by a high-beef, high-malt diet. Jameson's ability to relieve the pain of this condition with morphine (a pain-killing narcotic) won him the king's confidence. Jameson would play an important role as intermediary for the wealthy and powerful British mining magnate Cecil Rhodes and the British South Africa Company when they negotiated with Lobengula for rights to the region.

Lobengula was a huge man, over six feet in height and weighing more than 300 pounds. One well-known photograph shows him dressed in traditional clothing—a leopard or cheetah loin cloth, beaded anklets, and a Ndebele head ring—and carrying a tall spear in his right hand and a smoking pipe in his left. Another photograph shows 10 of his wives, although some sources claim he had as many as 68 wives. Polygyny—or having more than one wife—is practiced in many African societies. Under traditional law an African man may have as many wives at one time as he is able to support. Multiple marriages were often viewed as a measure of a man's wealth.

The discovery of gold

In 1886 gold was found in great quantities along the Witwatersrand, a ridge or reef in the Johannesburg area of South Africa. The discovery made some people think that the gold reef might run across the Limpopo River into southern Zimbabwe. Earlier, the European nations at the Conference of Berlin had carved up areas in Africa among themselves. At this conference the provinces of Mashonaland and Matabeleland (home to the Shona and Ndebele peoples, respectively) came under the British flag. Britain allowed other countries to explore the region's resources as long as the local chiefs agreed.

The Portuguese, the Germans, the Afrikaners, and Cecil Rhodes, a wealthy British industrialist (see box in Paul Kruger entry), all sought to negotiate with Lobengula for rights to the land. Rhodes wanted to claim the area for Britain, thereby extending Britain's domain from the Cape Colony at the foot of Africa to Cairo in Egypt at the very top. His chief goal was to become the only mining and farming operator in Mashonaland. Charles Rudd, a representative of Rhodes, ended up composing a contract for white settlement in the region; Lobengula cautiously accepted the terms of the agreement. The king found himself in an extremely difficult position, having to balance the demands of the Europeans against what was best for his own people. Clearly, the future of his kingdom rested on this all-important decision. Younger Ndebele warriors opposed European presence in the territory, but Lobengula knew that the Ndebele people could never win in a clash against European firepower.

On October 30, 1888, Lobengula officially agreed to Rudd's deal, giving Rudd alone control over all metals and minerals in the kingdom. In exchange, Rudd promised Lobengula 100 pounds sterling a month, 1,000 rifles, 100,000 rounds of ammunition, and a steamboat or 500 pounds sterling. The Europeans also made a verbal promise that no more than 10 whites would come into the country and that they would not interfere with or settle near the Ndebele community.

An uneasy arrangement

Other Europeans with interest in the region made Lobengula doubt the wisdom of his agreement with Rudd. Rhodes became increasingly worried about the situation and sent Dr. Jameson and Dr. Rutherford Harris to Bulawayo to try to set things right with Lobengula. They brought half the consignment of guns Lobengula was due to receive under the terms of the treaty. Still unsure about the deal and more suspicious than ever of the dealmakers, the king declined the guns and seemingly refused to honor the agreement with Rudd.

After much indecision, haggling, and even some intertribal violence, Lobengula reconsidered. Dr. Jameson praised Rhodes and convinced Lobengula that the Portuguese were eyeing Matabeleland from the East as were the Afrikaners from the South. Lobengula finally gave his permission to the British South Africa Company to build a road north to Mashonaland.

The British government granted the British South Africa Company a royal charter on October 10, 1889. Rhodes immediately put together a group of men he called the Pioneer Column to occupy the country to the north of Matabeleland and to prepare for a large and permanent white settlement. The flag of Great Britain was raised at Fort Salisbury (now Harare, the capital of Zimbabwe) in September 1890. British colonists named the area Southern Rhodesia, after Rhodes. In 1891 Rhodes appointed Jameson to act as administrator general of Mashonaland. The next year Lobengula lost all rights over the minerals and the land to Rhodes in a very complicated deal with a German financier. Apparently Lobengula did not realize that the German businessman was working in partnership with Rhodes.

Whites take the land

A disappointingly small amount of gold was mined in the region, so the Pioneer Column and the settlers began farming the rich and well-watered lands of the plateau south and east of the Zambezi River. In order to operate efficiently, these large farms required a considerable force of cheap labor. The Ndebele were a menace to the whites because their raiding practices scared off potential workers. The policy of the British South Africa Company was to avoid conflict—it wanted to attract new settlers, not frighten them off—and to discourage the involvement of the British government in company affairs. Lobengula also needed to avoid conflict because he knew his armies were not strong enough to take on the whites. Jameson and Lobengula had an unspoken agreement that the Umniati River and the Sashe River would be the borders between Matabeleland and Mashonaland.

Unavoidable clash

Despite their intentions to avert a full-blown confrontation, the two parties clashed. In desperation, Lobengula sent messengers to Cape Town, requesting the British High Commission to intervene and prevent the British South Africa Company from waging war on his people, but the friction only intensified. On one occasion, Lobengula's raid of a white settlement prompted Jameson to send 1,100 soldiers into Bulawayo. Although they outnumbered the whites by 18,000 to 1,100, the Ndebeles were no match for the Europeans' machine guns. Lobengula did as much damage as he could before the forces of the British South Africa Company entered Bulawayo.

After the defeat at Bulawayo, Lobengula fled northward. He sent an official with a bag of 1,000 gold coins and a message to his attackers. The note, recovered later, read: "White men, I am conquered. Take this and go back." The officers allegedly gave the message and the gold to police troopers, who stole the gold. The note was never delivered. Jameson ordered Lobengula's capture. The company sent out a special patrol and reinforcements under the command of Major Allan Wilson to pursue the king across the Shangani River. The river rose during the night, trapping Wilson and his men. Once the whites had run out of ammunition, the Ndebele warriors went in and killed all 36 of them. Lobengula died shortly after the Shangani patrol incident. The royal military leaders then surrendered, and the war was over.

The exact cause of Lobengula's death remains unclear, but it is known that he had three sons eligible to succeed him to the throne. The boys were attending school in Cape Town at Cecil Rhodes's expense; however, they were not allowed to return home after their father's death because officials of the British South Africa Company feared the Ndebele would proclaim one of them king. With Lobengula's death, the kingdom of the Ndebele ended.

Further Reading

Beach, D. N. *Zimbabwe before 1900.* Mambo Press, 1984.

Blake, Robert. *A History of Rhodesia.* Eyre Methuen, 1977.

Cary, Robert. *A Time to Die.* 1969.

Churchill, Lord Randolph. *Men, Mines, and Animals in South Africa.* Originally published in 1892. Reprinted. Books of Rhodesia, 1975.

Cooper-Chadwick, J. *Three Years with Lobengula.* Books of Rhodesia, 1975.

Depelchin, H., and C. Croonenberghs. *Letters of Journey to Gubuluwayo.* Books of Rhodesia, 1979.

Patrice Lumumba

Born July 2, 1925
Kasai province, Belgian Congo (now Democratic
Republic of the Congo)
Died January 17, 1961
Katanga province, Congo Republic (now Democratic
Republic of the Congo)

*First prime minister of independent
Congo Republic*

"We are not communist,
catholics, or socialist.
We are African
Nationalist. We retain
the right to be friends
with whomever we like in
accordance with the
principal of political
neutrality."

**—Lumumba, in a statement
defending his appeal to the Soviet
Union for help in unifying the
Congo, 1960**

n the 1950s throughout Africa, African colonies—lands ruled by European powers—began demanding their independence. Patrice Lumumba was a fierce nationalist who tried to overcome tribal and cultural differences to forge a united, centralized nation out of the Belgian Congo. A fiery speaker of endless energy, he addressed the various language groups of the central African region in their own languages. Lumumba became the first prime minister of the former Belgian Congo, now called the Democratic Republic of the Congo. The center of government fell away within days of independence, though, when two wealthy provinces declared their independence. In the turmoil that followed over the next six months, Lumumba was dismissed from his post, captured by the new military government, and beaten to death.

The Democratic Republic of the Congo was a Belgian colony from 1908 until 1960. Rich in mineral and water resources, it is the largest African country (in land mass) south of the Sahara Desert. When the region became independent in 1960, it was known as the Republic of the Congo. In 1971 President Mobutu Sese Seko (see entry) renamed it Zaire. Then, on May 17, 1997, after Mobutu was overthrown, it became known as the Democratic Republic of the Congo.

When Lumumba took office in 1960, the country was badly divided by powerful political interests. During the colonial period, the Belgians had prevented African advancement in the army and the civil (government) service, leaving the Congo unprepared for the inevitable day of transition to independent rule. When the Belgians realized they could no longer control Congolese demands for independence, the Belgian colonial office abruptly—and without adequate preparation—abandoned its colony. Their departure created a serious void in the Congo's power structure.

Youth in a colony

Patrice Hemery Lumumba was born July 2, 1925, in the village of Onalua in the Katako-Kombe territory of Kasai province. At that time the Congo was a colony of the Belgian government. Previously it had been the private preserve of King Leopold II (1835-1909) of Belgium. Lumumba said one of his earliest memories was of villagers gathering in the evenings or on stormy days listening to elders telling stories of the past. At one session the elders vividly retold how the Belgian soldiers of Leopold II would cut off the hands of natives when they failed to gather enough ivory or rubber.

Lumumba was one of four sons born to François Tolenga and his wife. They were poor farmers who belonged to the small Tetela tribe, famed for its fighting skills in war. Lumumba's parents were Catholics, and for a time they were able to send him to Catholic Mission schools. But, despite their wishes, Lumumba was enrolled in a Protestant Mission school called Wembo Nyama when he was 11 years old. Following government policy that Africans should learn manual labor, most mission schools spent only one hour each day on book instruction; the rest of the time the male students were taught farming and manual skills. Lumumba's formal education ended at the elementary school level, but he kept reading and learning on his own.

Life in the city

After holding some poorly paying, low-skilled jobs, in 1944 Lumumba went to Stanleyville (now Kisangani), considered the big city to the poor boys of northern Kasai. He landed a job there as a clerk in the post office. The European part of Stanleyville astounded him, with its beautiful parks, dazzling skyscrapers, handsome houses, and wide boulevards lined with palm and mango trees. Africans, however, could not use the restaurants, theaters, or hotels and had to sit at the back of buses and boats. Moreover, Africans could only live outside the center of the city.

Lumumba stayed in the township of Mangobo in the household of an elder named Paul Kimbala. There Lumumba joined the circle of *évolués,* Congolese youth like himself who had come from rural villages and been educated by Western mission schools. The group often got together to debate issues, listen to news on the radio, and exchange books. Lumumba took a correspondence course to improve his French; he also learned several Congolese languages, particularly Lingala, a trade language used along the Congo River, and Swahili, spoken in the eastern Congo and East Africa.

In 1951 Lumumba's father arranged for him to marry a girl from his home area named Pauline Opangu. No advocate of arranged marriages, Lumumba initially rebelled. Though Pauline was only 15 and could not read, write, or speak French, Lumumba eventually went along with tradition and married her. Within weeks he was completely captivated by her charm. In time they had at least eight children.

Joins Congolese intellectuals

In Stanleyville, Lumumba took an active role in the community. He did volunteer work in a nearby library and served as secretary and later as president of the African Government Employees Association. He also organized a club for postal workers and another club for African intellectuals and liberal Europeans to discuss how to improve race relations. Through his editorials and poems for *La Voix du Congolese* ("Voice of the Congo") and *La Croix du Congo* ("The Cross of the Congo")—two newsletters for the colony's *évolués*—Lumumba became known as one of a few who was willing to speak out.

To appease the growing demands of educated Congolese, the colonial administration announced in 1952 that they would grant registration cards to natives who could meet certain qualifications. This would, in theory, give them the same privileges as Europeans. One of the first to apply, Lumumba was granted the card in 1954. The next year he was one of a group of Congolese given the chance to meet with Belgian king Baudouin (reigned 1951 to 1953), who was on a tour of the colony. When the king asked questions, Lumumba was the only one fearless enough to answer. Lumumba's conversation with the king won him the admiration of the Congolese but brought on the contempt of administrators. He later went to Belgium as a member of the first Congolese delegation to discuss local political reform.

On his return to Stanleyville, the authorities charged Lumumba with stealing about $2,500 from his job at the post office. Judged guilty and given a two-year prison sentence, Lumumba continued to claim his innocence. The local *évolué* community raised enough funds to pay the stolen money back and provided for Lumumba's family during his jail term. He eventually won his appeal and was back in Stanleyville a year after his conviction.

Disheartened, Lumumba moved to Leopoldville (now Kinshasa) in 1957, where he took a job as a salesperson for Polar Beer. Within a year he had established several Polar Beer Clubs throughout the city and by August 1958 was sales manager for the entire brewery. Smith Hempstone, a journalist, author, and former U.S. ambassador to Kenya, wrote in *Katanga Report* that Lumumba, "the tall, thin, mercurial man with the small head and the smooth talk, the bright smile and the constantly fluttering hands, was soon a well-known figure in the bars of the native quarter."

Changes in the political climate

In the middle to late 1950s in Africa, sweeping political changes were taking place. Ghana, led by Kwame Nkrumah (see entry), had just become the first African colony south of the Sahara desert to win independence from colonial rule. Several French and British colonies had been given internal self-rule with the prospect of independence in the near future. In the Congo, Belgium reluctantly agreed to allow limited African participation in political affairs in the major cities and held elections in Leopoldville in December 1957.

Lumumba joined an action group called Mouvement National Congolais (the National Congolese Movement; MNC) started by

Joseph Ileo, editor of a publication called *Conscience Africaine*. Lumumba soon took control of the group, whose members included Kasai Baluba leader Albert Kalonji and the soldier-journalist Joseph Mobutu.

Several events took place in the second half of 1958 that built up Congolese demands for independence. In July the Belgian government sent representatives to the Congo to examine the situation and make recommendations for the future. In its first official act as a political party, the MNC petitioned the government to appoint Congolese to this fact-finding group. The next month General Charles de Gaulle, president of France, visited neighboring Brazzaville in the French Congo (now People's Republic of Congo) and offered independence for all territories under French rule. Spurred on by Brazzaville's freedom, the MNC members submitted a petition demanding independence throughout the Congo. Fluent in Swahili, Lingala, and French, Lumumba could communicate with people throughout the country, consolidating the MNC as a colony-wide political party.

Later that year the International Exposition in Brussels brought several hundred Congolese from all over the colony together, where they had a chance to voice their concerns. They came away from Brussels with a more militant attitude toward the Belgian colonials, indicating a greater likelihood of armed African rebellion. In December Lumumba attended the Pan-African Conference in Accra, Ghana, where he met nationalists from across the continent. He and Nkrumah became friends, and Nkrumah converted him to his Pan-Africanist ideas. (Pan-Africanism is a movement for cooperation among the African peoples.)

Over a dozen other political parties had sprung up in the Congo, also demanding independence. The most significant was ABAKO (Association des Ba-Kongo), a Kongo cultural group from Lower Congo. Its leader, Joseph Kasavubu, had already won election as mayor of Leopoldville. Another new party appeared named the Rassemblement Katangais, later called Confédération des associations tribales du Katanga (Confederation of Tribal Associations of Katanga; CONAKAT). It represented mainly the Lunda people of the mineral-rich Katanga province (Shaba province) in the southeastern section of the country. Moïse Tshombe (see entry), a member of the Lunda royal family, led CONAKAT in its demands for regional autonomy (self-rule).

Splits in the MNC

Both ABAKO and CONAKAT opposed the primary goal of Lumumba and the MNC—the goal of the unity of all the regions and tribes of the Congo. Lumumba sought to achieve unity through the formation of a strong central government—one that would be blind to regional and tribal differences. On the other hand, Kasavubu and Tshombe wanted the new government to reflect the Congo's rich heritage of strong, separate kingdoms. They favored a federal system that would give the regions or provinces as much control as possible over their own affairs, similar to the U.S. system of a federation of states. Lumumba ran the MNC with a heavy hand.

Disagreement within the ranks of the MNC tore the organization apart and ended any chance for development of a national party. One faction (group), the MNC/Kalonji—named after Kalonji, a Luba leader of the Kasai—identified with the idea of a Congo federation along ethnic lines. MNC/ Lumumba continued to insist on a strong central government. Increasing clashes between political factions led MNC/Lumumba to call for a delay in the national elections that would select a council to help in the transition to independence. Next, Lumumba delivered a highly charged speech at an MNC conference in Stanleyville, triggering rioting that resulted in the deaths of 20 people. Authorities arrested him and sentenced him to six months in jail. The Belgians then called for a conference in Brussels to discuss the future of the colony. When the Congolese delegates refused to attend unless Lumumba was present, the Belgian government released him—even though he had served only two days of his sentence—and then flew him to Brussels.

Forms a coalition government

The Brussels conference agreed to hold elections in May 1960 for provincial and national assemblies. Independence would follow the next month. As the time drew near, the Belgian government dispatched troops to protect the Congo's Belgian citizens and to ensure stability in the region. Though calm prevailed, the May elections revealed the divisions within the colony. Of the 137 seats in the national assembly, the federalists (Kasavubu of ABAKO, Tshombe of CONAKAT, and Kalonji of MNC/Kalonji) won a combined total of 38 seats. Lumumba's MNC won 33, making him the clear candidate for prime minister. The remaining seats were scattered among a dozen smaller parties. Although the MNC gained the most seats of any single party, Lumumba did not have enough votes to be elected prime minister. He tried to form a governing coalition (alliance or union for a common purpose) with Tshombe's CONAKAT but failed. Kasavubu also tried to form a government and failed. Finally, Lumumba and Kasavubu succeeding in establishing a coalition government on June 23, 1960, a week before independence: Lumumba would be prime minister and Kasavubu would be president.

In his acceptance speech at the independence day ceremony on June 30, 1960, Lumumba intentionally insulted King Baudouin. He reminded Baudouin of the "contempt, insults, hangings and shootings" that the Congolese had endured under Belgian rule. The situation was undeniably tense. Within four days the troops of the Force Publique (national army) rebelled against the remaining Belgian officers. By the end of the week the situation was out of control. Soldiers throughout the country took to the streets, looting, raping, and killing. The 40,000 white citizens who had stayed in Congo fled across the borders.

Chaos and political crisis

To try to stop the mayhem Lumumba fired the Belgian commander and promoted the entire army one rank. Kasavubu and Lumumba agreed to appoint Sergeant-Major Victor Lundula as the new army commander and Joseph Mobutu as his chief of staff. On the advice of Nkrumah and President Dwight Eisenhower of the United States, Lumumba appealed to the United Nations (UN; an international forum for global disputes) for help. On July 14 the UN agreed to send peacekeeping forces to restore order.

Lumumba hoped that the UN forces would not only maintain peace but also restore the secessionist Katanga province, which had split away from the rest of the Congo just after independence. (Tshombe, in league with the mining companies, had declared Katanga a separate state on July 6 and asked the Belgian troops to help maintain order.) When the UN refused to use its troops to bring Katanga back into the Congo, Lumumba appealed for help to the Soviet Union and its neighboring countries. Accused of being a Communist by Belgians and Americans, he replied: "We

Lumumba speaks to his troops; President Joseph Kasavubu stands next to him in the dark suit.

are not communist, catholics, or socialist. We are African Nationalist. We retain the right to be friends with whomever we like in accordance with the principal of political neutrality." (Communism is a system of government in which the state controls the means of production and the distribution of goods.)

Chaos and political crisis deepened when Lumumba used troops and supplies sent by the Soviet Union to crush a secession movement in Kasai province led by his old MNC rival Albert Kalonji. Angered by Lumumba's use of Soviet troops, President Kasavubu, with the support of the United States and Belgium, dismissed Lumumba as prime minister on September 5. Lumumba in turn dismissed Kasavubu as president. As the people of the nation took sides, both refused to resign their offices. Finally, on September 12, the 29-year-old commander of the Congolese troops stationed in Leopoldville, Joseph Mobutu, seized supreme power and ousted both Lumumba and Kasavubu from government. He ordered the Soviets out of the country and announced that the UN and United States had agreed to send assistance.

A brutal end

Lumumba was a prisoner in his official residence, surrounded by an inner ring of UN troops to prevent his arrest and an outer ring of Mobutu's soldiers to prevent his escape. By October 1960 Mobutu had reached an agreement with Kasavubu on an interim government. With support from the U.S. Central Intelligence Agency (CIA), he prepared to arrest Lumumba for treason. Fearing for his life, Lumumba escaped from his compound and fled toward his stronghold in Stanleyville. Before he reached there, however, Lumumba and two of his companions were captured and jailed in Thysville prison on a warrant signed by Kasavubu. Then, on the night of January 17, 1961, Lumumba and his companions were secretly beaten, removed from Thysville prison, and flown to Elisabethville (Lubumbashi) in Katanga, capital of his archrival Tshombe. According to an investigation conducted by the UN in later years, Lumumba was beaten to death—possibly on the same night—by Tshombe's soldiers. His companions were shot. For some weeks later the murders were kept secret. When Lumumba's death was finally exposed, it sparked worldwide protest against the failure of the UN to restore order in the region.

Further Reading

Dictionary of African Biography. Volume 2. Algonac, MI: Reference Publications, 1979.

Hempstone, Smith. *Katanga Report.* Winchester, MA: Faber, 1962.

Meredith, Martin. *The First Dance of Freedom.* New York: Harper, 1954.

Reshetnyak, Nikolai. *Patrice Lumumba.* Novosti Press, 1990.

Sarte, Jean Paul. *Lumumba Speaks.* Boston: Little, Brown, 1972.

Albert John Lutuli

Born c. 1898
Solusi, Rhodesia (Zimbabwe)
Died July 21, 1967
Groutville, South Africa

*President of the African National Congress and
winner of the Nobel Peace Prize*

lbert John Lutuli (surname sometimes spelled Luthuli; pronounced *loo-TOO-lee*), a humble Zulu chief who played a
key role in toppling white minority rule in South Africa, was the
first African to win a Nobel Peace Prize. He provided a historic
bridge between a cautious generation of African National Congress (ANC) leaders and the more militant post-World War II
(1939-45) South Africans led by Nelson Mandela (1918- ; see
entry). The ANC, founded in 1912 to promote African rights, is the
oldest black-dominated political organization in South Africa.

South Africa's white minority government banned and jailed
Lutuli during his 15 years as ANC president and may have even
killed him. Still, he never advocated the use of violence to fight
apartheid, a ruthless system of racial segregation imposed by the
whites and opposed by the ANC. Toward the end of his life,
though, perhaps out of frustration with increasingly vicious white

*"What we have aimed
to do in South Africa is
to bring the white man
to his senses, not
slaughter him."*

—Lutuli, in his 1952 Defiance
Campaign speech

violence against the black majority, Lutuli turned a blind eye to a guerrilla (independent fighting unit) war launched inside South Africa by Mandela and other young ANC leaders.

Lutuli always recognized that black South Africans would have to pay the price for freedom in their country. In his 1961 Nobel Peace Prize acceptance speech, he expressed "heartfelt appreciation" for the Nobel committee's support but added:

> We South Africans, however, equally understand that much as others might do for us, our freedom cannot come to us as a gift from abroad. Our freedom we must make ourselves. All honest freedom-loving people have dedicated themselves to that task. What we need is the courage that rises with danger.

In 1957 Lutuli told the ANC newspaper *New Age* that the road to freedom was "sanctified with the blood of martyrs—in other words, no cross, no crown." A devout Christian and advocate of passive resistance (nonviolent opposition to injustice), Lutuli sought equal rights—including voting rights—for all South Africans and the return of land that whites had confiscated from blacks. "What we have aimed to do in South Africa is to bring the white man to his senses, not slaughter him," he said in 1952.

Family background

According to his own calculations, Lutuli was born around 1898 at Solusi Mission, Rhodesia (in today's southwestern Zimbabwe). His mother, Mtonya Gumede, had spent her early childhood in the royal *kraal* ("enclosure") of King Cetshwayo (1827-1884; see entry). Cetshwayo was the last of the great, independent Zulu kings who reigned over Zululand in today's eastern South Africa, north of the city of Durban. When Lutuli's mother was young, her mother took Mtonya away from Cetshwayo's court to live in Groutville, a mission established in the mid-nineteenth century by the American Board of Commissioners for Foreign Missions near today's town of Stanger north of Durban. Groutville was named for American missionary Aldin Grout. Lutuli's grandfather, Ntaba, was the second chief of Groutville. Lutuli's grandfather and his wife, Titisi, also became the first Christians in the Lutuli family lineage.

At Groutville, Lutuli's mother had converted to Christianity by the time she met his father, John Bunyan Lutuli. He went to Rhodesia to assist the British in putting down the 1896 Matabele rebellion. (The Matabele were Zulus who migrated from Zululand in South Africa to southwestern Zimbabwe in the first half of the nineteenth century.) Afterward, the elder Lutuli stayed on at Solusi Mission. Mtonya then left Groutville to join her husband in Rhodesia. There, their third son, Albert John, was born. Their first son had died before Mtonya left Groutville for Rhodesia.

Tended mission mules

Lutuli's father died shortly after Albert John's birth. When Lutuli was about 10 years old, his mother moved with her two sons back to South Africa. They lived at a Seventh-Day Adventist mission near Vryheid in today's northern Natal. Lutuli was assigned to tend the mission mules. His mother was concerned that no school existed at the mission, so she sent Lutuli to Groutville to be educated and live in the house of his uncle, Chief Martin Lutuli. As a member of his uncle's household, young Lutuli observed the politics and demands of a chief—lessons that would prove useful 30 years later when he was elected Groutville's chief.

In 1914, after studying at Groutville's Congregationalist mission school, Lutuli went to a Methodist teacher training institution at Edendale, near Pietermaritzburg in eastern South Africa. Three years later he was qualified to take his first job as an elementary school teacher. Lutuli then attended Adams College on scholarship for two years to study for a higher teacher's degree. He taught at Adams for 15 years before being called home to Groutville as chief of an area populated by about 5,000 Zulus.

Lutuli met his wife, a teacher named Nokukhanya Bhengu, at Adams College. As the granddaughter of Zulu chief Khlokolo Bhengu, Lutuli's wife was of royal heritage, while he was considered a commoner. They were married in 1927. They had two sons and five daughters.

World opened up

Exposure to educated Africans and Europeans at the institutions away from Groutville opened Lutuli's mind to massive technological and economic changes taking place in the world at the beginning of the twentieth century. In his autobiography, published in 1962, Lutuli wrote of his early schooling:

We were thoroughly aware of the meeting of cultures, African and European, and of the disorganization of both—especially the African—as a result. We did not have the desire of the Nationalists [the white-only National party that imposed apartheid from 1948 to 1994] that we should return to the primitive. But we did have an intense wish to preserve what is valuable in our heritage while discarding the inappropriate and outmoded. Our people were ill-equipped to withstand the impact of the twentieth-century industrial society. Our task seemed to consist of relating the past coherently to the present and the future.

Christian missionary tours to India in 1938 and to the United States in 1948 further broadened Lutuli's insights into how different people of the world interacted, prospering together materially and intellectually. This stirred up his anger at those whites in his home country who tried to isolate people by tribes and educate blacks only as laborers and sweepers, reinforcing a master-servant relationship.

Lutuli emphasized the monumental mistake that whites had made in their campaign to bring Christianity, commerce, and civilization to the African continent. "Western civilization is only partly Western," wrote Lutuli. "It embraces the contribution of many lands and many races. It is the outcome of interaction, not apartheid. It is an inheritance, something received to be handed on, not a white preserve." As the industrial era flourished in the West, Africans were eager to incorporate into their culture those aspects of Western life that they found useful. But as Africans rose to take their places beside whites in this emerging African-Western culture, the whites denied blacks the right to grow and learn with the changing times. This provoked the wrath of black Africans, which led to rebellion, then independence. In far too many cases, poorly prepared leadership of new African countries resulted in disaster for both Africans and whites.

Elected in ANC crisis

Lutuli had joined the ANC in 1944. As Groutville chief, Lutuli became increasingly active in the ANC at a time when South Africa's whites were imposing tighter restrictions on blacks. In 1952, after the end of the Defiance Campaign—a long series of ANC-sponsored strikes throughout the nation—the ANC found itself locked in a leadership crisis between "go slow" conservative (traditional) leaders and revolutionaries (advocates of change) crying for violence. Backed by Mandela and the Johannesburg province, Lutuli was elected ANC president in 1952 as a compromise candidate. He favored firm but passive resistance to apartheid laws. As University of Witwatersrand political historian Tom Lodge put it in *Black Politics in South Africa since 1945,* Lutuli "was immediately at home in the world of popular politics, combining eloquence with personal warmth. His religious faith and training brought to his politics a principled belief in non-violence and a remarkable optimism about the capacity of whites to undergo a change of heart."

During Lutuli's 15 years as ANC president, the white government deprived him of his chieftainship, charged him with treason, jailed him for a year while awaiting trial at which the charge was dropped, and banned him to his home area much of the time. Nevertheless, the ANC continued to gain white supporters and members.

Sharpeville massacre

But the pressure the multiracial ANC was putting on the white government through passive resistance was unsatisfactory to nationalists. (African nationalism is the fight for independence and self-rule for Africans.) They contended that only black South Africans could bring black rule to the country. A group of former ANC members headed by Robert Sobukwe split off to form the Pan-Africanist Congress (PAC) on April 6, 1959. (Pan-Africanism is a movement for unity among Africans and freedom from colonial control.) Sobukwe called for "a government of the Africans by the Africans and for the Africans."

Competition between the PAC and ANC resulted in one of the tragic, defining events of the movement against apartheid. Late in 1959, the ANC decided to launch a campaign against the white laws that required blacks to carry identification passes restricting their access to many areas of the country. The campaign was scheduled for March 31, 1960, but the PAC staged demonstrations against the pass laws on March 21 in Sharpeville, a black township about 35 miles south of Johannesburg. Police panicked and fired on the demonstrators, killing 69 and wounding more than four hundred.

The ANC reacted with a show of strength. Lutuli, Mandela, and others burned their passes in public and called a national strike on March 28. Rioting broke out across South Africa. The government imposed martial law (military law declared in times of emergency). On April 28, 1961, the government outlawed the ANC and the PAC, effectively shutting off any legal black political opposition. In response, Mandela and others began to talk of using violence against the white government. According to Mandela, Lutuli refused to commit the ANC to a guerrilla war, but he did not object to the creation of a military organization separate from the ANC.

Don't touch his chickens

Luthuli was arrested during the state of emergency declared after the Sharpville attacks. In giving testimony during his treason trial in 1960, Lutuli made a distinction between the ANC's nonviolence and pacifism: pacifists refused to defend themselves when attacked; people acting nonviolently were not bound by the pacifists' code. Mandela wrote: "He ultimately agreed that a military campaign was inevitable. When someone later insinuated that perhaps the chief was not prepared for such a course, he retorted, 'If anyone thinks I am a pacifist, let him try to take my chickens, and he will know how wrong he is.'"

By this time, Lutuli was ill with a heart problem and suffering from high blood pressure. He seemed to have been tired of waiting, perhaps recalling an earlier statement he had made: "Who will deny that thirty years of my life have been spent knocking in vain, patiently, moderately and modestly at a closed and barred door." In December 1961, the South African government agreed to lift Lutuli's banning order to allow him and his wife to travel to Oslo, Norway, for the award of the Nobel Peace Prize.

"I, as a Christian, have always felt that there is one thing above all about 'apartheid' or 'separate development' that is unforgivable," Lutuli noted in his Nobel acceptance speech. "It seems utterly indifferent to the suffering of individual persons, who lose their land, their homes, their jobs," all because of "the deliberate policy of a government." But this type of government—"supported actively by a large part of the white population, and tolerated passively by an overwhelming white majority"—showed signs of weakening throughout the sixties. "An encouraging white minority have thrown their lot with non-whites who are overwhelmingly opposed to so-called separate development," declared Lutuli. He returned with the prize to South Africa on December 15, 1961.

The next day, Mandela's guerrilla Umkhonto we Sizwe (means "Spear of the Nation") units made their first sabotage attacks against the white minority government, blowing up electric power stations and government buildings, announcing to the world: "The time comes in the life of any nation when there remain only two choices: submit or fight. . . . We shall not submit." The ANC had a long battle ahead, but Lutuli would not live to see the victory more than three decades later.

Lutuli (right) receives the 1960 Nobel Peace Prize from Gunnar Jahn, president of the Nobel Committee.

The death of a statesman

By 1967 more and more whites were listening to the reasoning of this strong-minded, charitable black South African: "To the Government Lutuli was a peculiarly dangerous man: he, more than any other African leader in the country's history, had profoundly affected the whites," wrote Mary Benson, one of the leading chroniclers of the ANC, in 1966. "The Government dreaded that whites should come to know and understand Africans as individuals, and therefore should lose their fear of them."

That would have been reason enough for Lutuli's "elimination." His death in 1967 is shrouded with mystery. Some ANC leaders suspect a conspiracy in which white authorities assassinated Lutuli and made his death look like an accident. Police reported Lutuli died when struck by a freight train as he walked along a trestle over the Umvoti River near his home. "The circumstances were curious: he had been hit by a train in an area near his farm where he often walked," wrote Mandela in his autobiography published in 1994. "Luthuli's death left a great vacuum in the organization [the ANC]; the chief was a Nobel Prize winner, a distinguished, internationally known figure, a man who commanded respect from both black and white. For these reasons, he was irreplaceable."

In 1960, seven years prior to his death, Lutuli had sent one of the ANC's strongest leaders and Mandela's law partner—Oliver Tambo (1917-1993)—into exile when it became evident that the white government was going to ban the ANC. Lutuli apparently feared for Tambo's safety and freedom and felt he would be better off conducting ANC business from outside South Africa. Mandela had been isolated in South Africa's Robben Island prison, and so Tambo was elected Lutuli's successor in 1967. From outside the country, Tambo directed the ANC's campaign that eventually led to South Africa's first democratic elections in 1994—the election that made Mandela president.

Further Reading

Benson, Mary. *African Patriots: The Story of the African National Congress.* 1963.

Benson, M. *Chief Albert Luthuli of South Africa.* 1963.

Benson, M. *South Africa: The Struggle for a Birthright, International Defence, and Aid Fund for Southern Africa.* 1966.

Lodge, Tom. *Black Politics in South Africa since 1945.* Ravan Press, 1990.

Luthuli, Albert. *Let My People Go.* Collins, 1962.

Mandela, Nelson. *Long Walk to Freedom.* Boston: Little, Brown, 1994.

Sampson, Anthony. *The Treason Cage: The Opposition on Trial in South Africa.* 1958.

Sparks, Allister. *The Mind of South Africa.* North Pomfret, VT: William Heinemann, 1990.

Wangari Maathai

Born April 1, 1940
Nyeri, Kenya

Kenyan environmentalist and political activist

o make Kenya green again" is the objective of the Green Belt Movement in Kenya, founded by Wangari Muta Maathai (*MATH-eye*) in 1977. Since then Maathai has become internationally known as an environmentalist and has received many awards and honors for her work. (An environmentalist is someone who is concerned with preserving and protecting nature.) At home she is controversial. The president of Kenya, Daniel arap Moi (see entry), has called her a "mad woman" and "a threat to the order and security of the country." A member of parliament even threatened her with physical violence if she came into his electoral district.

Maathai has provoked the president and the parliamentarians because she has gone beyond the boundaries set by tradition for a Kenyan woman. Not only is she intelligent, highly educated, and outspoken, she has publicly challenged the government on its

"African women in general need to know that it's OK for them to be the way they are—to see the way they are as a strength, and to be liberated from fear and from silence."

human rights abuses and insensitivity to the poor. In addition, she personally challenged the ruling political party when she prevented construction of an office tower in a Nairobi public park.

Basing her program on the simple idea of tree planting, Maathai has found a solution for many environmental and humanitarian problems in eastern Africa. Called the Green Belt Movement, it encourages people in rural areas to plant trees. Since it began in 1977, the 50,000 people involved in the effort have planted an estimated 10 million trees. The trees provide people with firewood for cooking and prevent soil erosion or loss, which eventually turns productive areas into deserts.

Breaks barriers in Kenya

Wangar Maathai was born on April 1, 1940, in Nyeri, a rich agricultural area in the so-called "White Highlands" of Kenya. As the oldest daughter of Kikuyu farmers, Maathai would traditionally have been assigned many of the chores in her family's rural household. But Maathai's older brother convinced their parents that she should be allowed to attend school. She went to the Loreto Limuru School for girls and in 1960 won a scholarship to study in the United States. Maathai graduated from Mount St. Scholastica College in Kansas with a bachelor of science degree in biology in 1964. She earned a master's degree from the University of Pittsburgh in 1965.

When Maathai returned to Kenya in 1966, the University of Nairobi hired her as a research associate in the Department of Veterinary Medicine. At that time, few women held such jobs in Kenya. Women were expected to be submissive (to yield to authority) and not seek higher education or employment. Maathai's male colleagues did not believe she was qualified to work in a university department. Slowly, though, she overcame the obstacles, and by 1971 she had earned a doctorate of philosophy from the University of Nairobi. Continuing at the university, she went on to become a lecturer, then an assistant professor, and finally head of the faculty of veterinary medicine. She was the first woman ever to reach such a level of authority at the university.

The Green Belt Movement

Maathai became involved in environmental and humanitarian topics when her husband, a Nairobi businessman, ran for a seat in the Kenyan parliament in the early 1970s. While helping with his campaign, Maathai became aware of the poverty and unemployment that affected many people in the capital city of Nairobi. Her husband made a campaign promise to create more jobs for the city's poor. After he won the election, Maathai began working on the problem of putting people to work. She opened an agency that paid poor people to plant trees and shrubs. Although the original company went out of business, Maathai did not abandon her plan. In 1977 she took the idea to a women's group called the National Council of Women of Kenya. With the group's support, Maathai turned her idea into a nationwide grass-roots (operated by people at the local level) organization known as the Green Belt Movement.

Maathai based her organization on the idea that the quality of the natural environment was closely related to the quality of life of the people living in that environment. Trees, for example, play a key role in the lives of many Africans. Ninety percent of the African population depends on wood as a cooking fuel. Because so many trees in Kenya had been cut down for fuel or for making charcoal, women found it increasingly difficult to get enough wood for their various domestic needs. As a result, they had to walk longer distances to find new supplies. So even though food was available, the shortage of fuel meant that women could not cook enough food to satisfy their families' needs. Because of this, nutritional problems developed.

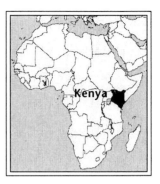

International attention

By offering free seedlings for communities to plant and tend, the Green Belt Movement helped local people reforest their land. The movement paid workers a small amount for every tree they planted and preserved for more than three months. Maathai's efforts to fight the deforestation of Kenya have been successful over the years, resulting in the planting of more than 10 million native trees such as acacias, cedars, baobabs, and cotton trees. The Green Belt Movement has also employed about 50,000 workers.

Maathai's crusade has gained worldwide attention. About a dozen other African countries modeled similar programs after it.

The United Nations and several European countries have contributed financial support for Maathai's work. In 1988 Maathai published a small book called *The Green Belt Movement: Sharing the Approach and the Experience.* She has been honored for her efforts. Her awards include the 1989 Windstar Award for the Environment, the prestigious Goldman Environmental Prize of 1991, the 1991 Africa Prize for Leadership, and the 1993 Jane Addams International Women's Leadership Award.

In a reflective mood about her struggles against the authorities, she was quoted as saying:

> I believe that I was on the right path all along, particularly with the Green Belt Movement, but then others told me that I shouldn't have a career, that I shouldn't raise my voice, that women are supposed to have a master. That I needed to be someone else. Finally I was able to see that if I have a contribution I wanted to make, I must do it, despite what others said. That I was OK the way I was. That it was all right to be strong. African women in general need to know that it's OK for them to be the way they are—to see the way they are as a strength, and to be liberated from fear and from silence.

Encounters conflict with government

Maathai's involvement with political issues and her refusal to accept the traditional role of Kenyan women created conflict both in her personal and public life. Unhappy with her high-profile position, Maathai's husband, with whom she had three children, divorced her in the early 1980s. In 1989 Maathai angered political leaders when she led an environmental campaign to stop construction of an office building in Uhuru Park, one of the few natural areas in Nairobi. Sneeringly referred to as the Tower of Babel, the proposed 60-story skyscraper would have housed the offices of Kenya's ruling political party. She asked the government in public, "We can provide parks for rhino and elephants, why can't we provide open spaces for the people? Why are we creating environmental havoc in urban areas?" The publicity of Maathai's fight caused foreign investors to pull out of the project, saving the park for Nairobi's citizens.

Displeased government officials—unaccustomed to being challenged—started speaking out against Maathai and her Green Belt Movement. They eventually forced the organization to leave its office in a government-owned building and to move to her home. Determined to fight for changes in Kenya's political system

Winnie Madikizela-Mandela

Born 1934
Bizana, Pondoland (Transkei), South Africa

Social worker and political activist

Winnie Madikizela-Mandela (*mah-deek-ee-ZELL-ah*) is a South African political activist, a member of parliament, and the former wife of Nelson Mandela, the country's first black president (see entry). Upon her marriage to Nelson Mandela in 1958 Madikizela-Mandela became a symbol for the political goals and ideals of the black people of South Africa. For many years she was idolized by those opposed to the apartheid system and vilified (defamed or slandered) by supporters of the apartheid government. (Apartheid is an Afrikaans word meaning apartness or separateness. It is a system of segregation based on race that favors whites and restricts blacks to labor reserves.)

Madikizela-Mandela showed great courage as the South African government tried to break her defiant spirit. With her husband in prison since 1962, she had full responsibility for raising

"The difficult part was finding myself with a spotlight on me. I wasn't ready for that."

—Madikizela-Mandela describing her life after husband Nelson Mandela was sentenced to life imprisonment their two daughters, Zindziswa and Zenani. The government harassed her, arrested her and put her in prison—in solitary confinement—for months, and then banned her. (During the apartheid government years, a person could be banned arbitrarily with no right to appeal. Under banning orders Madikizela-Mandela was restricted to a specified district; she was not allowed to be quoted in the South African press; she could not enter schools or universities, publishing houses or courts; she could not communicate with more than one other person at a time; and sometimes she was not allowed to leave her home at all. For more than eight years, the authorities banished her to a small Afrikaner town about 250 miles from Johannesburg.

While Madikizela-Mandela's defiance toward the authorities earned her the adoration of the black youth, who called her "the mother of the nation," by the 1980s her defiance seemed to turn into arrogance, and her militancy became controversial even among her peers. In 1986 she found herself publicly reprimanded by her own and her husband's organization, the African National Congress (ANC). In 1991 the courts convicted her of kidnapping and assaulting a young boy, though the conviction of assault was overturned on appeal. Despite her criminal conviction and her divorce from President Mandela, Madikizela-Mandela continues to hold a leading position in the ANC as head of its women's league. She is a member of parliament and serves on the national executive committee of the ANC, its policy-making body.

Arrives in the city

Nothing in Madikizela-Mandela's upbringing prepared her for the life she would lead as Nelson Mandela's wife. She was born in Bizana in rural Pondoland in the Transkei, in 1934. Her parents named her Nomzamo Zaniewe Winnifred Madikizela. Her mother, a domestic science teacher and religious fundamentalist, died when Winnie was nine years old. She left nine children; the youngest of which was three months old. Her father, Columbus Madikizela, taught history and later worked for the ministry of agriculture and forestry in the Transkei government. Madikizela-Mandela attended Bizana and Shawbury schools in the Transkei. She graduated from Jan Hofmeyr in 1955 and took a job at Baragwanath Hospital in Soweto, becoming the first black medical social worker in South Africa.

Madikizela-Mandela first went to Johannesburg in 1953 at the age of 19 to continue her studies at the Jan Hofmeyr School of Social Work. The year before she moved to Johannesburg, Nelson Mandela and others in the ANC had led the nationwide Defiance Campaign against government apartheid regulations. Many people, especially in the urban areas, became more actively political because of the campaign. When Winnie arrived in Johannesburg she made many friends who were members of the ANC. One of her closest friends was Adelaide Tsukudu, the wife-to-be of Oliver Tambo, who would later be the ANC's president in exile. In 1957 friends introduced her to Nelson Mandela, a 39-year-old lawyer, member of the ANC executive committee, and one of the accused in a treason trial, which was then going on. They had a brief and rather unorthodox courtship because of the time taken up by his court case and his law practice. Nevertheless, on June 14, 1958, Nelson Mandela received permission to go to the Transkei where he and Winnie were married; Madikizela-Mandela was 18 years younger than her husband.

Confrontations with the authorities

That year also marked the beginning of Madikizela-Mandela's encounters with the security police. In September 1958, she and thousands of other women were arrested and held for demonstrating against the government for issuing passes to women. (Under the pass law system, Africans had to carry documents that identified them and certified that they had authorized jobs in white areas.) Because of her arrest, she lost her job at Baragwanath Hospital. This was a real hardship because she was the wage earner in the family.

In 1960 police fired on a group of people protesting the pass laws in the small town of Sharpeville. They killed 68 unarmed demonstrators and injured hundreds more. With the nationwide and worldwide demonstrations that followed the Sharpeville Massacre, the government declared a state of emergency, detained thousands of people, and outlawed the ANC. Although Nelson Mandela was already out on bail awaiting the treason trial, the government detained him and other defendants for nearly five months.

In March 1961, after a trial that lasted four and one-half years, the court found the defendants in the treason trial not guilty. The few months between March and the following December were the only time Nelson and Winnie and their two small girls would have any semblance of a family life. In December Nelson Mandela decided to go into hiding so that he could organize a military wing of the ANC. In August 1962, he was picked up and charged with encouraging Africans to strike in the 1961 work stoppage and with leaving the country illegally. While he was serving a five-year sentence on these charges, he was accused of sabotage, put on trial, and found guilty. In 1964 the courts sentenced him to life in prison.

In 1962 the government placed banning orders on Madikizela-Mandela. Because of these orders she had to get special permission to attend her husband's trial, which was held in Pretoria, outside her restricted area. The wives of the men on trial wore traditional dress to court as a symbol of resistance and inspiration to the people. When the authorities banned the dress, in a gesture typical of her defiance, Madikizela-Mandela began wearing gold, green, and black, the colors of the outlawed ANC.

On her own

After the trial, Madikizela-Mandela was alone, without an income and with two small children to care for. Although she had visitation rights, she was not to have any physical contact with her husband for the next 22 years. In an interview with Anne Benjamin for the book *Part of My Soul Went With Him,* she said of those times: "The difficult part was finding myself with a spotlight on me. I wasn't ready for that." Mandela, a beautiful woman who photographs well, became a symbol of defiance in her traditional dress. She drew attention to herself and became a focal point for the international media. In the same interview she said: "I had to think so carefully what I said as his representative. I don't mean careful because of my banning orders but because of the responsibility."

Banned in 1962, and with more stringent restrictions imposed on her in 1965, Madikizela-Mandela was forced to leave her job with the Child Welfare Society because she could not travel outside of Orlando in Soweto. The authorities placed additional restrictions on her and she remained banned, except for two weeks in 1970, until 1975.

On several occasions between 1962 and 1975 Madikizela-Mandela was charged with violating her banning orders. In May 1969 she and 21 others were detained under the Suppression of

Communism Act and accused of promoting the aims of the out-lawed ANC. The charges were withdrawn in 1970 but she was immediately detained again on the same charges and placed in solitary confinement in Pretoria Central Prison. On these charges, she spent 17 months, 491 days, in prison—most of that time in solitary confinement. She described her confinement to Benjamin:

> Those first few days are the worst in anyone's life—that uncertainty, that insecurity. . . . The whole thing is calculated to destroy you. You are not in touch with anybody. And in those days all I had in the cell was a sanitary bucket, a plastic bottle which could contain only about three glasses of water, and a mug. . . . The days and nights became so long I found I was talking to myself. . . . Your body becomes sore, because you are not used to sleeping on cement.

Because of her circumstances, Madikizela-Mandela had to send her daughters away from her, to a school in Swaziland. The girls had to leave the country because headmasters in private South African schools, after visits from the security forces, invariably found reasons to dismiss them.

Authorities put on more pressure

On her release in September 1970, the government renewed Madikizela-Mandela's banning orders for five years, only two weeks after they expired. They restricted her to her home in Orlando at night and on weekends and public holidays. In 1975 her banning orders expired and the authorities did not renew them for ten months. After 13 years of banning she tasted "freedom" for nearly a year. During this time Madikizela-Mandela helped organize the Black Women's Federation and, after the 1976 Soweto riots, she helped establish the Black Parents' Association to assist people with medical and legal problems caused by police action during the uprising.

Mandela's freedom was brief, however; in August, after the riots, the police arrested her and thousands of others under the Internal Security Act and held them until December 1976. On December 28 she received new banning orders, which were amended in May 1977. This time the authorities banned her from her Orlando home and restricted her to Phatakahle, a black township of about 5,000 people on the outskirts of Brandfort, an Afrikaner town of 1,900 in the Orange Free State.

The banning orders confined Madikizela-Mandela to the Brandfort area for eight years. Because she was a figure of inter-

national standing, she received many foreign visitors in her isolated farm community. Through her contacts and training she
helped the local black community establish a nursery school or
creche, a soup kitchen for the school children, a mobile health
unit, and self-help projects that ranged from growing vegetables to
knitting clothes to sewing school uniforms. While in Brandfort,
the police kept watch over her 24 hours a day; she could entertain
no visitors in her home and could only be in the company of one
person at a time.

Returns to Johannesburg and controversy

In August 1985, someone firebombed Madikizela-Mandela's
Brandfort house. She accused the government of responsibility for
it and, defying her banning orders, left Brandfort to return to her
home in Orlando. The government eventually lifted her restrictions. Mandela then moved out of her Orlando house into a large
house she had constructed in an exclusive area of Soweto.

It was in the 1980s that Madikizela-Mandela became a controversial figure in Soweto. In 1988 other anti-apartheid groups took steps to distance themselves from her. She first alienated many supporters when she endorsed "necklacing," the practice of killing suspected government collaborators by hanging a tire filled with gasoline around their necks and burning them alive. More problems resulted from the so-called Mandela United Football Club, a group of young men who lived in Mandela's house and acted as her bodyguards. Shortly after the killing of a teenage activist in December 1988, for which the leader of the football club was jailed, an influential group of African National Congress members publicly reprimanded her. Eventually, the police charged Mandela with the assault and kidnapping of the young activist. A South African court found her guilty of both charges, but on appeal dropped the assault charge.

The rebuff by the ANC was forgotten when Madikizela-Mandela walked alongside her husband on his release from prison in February 1990. Their marriage, however, could not sustain the difficulties of the past. In 1996 Nelson Mandela divorced her, citing

Winnie and Nelson Mandela after his release from prison, 1990.

| Winnie Madikizela-Mandela

cruelty and infidelity. Many political observers thought she would lose her support once she was no longer Mandela's wife, but to her supporters she was still the champion of the "impoverished masses." She adopted her maiden name after her divorce, calling herself Madikizela-Mandela.

Madikizela-Mandela won election to the new South African parliament as a member of the ANC in 1994 and briefly held a cabinet post. She was also elected president of the ANC women's league in 1994. In 1997, despite public accusations against her at the Truth and Reconciliation Commission, the party members elected her to the National Executive Committee, the decision-making body of the African National Congress.

Further Reading

Benson, Mary. *Nelson Mandela: The Man and the Movement.* New York: Norton, 1986.

Contemporary Newsmakers. Detroit: Gale, 1989.

Gilbey, Emma. "The Lady: The Life and Times of Winnie." *New York Times Magazine,* May 14, 1995, pp. 24-29.

Mandela, Winnie. *Part of My Soul Went with Him.* Edited by Anne Benjamin. New York: Norton, 1985.

Meltzer, Milton. *Winnie Mandela: The Soul of South Africa.* New York: Viking Kestrel, 1986.

Rolling Stone. October 20, 1994, pp. 55-56.

UXL Biographies CD. Detroit: UXL, 1995.

Vail, John J. *Nelson and Winnie Mandela.* New York: Chelsea House, 1989.

The Mahdi, Muhammad Ahmed

Born c. 1844
Dongola province, North Sudan (Sudan)
Died 1885
Omdurman, Mahdia (Sudan)

Islamic prophet and leader

n 1881 a young Muslim visionary named Muhammad Ahmed Ibn el-Sayyid Abdullah declared himself the Mahdi—the successor to the prophet Muhammad, who founded Islam in the seventh century. (Islam is the religion of those who worship the god Allah). Muhammad Ahmed raised an army and purged the northern Sudan of foreign influences. He led his committed believers in an uprising against the Egyptian overlords and their British administrators. To his followers today, the Mahdi is remembered as a nationalist leader (one who fought for self-rule) who liberated the people of the Sudan from outside oppression and paved the way for the modernization of the country.

From a successful strike against a British-led expeditionary force in the desert in 1883, the Mahdi's reputation and strength

"God has guarded you by His angels and prophets. No nation shall be able to face you in battle, whether of the human race or of the race of genii [demons]."

—The Prophet Muhammad's words upon handing the Mahdi a crown from God in the Mahdi's vision

grew. His forces overthrew famed British general Charles Gordon and his troops at Khartoum in 1884, after surrounding the city for months. With the approach of British troops, the Mahdi's forces stormed the city, beheaded Gordon, and displayed his head outside the governor's palace. Although the Mahdi died a few months after Khartoum fell, his chosen successor, the Khalifa Abdallahi, established an Islamic state called Mahdia. Mahdia lasted until 1898, when a British force led by Horatio Herbert Kitchener (1850-1916) defeated its forces at Omdurman and returned the Sudan to Egyptian control.

Foreigners in control

At the time of the Mahdi, the Sudan was a colony of Egypt, although Egypt was still technically part of the Turkish Ottoman empire. Egypt had reached its peak of expansion in Africa, claiming control of the southern areas along the Nile River, the longest river in the world. It runs northward through the northeast African countries of Ethiopia, Uganda, Sudan, and Egypt. From the west, Egypt's territory ran from Darfur province to the Red Sea Coast in the east, controlling several hundred thousand square miles of what is now the Sudan.

The *khedive* (Egyptian ruler) Ismail (reigned 1863-79) and his grandfather Mohammed Ali (reigned 1805-49) had taken huge steps to modernize Egypt, including building the Suez Canal and the Cairo Opera House. They had borrowed enormous sums of money to do it and had amassed a debt they could not repay. To raise funds in the late 1870s, Ismail imposed real hardships on the *fellaheen,* peasant farmers, by over-taxing them. People lost their farms because they could not pay the taxes. And when the government nationalized (took over) farms and made them properties of the state, many ordinary people lost access to farmland.

Western influence in Egypt had grown steadily since the Suez Canal was completed in 1869. Thousands of tourists came from the West each year to the capital city of Cairo. To make room for them, Egyptian authorities tore down mosques (Muslim houses of worship) and replaced them with hotels for Westerners. Europeans held bureaucratic posts (positions held by nonelected government officials) and even took control of the country's finances because of the government's huge debt to European bondholders. By 1875 about 80,000 Europeans were living and working in Egypt. In

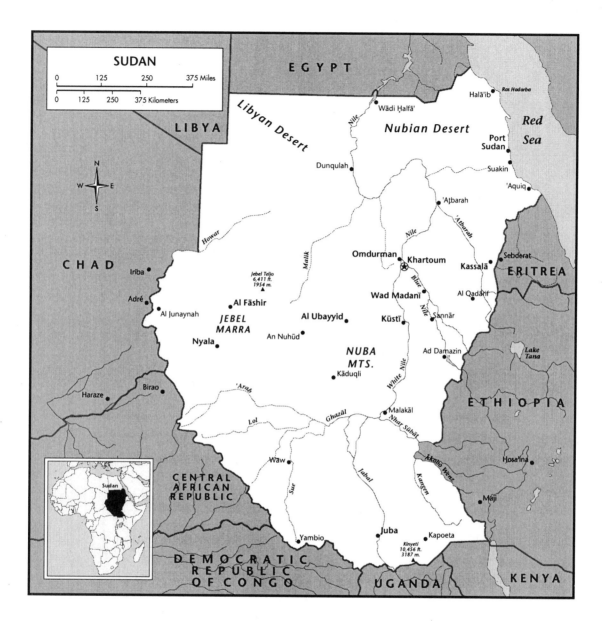

addition, the Egyptian government appointed Europeans as governors-general to administer its provinces.

Agitation grows

Within Egyptian society and in its areas of control, resentment of European presence and influence was growing. Young Egyptian intellectuals began calling for a regeneration of Islamic values, a return to the basic tenets of their faith, and a renewed sense of Muslim unity. Army officers were also unhappy with the system that prevented them, the officers of *fellah* origin, from advancing; all senior posts in the military were reserved for Turks.

When the European-controlled finance ministry stepped up measures to reduce spending, Khedive Ismail saw his opportunity to get rid of the Europeans. The ministry recommended that the government reduce spending on the military by putting 2,000 officers on half pay. The khedive sided with the soldiers and dismissed the head of the finance ministry and the European ministers. Realizing that Ismail was not going to support their financial reforms, the Europeans asked the Ottoman sultan (the khedive's boss back in Turkey) to force Ismail to abdicate, or give up his rule. He did. Ismail was then succeeded by his weak and inexperienced son Tawfiq. The Europeans again imposed their will—they called it Dual Control—as a means of getting back the money the Egyptians owed them. They did not, however, address the growing discontent within society.

The Coming of the Mahdi

Preoccupied with matters of finance, Britain did not pay much attention when a young Islamic leader declared in 1881 that he was the Mahdi, "the Rightly Guided One," whose coming had been foretold in many Muslim prophecies. In popular Muslim belief the Mahdi was the messiah, or savior, who would restore the unity of Islam before the Day of Judgment at the end of the world. Muhammad Ahmed claimed he was the "divine leader sent by God at the end of time to fill the world with justice and equity, even as it had been filled with oppression and wrong." He preached primarily about turning away from worldly pleasures and renewing faith in God. The key to his message, according to Benjamin C. Ray in *African Religions,* was that he truly believed he had been appointed the Mahdi: "The Prophet [Muhammad] then repeated several times that if any man doubts my message, he sins against God and His Apostle. And should anyone oppose me, destruction will come upon him, and he will lose all hope in this world and in the world to come."

A man of vision

Muhammad Ahmed was born near Dongola along the Nile River in what is now the northern Sudan. Most historians believe his father was a boat builder. Ahmed took an early and intense interest in Islamic mysticism and asceticism (spiritual discipline through self-denial). He trained in the Sufi order (called *Sammaniya*) and became a religious teacher, setting up a place of study on Aba Island in the White Nile south of Khartoum. (The White Nile runs out of Lake Victoria in Uganda and the Blue Nile flows from Lake Tana in Ethiopia. The two rivers meet at Khartoum to form the Nile, which flows north and empties into the Mediterranean Sea near Alexandria, Egypt.) Among his followers, he earned a reputation for holiness and mystical powers. Ahmed claimed he learned through a vision that he had been chosen as the Mahdi. He described his vision this way:

> An angel descended from Heaven bearing in his hand a green crown. He saluted the Prophet [Muhammad] and addressed him as follows: "Your Lord salutes you and sends you His blessings and He informs you that this is His crown of victory, and He orders you to give it to him [Muhammad Ahmed] with your own hands." Thereupon the Prophet presented it to the Mahdi, saying "there is no victory save from God. . . . God has guarded you by His angels and prophets. No nation shall be able to face you in battle, whether of the human race or of the race of genii [demons]."

Ahmed believed Allah, the god of Islam, had called him to battle against immorality and corruption in society. He saw himself as being sent by Allah to purify Islam and rid it of its evils. Various religious, political, and economic factors were key to Ahmed's rise in popularity throughout central and northern Sudan in the 1880s. The Muslim population in the area was conservative (traditional), and they deeply resented the corruption and oppression of their Turkish and Egyptian overlords. In addition, the fellaheen resented the heavy taxes they were forced to pay. And regional slavers opposed the efforts of the Egyptian khedive Ismail and General Charles Gordon to eliminate the slave trade.

The movement for reform and reorganization under Ahmed had wide appeal and spread rapidly following his public appearance as the Mahdi in June 1881. But the weakness and indecisiveness of Egyptian authorities also played a major role in the success of the Mahdi's campaign. The Egyptian government declared bankruptcy in 1876, in part because of Khedive Ismail's efforts to build a vast Egyptian empire in the Sudan and Upper

Seeing the Mahdi

Nile area. By 1878 the government owed its foreign creditors 80 million pounds sterling. At the same time, the nationalist movement against foreign presence in Egypt was on the rise. This movement reached its peak with the military coup (overthrow of an existing government) of early 1882 and the consequent British intervention and occupation later that year. The British occupation of Egypt (the presence of British forces that assumed control over the Egyptian government) gave Britain responsibility for the Egyptian empire in the Sudan. Britain sent out 40,000 soldiers to hold the Sudan and appointed foreign governors-general to oversee the various provinces.

Military victories

The Mahdi's movement gained followers because people saw that the Egyptians were unable to overcome it. In 1881 the Egyptian government sent Abu Saoud to Aba Island to bring the Mahdi to Khartoum. The authorities wanted to punish the Mahdi for saying that the Sudan should be purged of corrupt Egyptians. When Saoud's forces approached the island, the Mahdi's supporters pelted them with stones and attacked with swords. They defeated Saoud's forces and sent him fleeing, in the process confiscating much military equipment. After the skirmish, the Mahdi left the island and took his followers to the Nuba Mountains of southern Kordofan province. To his followers, his victory over the better-equipped government troops gave proof of Allah's support.

Siege of El Obeid and its consequences

Kordofan province was the richest agricultural area in the Sudan, and the fall of its capital, El Obeid, was the turning point in the Mahdi's campaign. In August 1882 the Mahdi's forces surrounded the town, which was protected by an Egyptian garrison (troops stationed at a military post). In January 1883, after nearly six months, the town surrendered because its 100,000 residents were starving. The Mahdi took a large supply of arms and money—about 100,000 pounds sterling. After the fall of El Obeid, the intensity of the war increased.

For the followers of the Mahdi, the defeat of El Obeid offered concrete proof of his righteousness and his holiness. They began to worship him as the new prophet and even clothed themselves in a special uniform called a *jibbeh*—a white cotton shirt and skirt with patches sewn on as a mark of virtuous poverty, and a white turban wound around their heads. The Mahdi called them *Ansars,* his "helpers." The British soldiers called them "Dervishes," a word of Middle Eastern and Indian origin that describes their whirling dances of devotion.

Following the fall of El Obeid in January 1883, Lord Cromer (Sir Evelyn Baring, the British consul general in Cairo) sent out troops to crush the Mahdi. Colonel William Hicks of the Bombay Army, a freelance soldier who had joined the Egyptian Service, led the force. He assembled a group of 7,000 infantrymen, 1,000 cavalry (soldiers on horseback), and 5,000 camels to carry their supplies, including mountain and machine guns and millions of rounds of ammunition. Once the expedition was about 100 miles out of Khartoum, it turned westward and marched across the dry plains to El Obeid. Along the way, the soldiers lost their way in the desert and ran out of water. The Mahdi's forces took advantage and swooped down on them at Shaykan in November 1883. Of the thousands of men Hicks started with, only 200 to 300 survived. The victorious followers of the Mahdi occupied most of the Sudan.

The British react cautiously

When the British Cabinet met in January 1884 to discuss the situation in Sudan, it acknowledged that it could not win a war in the desert and did not want the expense of trying. Instead, British authorities sent General Charles Gordon to Khartoum in February

Charles George Gordon, English soldier and adventurer, killed and beheaded by the Mahdi's forces in 1885.

1884 under orders to evacuate all Egyptian troops. Gordon, however, became obsessed by the Mahdi and was determined to smash him at all costs. He cleverly appealed to the British press, calling on his countrymen "to shoulder the burden of civilization and save the Sudan from being overwhelmed by the forces of darkness," according to Lawrence James in *The Rise and Fall of the British Empire.*

In the following month, the Mahdi blocked the Egyptian traffic on the Nile River. No messages or supplies could get through to Khartoum. Nearly 30,000 of Mahdi's forces surrounded the town. Gordon's soldiers were still able to slip out to get cattle and corn for food, but little communication got through and when it did it was months out of date. Soon, Khartoum was impossible to evacuate. In September the Mahdists converged on the city, and in October the Mahdi himself came to take command of the siege (forcing an opponent to surrender, through long-term blockades or persistent attacks).

Meanwhile, the British government sent a relief expedition headed by Sir Garnet Wolseley to rescue Gordon. Wolseley had 7,000 soldiers and equipment and had to cover 1,500 miles of desert. The main body of his forces was going to march across the desert at Matamma. Gordon tried to get word to Wolseley about his situation by sending his small steamboat, the *Abbas,* down river, but the Mahdi's forces captured the sailors and confiscated all of Gordon's correspondence. When these papers fell into the Mahdi's hands, he realized how weak Gordon really was and moved in on Khartoum. Gordon, however, would not surrender.

Fearing that the British forces were getting closer, the Mahdi ordered an attack on Wolseley's relief expedition. The British were not expecting the attack and were quite unprepared for it. The battle was over in 20 minutes with heavy casualties on both sides. After learning that the British were sending back-up forces to Khartoum by steamboat, the Mahdi ordered 50,000 of his soldiers to attack the city on the night of January 25, 1885. They killed nearly 4,000 people, including Gordon, who was speared to death. The Mahdi's soldiers then cut off Gordon's head and presented it to the Mahdi. The ship with the British soldiers arrived three days too late.

The Mahdi died a few months later, probably of typhus (a bacterial disease). His chosen khalifa, Abdallahi, maintained the Islamic state of Mahdia for 13 years until British general Kitchener reoccupied the Sudan, primarily with Egyptian troops, in 1898.

Further Reading

Bermann, Richard A. *The Mahdi of Allah.* 1931.

Farwell, Byron. *Prisoners of the Mahdi: The Story of the Mahdist Revolt Which Frustrated Queen Victoria's Designs on the Sudan.* New York: Norton, 1989.

Hallet, Robin. *Africa since 1875.* Ann Arbor: University of Michigan Press, 1974.

Holt, P. M. *The Mahdist State in the Sudan: 1881-1898.* 1958.

Holt, P. M. *A Modern History of the Sudan.* 1966.

James, Lawrence. *The Rise and Fall of the British Empire.* Boston: Little, Brown, 1994.

Moorehead, Alan. *The White Nile.* New York: Harper, 1971.

Ray, Benjamin C. *African Religions.* Englewood Cliffs, NJ: Prentice Hall, 1976.

Shibeika, Mekki. *The Independent Sudan,* 1959. and P. M. Holt

Theobald, A. B. *The Mahdiya: A History of the Anglo-Egyptian Sudan, 1881-1899.* 1951.

Wingate, F. R. *Mahdism and the Egyptian Sudan.* Originally published in 1891. 2nd ed. London: Frank Cass and Co., 1968.

Samuel Maherero

Born c. 1854
Okahandja, South West Africa (Namibia)
Died March 14, 1923
Lake Ngami, Bechuanaland (Botswana)

Herero chief

"Let us die fighting rather than die as a result of maltreatment, imprisonment or some other calamity."

—Maherero, in a letter seeking support for his rebellion against the Germans

t the Conference of Berlin held in 1884 and 1885, as several powerful European nations carved up Africa among themselves, they brought tragedy to many, including the Herero people of present-day Namibia. The German imperial government wanted its own piece of Africa, and it claimed the territory along the Atlantic Ocean coast that lay between British- and Afrikaner-settled South Africa and Portuguese Angola. In this territory lived the strong and prosperous Herero population. Samuel Maherero, the supreme chief of the Herero nation, made a brave but ultimately hopeless attempt to get the land back from the Germans. The Germans had superior military strength and followed a ruthless racist policy, almost eradicating the Herero nation. When the Herero revolt began in 1904, the population stood at about 80,000. In one year's time more than 65,000 were killed in battle or died of thirst or starvation in the desert where the German troops had chased them.

German policy changes

Before 1884 the only Germans in South West Africa were German missionaries. They had arrived there in the early 1800s with the London Missionary Society. German and British prospectors came later searching for gold and diamonds. In 1884 the German government claimed the territory along the coast to keep the British from advancing into the center of the country. At that time the Herero controlled most of the central territory, running from the Atlantic Ocean to the Kalahari Desert. The most populous and the wealthiest of the peoples of South West Africa, the Herero ran their cattle over vast areas. Cattle raiding was a major occupation, since the measure of a man's wealth was the size of his cattle herd.

The German foreign office did not want to spend a lot of money on its project in South West Africa. It sent out some troops and a few civil servants as representatives. (Heinrich Goering, the father of Nazi leader Hermann Goering, was the high commissioner to the region.) Rather than come into conflict with the local people, the Germans offered to support the chief and protect his clan—but only if the chief promised them exclusive rights to his land and pledged not to engage in any other treaties without German approval. Samuel Maherero's father signed a treaty with the Germans, hoping to get German protection from the Nama people who lived to the south across the Swakop River. But the Germans never intended to get mixed up in any feuds. They were more interested in playing one group off against another.

In 1888, following a report of a gold find in the territory, Germany changed its goals in South West Africa. German miners started to settle in the area, and in 1889 the government sent more troops. Germany was starting to worry about Great Britain's plans: Britain had recently agreed to protect South West Africa's neighbor, Bechuanaland (now Botswana). The Germans wanted to stop the British from gaining more territory in Africa, so they sent a small force of soldiers under Curt von Francois into the German South West. Von Francois was under orders not to upset the Herero. Within six months, however, 200 more German soldiers arrived.

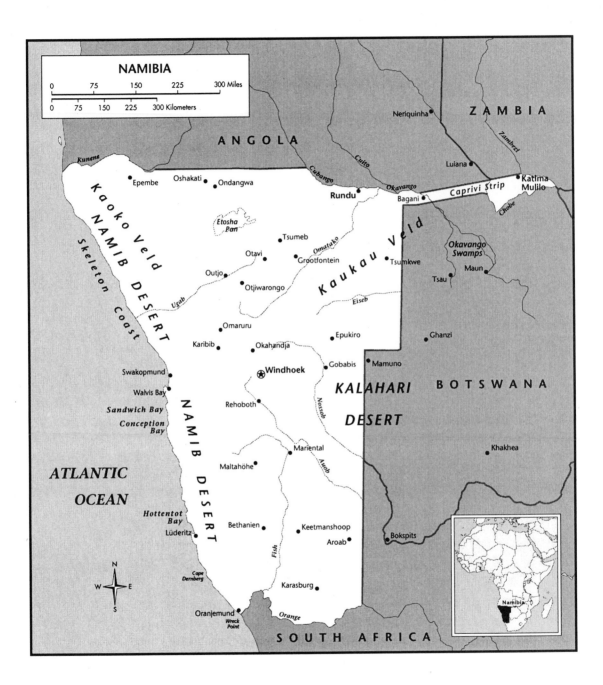

NAMIBIA

0   75   150   225   300 Miles

0   75   150   225   300 Kilometers

ANGOLA

ZAMBIA

Neriquinha

Luiana

Kunene

Cubango

Cuito

Okavango

Zambezi

Katima Mulilo

Bagani

Caprivi Strip

Chobe

Epembe

Oshakati

Ondangwa

Rundu

Kaoko Veld

NAMIB DESERT

Skeleton Coast

Etosha Pan

Tsumeb

Otavi

Grootfontein

Omatako

Kaukau Veld

Tsumkwe

Okavango Swamps

Maun

Tsau

Outjo

Otjiwarongo

Ugab

Eiseb

Omaruru

Epukiro

Ghanzi

Karibib

Okahandja

Windhoek

Gobabis

Mamuno

BOTSWANA

Swakopmund

Walvis Bay

Sandwich Bay

Conception Bay

Rehoboth

Nossob

KALAHARI DESERT

NAMIB DESERT

Mariental

Maltahöhe

Auob

Khakhea

ATLANTIC OCEAN

Hottentot Bay

Lüderitz

Bethanien

Keetmanshoop

Aroab

Bokspits

Cape Dernberg

Fish

Karasburg

N
W   E
S

Oranjemund

Wreck Point

Orange

SOUTH AFRICA

Namibia

Infighting causes problems

Samuel Maherero was born around 1854. His father was the Herero Supreme Chief KaMaherero, and his mother, Kataree, was his father's main wife. Samuel's father had about 60 wives, most of them daughters of Herero chiefs. He took the chiefs' daughters to build support for his role as paramount chief and to unite the Herero. (Polygyny is practiced in many African societies. Under traditional law, a man may have as many wives at one time as he can support.)

Samuel and his brother, Wilhelm, were both baptized Christians. In October 1890, when Samuel was in his mid-thirties, the Herero moved south to fight the Nama. During this time KaMaherero died. Under ordinary circumstances his first son, Wilhelm, would have succeeded him. Wilhelm, however, had been killed in a battle 10 years earlier, and KaMaherero had remained undecided about naming his successor. Samuel's mother was instrumental in having Samuel named successor to KaMaherero.

The fighting between the Nama and the Herero continued, but the Germans remained uninvolved for a time because German settlers were not being affected. The fighting did frighten potential new settlers away from the territory, though. Because of this, Commissioner Goering wrote to Hendrik Witbooi, an educated leader of a Nama subgroup, and asked him to stop attacking the Herero (who were under German protection). Witbooi then wrote to Samuel Maherero and suggested they resolve their differences—that peace between the Nama and the Herero was always a possibility. In November 1892, when the Herero learned that farmers from South Africa were heading north to settle, Samuel Maherero finally agreed to a treaty with Witbooi. The treaty ended nearly 100 years of fighting between the two peoples.

German influence

The peace treaty between the two rival chiefs worried the Germans; they planned a strike against Witbooi. In preparation, the German foreign office sent out 214 more men and two more officers. The fresh troops arrived in March 1893. The next month von Francois made a surprise attack on Hoornkrans, Witbooi's capital. Other Nama tribesmen soon joined Witbooi, and his numbers swelled from 250 to 600 men. Witbooi started with 100 rifles and 120 horses. Within six months they had taken 400 rifles and 300 horses from the Germans. After this defeat the German foreign office sent von Francois home and replaced him with Major Theodor Leutwein.

The Nama people

In the 1700s in southern Africa, the Nama, or Namaqua—a nomadic cattle-herding people—lived on both sides of the Orange River, which borders Namibia and South Africa. The Nama were Khoikhoi, the original peoples of that area. Nama hunters often ventured far to the north, where the Herero pastured their cattle. During droughts the Herero drove their herds south into Namaqualand. This infringement on each other's land caused conflict between the Herero and the Nama.

South of the Orange River, Afrikaner farmers had pushed north from the Cape Colony and occupied land belonging to the Khoikhoi. They forced the Khoikhoi to work for them; over time the Khoikhoi and the Afrikaners intermarried and had children. These people of mixed descent came to be called Orlams. They adopted Western ways and clothing, took up manual crafts, and learned to speak Dutch. Some became Christians. The Orlams received guns and horses in exchange for their labor on the farms.

With their guns and horses they raided cattle, pressing north into land occupied by the Namas across the Orange River. The first major *kapitein* (captain) of an Orlam group was Jaeger Afrikaner. His son Jonker Afrikaner succeeded him in 1823. Jonker settled in central Namibia and called his capital Windhoek. The better-armed Orlam raided the Nama and Herero cattle to trade for more guns and horses. The years following their arrival were marked by ongoing strife between the three communities. But by the time the Germans occupied South West Africa, the power of the Orlams had weakened and the Herero were the dominant group.

In the beginning Leutwein attacked the smaller tribes, leaving Witbooi alone. Late in 1894, Leutwein concocted a scheme to take Herero land without any fighting. First, he paid Samuel Maherero 2,000 German marks to agree to a new southern boundary of Hereroland. Then he obtained Maherero's permission to establish a so-called crown territory (land controlled by the German governor) in the North. These agreements with the Germans angered most of the Herero chiefs. Fearing for his own safety, Maherero asked Leutwein to establish a German military post at Okahandja to protect him. Thus, without a shot being fired, German troops occupied the Herero people's capital. In a letter to the foreign office, Leutwein bragged of his success with Samuel Maherero:

> His friendship has enabled us to remain masters of Hereroland despite our modest protective force. In order to please us, he did more harm to his people than we could ever have done by relying on our strength alone.

With the Herero no longer a threat, Leutwein turned back to the job of bringing Witbooi's forces under control. When more troops arrived, he went after Witbooi, who had hidden out in the mountains. The Germans lost many men, but after 18 months of fighting they finally forced Witbooi to surrender. In September 1894 Witbooi signed a Treaty of Protection and Friendship with the Germans. The Germans took all their cattle and, without food, Witbooi's clan had no choice but to agree to fight against any German enemy.

Inevitable conflict

Leutwein's policy of division was working. Two subgroups, the Herero Mbandjeru and the Nama Khauas, rose up against German settlers and forces. Samuel Maherero—under German protection—was obligated to fight against his fellow Herero in support of the Germans. And Hendrik Witbooi, in honor of his treaty with the Germans, did not support the Nama forces. Leutwein took all the cattle belonging to the Mbandjeru and gave them to the settlers and his troops. Several years later he admitted that he had taken a total of 12,000 head of cattle from Mbandjeru between 1896 and 1897.

In 1897 the Herero suffered even more when rinderpest, a disease of cattle, killed most of their remaining herds. (The Germans had vaccinated their own herds and did not lose many to the disease.) In a few years' time the settlers had nearly 50,000 head of cattle. Many Herero were forced to work for the Germans on the railway or in the mines in South Africa.

Between 1901 and 1903 the white population increased from 310 to 3,000, and more and more often the settlers clashed with the African people. The whites cheated the Africans out of their cattle, took their land, tricked them in business deals, raped women, and lynched men. The last straw for Maherero came when the Germans were completing a railway from Swakopmund on the coast to Windhoek. Samuel Maherero had already granted them the land for building the railway. When they demanded a strip on either side of the line 12 miles wide—and water rights—Maherero refused.

In 1903 a subclan of the Nama, the Bondelswarts, rebelled against the Germans in the southern part of the country. In response to the uprising, Leutwein moved most of his troops from

Hereroland to the South to put down the Nama group. With the soldiers away, Maherero urged his people to rise up against the Germans. The Herero uprising began on January 12, 1904. In one brave move, Samuel Maherero renounced his policy of cooperation with the Germans and united the Herero people. The Herero revolt forced Leutwein to make a hasty peace treaty with the Bondelswarts so he could move his troops back north.

Help too late

In planning for the revolt, Maherero decided to send a letter by messenger to Witbooi, asking him to join the Herero against the Germans. But the letter never made it to Witbooi; the messenger betrayed Maherero and gave the note to the German military leader. The message read:

> I appeal to you my brother, not to hold aloof from the uprising, but to make your voice heard so that all Africa may take up arms against the Germans. Let us die fighting rather than die as a result of maltreatment, imprisonment or some other calamity. Tell all the kapiteins [chiefs] down there to rise and do battle.

Unaware of Maherero's plea, Witbooi honored his treaty with the Germans, giving them time to concentrate on fighting the Herero.

For the first six months, the Herero made strides. They had caught the Germans off guard. In April 1904 the Herero encircled the main German troops and forced Leutwein and his troops to retreat from Oviumbo. The casualty list of German soldiers and settlers grew as the Herero took back their land. In Herero attacks, all German men were killed, but on Maherero's orders, women, children, missionaries, English, and Afrikaners were spared. Toward the end of May the Herero moved to the northeast of the Waterberg plateau, away from the railway and the German supply lines.

The German foreign office criticized Leutwein for retreating at Oviumbo, and he resigned his post. His replacement, Lieutenant-General Lothar von Trotha, described as a "butcher in uniform," arrived in June. He issued what are called "Extermination Orders," in which he demanded: "The Herero people must depart from the country. If they do not, I shall force them to, with large cannons. Within the German boundary every Herero, whether found armed or unarmed, with or without cattle, will be shot."

Hendrik Witbooi (1830-1905) had become a Christian as a young man and claimed that God had chosen him to be the messiah, or savior, of his people. Witbooi was an educated man, fluent in the languages of both the Nama and the Cape Dutch. He wrote letters to friends and enemies and recorded his experiences in his diary.

When the Germans occupied South West Africa, Witbooi was the leader of a large Nama community. The Nama were skillful cattle raiders who increased their herds by attacking Herero cattle posts. In 1893 Witbooi refused German demands that the Namas sign a protection treaty with them. In retaliation, 200 German troops surrounded his capital and opened fire, killing 78 women and children but few fighters. Witbooi and his men escaped to the mountains, where they continued to harass the Germans, cutting off their supply lines from the coast and capturing their horses. Finally, the Germans chased them out of the mountains and forced them to sign the treaty. Witbooi and his people returned to Gibeon where they reestablished their community. For the next 10 years they lived in peace with the Germans—even giving them military support when needed.

When Samuel Maherero rose against the Germans in January 1904, Witbooi at first honored his agreement and sent 100 men to support the Germans. By October, however, he had changed his mind. (This 10-month delay—between January and October of 1904—probably cost thousands of Herero people their lives.) Witbooi urged all Nama communities to rise up against the Germans and wrote to the Nama chiefs: "I have now stopped walking submissively and will write a letter to the Kapitein saying that I have put on the white feather [the sign of the time for war] and that the time is over when I will walk behind him."

Most of the Nama groups answered Witbooi's appeal and attempted to fight off the Germans, who were at a disadvantage because they knew little about the countryside or the location of water sources. On April 22, 1905, when the Germans asked Witbooi to surrender, he refused. Witbooi died that October, still fighting at the age of 75. In their resistance to the Germans, nearly 10,000 Nama had been killed—about half the population. The survivors became laborers on German farms. Witbooi's challenge to the Germans had come too late. Most historians feel that if he had supported Maherero back in January 1904, together they might have prevented the terrible plight of the Herero.

Herero fight a losing battle

Once fresh troops arrived, von Trotha decided to go after the Herero at Waterberg. The Waterberg plateau looms up out of the flat Namibian landscape like a bowl turned upside down. Steep walls protect the plateau on three sides. The southeastern side dips into the Omaheke Desert in Botswana. Von Trotha ordered six

German detachments (separate units of troops) to spread out on the three sides of the plateau, with the smallest group in the southeast. They began their attack on August 11 from the west. With their superior weaponry, the Germans overwhelmed the Herero, leaving them no choice but to flee onto the plateau and then southeast into the desert. German troops killed those who tried to go northward. Most Herero died in the desert; the Germans had formed a line 150 miles long, denying the Herero access to all wells and waterholes until mid-1905.

Von Trotha's extermination order at the time of the attack was brutal:

> Within the German borders, every Herero, whether armed or unarmed, with or without cattle, will be shot. I shall not accept any more women or children. I shall drive them back to their people—otherwise I shall order shots to be fired at them."

Out of a population of 80,000, about 65,000 Herero died, most of them from thirst and starvation in the desert. German soldiers hunted down and killed most survivors. Reports reached Witbooi of how horribly the Germans were treating the Herero. Witbooi and the entire Nama nation took up arms against the Germans in October 1904. A year later Hendrik Witbooi was killed. The Namas continued to fight, engaging 14,000 German soldiers in combat for two more years, but the Nama revolt came too late to help the Herero.

Following Witbooi's death, von Trotha left South West Africa. With von Trotha gone and the Germans realizing they could not win against the Nama, they finally agreed to end the war in 1907. By then half the Nama population of 20,000 had died.

Samuel Maherero and his three sons survived the desert. They made their way to British territory and eventually settled at Lake Ngami in Botswana. Maherero died in exile in 1923. His remains were returned to South West Africa, and he was buried with his grandfather and father in Okahandja. Every year, the Herero gather at the grave site to commemorate their leaders.

Herero today

German-speaking ranchers in Namibia still own much of the prime land taken from the Herero and other groups in the first decade of the twentieth century, while poverty is severe in many of the tribal areas. The once-powerful Herero, their numbers greatly reduced, are a minor ethnic group in Namibia today. In the late 1990s they asked for a national apology and reparations (payment for their losses) from the German government for the genocide it ordered in 1904.

Further Reading

Drechsler, Horst. *Let Us Die Fighting.* Akademie-Verlag, 1966.

Helbig, Ludwig, and Werner Hillebrecht. *The Witbooi.* Longman Namibia, 1992.

Jenny, Hans. *South West Africa: Land of Extremes.* Southwest Africa Scientific Society, 1976.

Knight, Virginia Curtin. "Samuel Maherero." In *Historic World Leaders.* Edited by Anne Commire. Volume 1. Detroit: Gale, 1994.

Lau, Brigitte. *Namibia in Jonker Afrikaner's Time.* Namibia Archives, 1987.

McNeil, Donald G. Jr. "Its Past on Its Sleeve, Tribe Seeks Bonn's Apology," *New York Times,* May 31, 1998.

Soggot, David. *Namibia: The Violent Heritage.* Rex Collings, 1986.

Miriam Makeba

Born March 4, 1932
Prospect, Johannesburg, South Africa

Anti-apartheid activist and singer

"I have love, but I also have suffering. I am a South African. I left part of me there. I belong there."

—Makeba, commenting on her 31-year-long exile from South Africa

Singer-activist Miriam Makeba made the struggle for freedom in South Africa real for the people in the West. In a career spanning more than four decades, she established herself as a powerful voice in the fight against apartheid—the system of economic and social separation along racial lines. Known as "Mamma-Afrika" and "The Empress of African Song," Makeba brought the rhythmic and spiritual tones of Africa to the rest of the world and in the process introduced non-Africans to the unique clicking sounds of her first language, Xhosa. Her more mainstream music is a soulful mix of jazz, blues, and traditional African folk songs shaded with political overtones. Using music as a primary forum for her social concerns, Makeba stands as a lasting symbol in the fight for racial equality.

Early encounter with the system

In all, Makeba spent more than 30 years of her life in exile (a period of forced absence from one's home country). She had her first run-in with the white government when she was just 18 days old. The police arrested her mother, a Xhosa domestic worker, for the illegal sale of home-brewed beer, and the infant Makeba served a six-month jail term in Nelspruit with her. Makeba was one of five children and her childhood was difficult. Her father, a Swazi, died when she was five years old, and her mother could not afford to keep the family together on her own. So young Zenzie (the name Makeba went by as a child) was sent to live with her grandmother in a township in the administrative capital city of Pretoria. She claims that her interest in music was first sparked by the sounds of people known as Pedi, from the northern Transvaal, playing music and dancing in a field in the township.

After primary school Makeba went to the Kimerton Training Institute in Pretoria. As a teenager she earned money working as a house cleaner for white families. But Makeba found comfort and a sense of community in her music and her religion. Singing first in a church choir, she soon branched out and began singing with local bands, achieving success on the regional club circuit. She sang with Nathan Mdlendlhe's band, the Manhattan Brothers, in the early 1950s. It was at this point that she took her professional name, Miriam Makeba.

Makeba toured the southern Africa region (Rhodesia and the Belgian Congo) as a vocalist with the Black Mountain Brothers between 1954 and 1957 and played the female lead in the musical show *King Kong.* She drew international attention with her role in the pseudo-documentary *Come Back, Africa,* a controversial anti-apartheid film released in 1959. Following the film's showing at the Venice Film Festival, Makeba traveled to London, where she met respected American entertainer and activist Harry Belafonte. Impressed with her unique and profound renderings of traditional African song, he served as her mentor and promoter in the United States. He arranged shows for her in New York City clubs and a guest spot on a popular talk show, *The Steve Allen Show.* The exposure brought her worldwide acclaim and launched her musical career.

Makeba, accompanied by Zambia president Kenneth Kaunda (see entry) on the piano, sings Zambia's national anthem, 1969.

Exiled from South Africa

The 1960s were especially tumultuous years for Makeba. Her outspoken opposition to the repressive political climate in South Africa provoked harsh government retaliation. As Makeba's call for an end to apartheid became increasingly powerful, the South African government banned her recordings in South Africa. More than three decades of exile began for the singer in 1959, when she tried to return to South Africa for her mother's funeral. The authorities refused her entry, saying she was an "undesirable person," and they nullified her passport. Around the same time, Makeba endured additional turmoil in her personal life. Between 1959 and 1966 she had two failed marriages, one to singer Sonny Pilay, which lasted for only three months, and another to South African trumpeter Hugh Masekela. Makeba suffered physical abuse at the hands of her first husband, Pilay, who was the father of her only child, a daughter she called Bongi. When that marriage ended, Makeba was left to raise their baby by herself. In the early 1960s she also faced threats to her health, battling cervical cancer through radical surgery.

Marries black activist

Perhaps the biggest blow to Makeba's career came with her 1968 marriage to American black activist Stokely Carmichael (1941-). A self-avowed revolutionary, Carmichael took a militant (aggressive) Black Power stance that frightened many Americans. Having long used song as a vehicle to raise social and political awareness, Makeba was stunned by the devastating effect her marriage had on her musical career. In her autobiography, *Makeba: My Story*, she recalled her disappointment at the way people in the United States regarded her after she had married Carmichael: "My concerts are being canceled left and right. I learn that people are afraid that my shows will finance radical activities. I can only shake my head. What does Stokely have to do with my singing?"

When her record label, Reprise, refused to honor her contract in the United States, Makeba moved with Carmichael to the West African nation of Guinea. In 1968 she represented Guinea at the United Nations. Although Makeba's marriage to Carmichael ended in 1978, she remained in Guinea for several more years. She continued performing in Europe and parts of Africa, promoting freedom, unity, and social change. During the singer's time in Guinea, though, misfortune again touched her life. Her youngest grandson became fatally ill, and her only child, Bongi, died after delivering a stillborn baby.

Tour renews popularity

In the spring of 1987 Makeba joined American folk-rock legend Paul Simon's phenomenal *Graceland* tour in newly independent

Zimbabwe (formerly Rhodesia). The concert focused attention on the racist policies in South Africa and gave South African musicians a chance to be seen by a worldwide audience. Following the success of the *Graceland* tour, Makeba recorded a collection of South African tribal songs. The solo album—titled *Sangoma,* which means "diviner-healer"—was her first American release in two decades. Featuring African chants that Makeba had learned in her youth from her mother, *Sangoma* casts a new light on the soulful, spiritual sounds of the singer's native land. Her follow-up album, 1989's *Welela,* blends traditional songs with newer pop pieces.

Returns home

In a *Chicago Tribune* interview with Leigh Behrens, Makeba summarized her thoughts on her life in exile since 1959: "I have love, but I also have suffering. I am a South African. I left part of me there. I belong there." In June 1990 Makeba finally returned to South Africa after 31 years' absence. The following year she released *Eyes on Tomorrow,* an upbeat protest album recorded in a Johannesburg studio. Featuring pioneering jazz trumpeter Dizzy Gillespie, rhythm and blues singer Nina Simone, and Makeba's ex-husband Hugh Masekela, *Eyes on Tomorrow* is generally considered a more commercial mix of pop, blues, and jazz than the singer's previous efforts.

A spokesperson for civil rights throughout the world, Makeba continues to stand as the embodiment of the black South African condition. As Robert Farris Thompson put it in the *New York Times,* "She is a symbol of the emergence of Afro-Atlantic art and a voice for her people. Her life in multiple cultural and political settings—and her rich musical career, drawing on traditional and contemporary sources—have resonance for us all."

Further Reading

Chicago Tribune, March 20, 1988.

Contemporary Black Biography. Volume 2. Detroit: Gale, 1992.

Makeba, Miriam, and James Hall. *Makeba: My Story.* New York: New American Library, 1987.

New York Times, March 8, 1988; March 13, 1988; June 11, 1988.

Nelson Mandela

Born July 18, 1918
Mvezo village, Transkei, South Africa

*First democratically elected
president of South Africa*

A herd boy from an isolated mountainous area who did not wear shoes until age 16, Nelson Rolihlahla Mandela rose against overwhelming odds to be president of the richest, most culturally diverse country in Africa. He endured more than 27 years in jail for trying to overthrow a white police state, becoming the world's most famous political prisoner. He led voteless black South Africans from the racist apartheid period into a democratic era in 1994. (Apartheid is an Afrikaans word meaning apartness or separateness. It is a system of segregation based on race that favors whites and restricts blacks to labor reserves.) Celebrated as an international hero upon his release from prison in 1990, Mandela will be remembered as one of the twentieth century's towering leaders.

"You had no doubt when you were with him that he had what we call in our language 'shadow'—substance, presence. He was regal."

—Desmond Tutu describing Mandela

Mandela also will be remembered as the precedent-setting African head of state who announced his retirement at the peak of his power after only one five-year term in office. By retiring, he passed "the baton" to a new generation, leaving behind a reputation untarnished by corruption and brutality that besmirched so many long-term African leaders. More than anyone else, Mandela bridged African and European cultures—taking the best from each. He was an educated man, a lawyer, a democrat, a shrewd observer of human behavior, a conservative politician who led a military uprising against an inhuman system, a best-selling and wealthy author, a winner of the Nobel Peace Prize, a connoisseur of food, and a president daring enough to wear colorful, dashing shirts rather than stuffy suits and ties.

Sparkling streams, green mountains

Though he became the toast of Western countries, outshining European and North American leaders of his era, Mandela kept in touch with a royal African heritage that molded him into a self-confident leader at an early stage in life.

Mandela was born in Mvezo, a small, isolated Thembu village on the Mbashe River near Umtata, the Transkei capital. The Transkei is a land of sparkling streams and rounded green mountains in today's eastern South Africa. An area as large as Switzerland, the Transkei was home to the Xhosa people before whites arrived in the seventeenth century. The Thembu form one of seven groups that make up the Xhosa nation.

Mandela's father, Gadla Henry Mphakanyiswa, gave him the first name Rolihlahla, and he got his last name from his grandfather Mandela. As a show of respect, he is often called Madiba, his clan name. The name Rolihlahla means literally in Xhosa "pulling the branch of a tree." But Mandela said its informal meaning is more accurate: "troublemaker." On his first day in school, his British-trained African teacher gave each student an English name. Mandela was named Nelson. "Why she bestowed this particular name upon me I have no idea," Mandela wrote later. "Perhaps it had something to do with the great British sea captain Lord Nelson [1758-1805], but that would be only a guess."

Mandela's father was a gifted orator, custodian of Xhosa history, and a tribal priest. He could not read or write, but he placed great emphasis on education for young Mandela. Mandela's father had four wives who lived at homesteads spaced miles apart. His wives had 13 children—nine girls and four boys—among them. Mandela was the youngest of the four boys. His mother was his father's third wife, Nosekeni Fanny. In Thembu lineage, Mandela was in line to become counselor to the tribal rulers, but never a ruler. Ironically, social and political upheavals would not only make him ruler of his Transkei people, but also of the more than 40 million people living in South Africa when he was elected president in 1994.

South Africa

A "stubborn sense of fairness"

Shortly after Mandela's birth, his father became embroiled in a dispute with a British magistrate that would have a lifelong effect on Mandela. The magistrate summoned Mandela's father in a complaint involving an ox. Mandela's father refused to appear before the magistrate, sending him a message informing him that, as a chief, he was governed by Thembu customs and not by the laws of the king of England. Without an inquiry or hearing, the offended magistrate deposed (removed from power) Mandela's father as a chief.

"My father, who was a wealthy nobleman by the standards of his time, lost both his fortune and his title," Mandela recalled. "He was deprived of most of his herd and land, and the revenue that came with them." Mandela credits the incident with instilling in him his father's "stubborn sense of fairness."

With the family impoverished, Mandela's mother moved a short distance to a larger village and Methodist mission station, Qunu, where she had relatives and could count on support. Mandela's memories of Qunu were fond enough to prompt him to build his retirement home there many years later.

At Qunu, his mother became a Methodist and was given the Christian name Fanny. Mandela also was baptized a Methodist. The Methodist community persuaded Mandela's mother and father to send him to Qunu's one-room, Western-style school. He was the first member of his family to attend school.

The Great Place

When Mandela was nine years old, his father died. After that, Mandela was raised at Mqhekezweni, the Thembuland capital in the Transkei, in the Great Place of Chief Jongintaba Dalindyebo, acting regent (ruler) of the Thembu people. As a local chief and counselor to Thembu kings, Mandela's father had been instrumental in getting Jongintaba chosen acting regent to rule until an infant prince came of age. Jongintaba repaid the counselor's favor by taking his son into the Great Place. Mandela was taken by his mother to the Great Place at Mqhekezweni where he was to be integrated into Chief Jongintaba's court and treated as a member of the royal family. Mandela remembers his mother's parting words as she left him in the majestic new world of the royal house (the chief even had a V-8 Ford): "Brace yourself, my boy!" It was motherly advice that Mandela could use for the rest of his life.

In the Great Place as a boy Mandela watched Jongintabe hold court on public affairs. Thembu men, no matter what their standing, were free to speak and make their arguments until a consensus (general agreement) could be reached—with Jongintabe summing up at the end of debate. "It was democracy in the purest form. . ." Mandela recalled. He added in his book *Long Walk to Freedom*:

> As a leader, I have always followed the principles I first saw demonstrated by the regent at the Great Place. I have always endeavoured to listen to what each and every person had to say before venturing my own opinion. Oftentimes, my own opinion will simply represent a consensus of what I heard in a discussion. I always remember the regent's axiom [rule or principle]: a leader, he said, is like a shepherd. He stays behind the flock, letting the most nimble go ahead, whereupon the others follow, not realizing that all along they are being directed from behind.

At Mqhekezweni, Mandela continued his education at Christian schools, where he learned about British ideas, culture, and institutions. From Chief Jongintaba's Great Place he learned tribal culture and stories of past Xhosa heroes and glories. At the Christian church, Mandela learned another thing: how to eat with a knife and fork.

A promise to be fulfilled

At 16, Mandela went through an elaborate Xhosa circumcision ceremony, a ritual that declared him a man. At the end of the ceremony, Mandela listened to a lamentation (an expression of grief) by Chief Meligqili:

There sit our sons, young, healthy and handsome, the flower of the Xhosa tribe. . . We have just circumcised them in a ritual that promises them manhood, but I am here to tell you that it is an empty, illusory promise, a promise that can never be fulfilled. For the Xhosa, and all black South Africans, are conquered people.... They will go to cities where they will live in shacks and drink cheap alcohol, all because we have no land to give them where they could prosper and multiply. They will cough their lungs out deep in the bowels of the white man's mines.... Among these young men are chiefs who will never rule because we have no power to govern ourselves; soldiers who will never fight because we have no weapons to fight with; scholars who will never teach because we have no place for them to study. . .

Shortly after Mandela's circumcision, Chief Jongintaba told the young man he was being sent to school in a wider world. "It is not for you to spend your life mining the white man's gold, never knowing how to write your name," the chief told Mandela.

In his royal V8 Ford, the chief drove Mandela to Clarkesbury Boarding School at Engcobo, one of the oldest Methodist missions in the Transkei. The chief left the young scholar with pocket money and a new pair of boots. In *Long Walk to Freedom* Mandela remembers his first days at the school:

On this first day of classes I sported my new boots. I had never worn boots before of any kind, and that first day I walked like a newly shod horse. I made a terrible racket walking up the steps and almost slipped several times. As I clomped into the classroom, my boots crashing on the shiny wood floor, I noticed two female students in the first row were watching my lame performance with great amusement. The prettier of the two leaned over to her friend and said loud enough for all to hear: 'The country boy is not used to wearing shoes,' at which her friend laughed. I was blind with fury and embarrassment."

His world widens

In 1937, Mandela transferred to Healdtown, a Wesleyan college at Fort Beaufort, near East London, South Africa, still in the Transkei but 175 miles from home. His world was getting larger. Two years later at the age of 21, Mandela entered University College of Fort Hare at the Transkei town of Alice, also near East London. Fort Hare, the only residential (live-in) center of higher education for blacks in South Africa at the time, had been founded in 1916 by Scottish missionaries. By the time Mandela arrived for study in 1939, the university had evolved into a training ground for the African elite—some of them later to be heads of state—from southern, central, and eastern Africa.

At the end of his second year at Fort Hare, Mandela's studies were cut short by a tribal tradition. Chief Jongintaba decided it was time for Mandela to marry, picked out a wife for him, and set a wedding date. "He loved me very much and looked after me as diligently as my father had," Mandela said in a quote from May Benson's book *Nelson Mandela: The Man and the Movement.* "But he was no democrat and did not think it worth while to consult me about a wife. He selected a girl, fat and dignified. . . ."

To escape the arranged marriage, Mandela really opened up his world. He fled 550 miles north to Johannesburg, the city of gold where tens of thousands of people hurried to and fro all hours of the day and night. Mandela got a job on the police force at a gold mine. But Chief Jongintaba's agents soon found him, and he fled to Alexandra, a black township north of Johannesburg. There he met Walter Sisulu (1912-), a one-time teacher from the Transkei and a real estate dealer in Alexandra, who was bent on overturning the white-minority government.

The African National Congress

Sisulu sent Mandela to law school and made it possible for Mandela and Oliver Tambo (1917-1993) to establish South Africa's first black law firm in Johannesburg in 1952. Besides helping Mandela to start a legal career, Sisulu introduced him to the African National Congress (ANC). The ANC had been organized in 1912 by a group of black lawyers for the purpose of promoting the interests of blacks in the newly created Union of South Africa. In 1944, Mandela, Sisulu, Tambo, and other young ANC members who were ready to fight for the rights of black Africans formed the core of a militant ANC Youth League movement. They removed the ANC's conservative leadership, helped elect Zulu Chief Albert Lutuli (c. 1898-1967; see entry) ANC president, and embarked on non-violent mass action campaigns of defiance by promoting work stoppages throughout South Africa. The militants, including Mandela, opposed cooperating with other racial groups. Mandela became president of the Youth League in 1950.

In 1952 the ANC leadership appointed Mandela "volunteer-in-chief" of a "defiance campaign," by which the ANC hoped to combat apartheid through strikes and civil disobedience. Mandela traveled around the country recruiting volunteers to break

apartheid laws through such acts as passing through "whites only" entrances to railroad stations, defying curfews, and burning passes. On June 26 he and 51 others started the campaign by breaking a curfew.

Mandela in his law office, 1952.

From the time Mandela joined the ANC in 1942 until he went underground after the organization was banned in 1960, the white government beat, banned, jailed, and tried him, unsuccessfully, for treason. In 1952 he and other ANC leaders were arrested under South Africa's Suppression of Communism Act. Mandela was given a suspended sentence, but was then served with an order prohibiting him from attending meetings or leaving the Johannesburg area. The banning order would be continually renewed. At that time Mandela was deputy national president of the ANC, but forced to resign in 1953 because of the banning orders, he had to lead the organization secretly. In 1955 Mandela and 155 others were charged with treason. The case did not go to trial for three years. Mandela helped to conduct the defense, and it was largely through his efforts that he and all of his co-defendants were acquitted.

Umkhonto we Sizwe

By mid-1961, Mandela, Sisulu, and other ANC members concluded that the white government of South Africa would respond only to violence. They set up *Umkhonto we Sizwe* (known by the initials MK), or "Spear of the Nation," which would become the military wing of the ANC to carry out sabotage and guerrilla warfare. Mandela was made commander of the MK. The military unit launched a campaign of sabotage on December 16, 1961, with the announcement: "The time comes in the life of any nation when there remains only two choices: submit or fight. . . We shall not submit and we have no choice but to hit back by all means within our power in defense of our people, our future and our freedom."

Travels across Africa to London

In January 1962, Mandela left South Africa for the first time—and the only time until he was released from prison 28 years later. Leaving secretly because police sought him on a charge of organizing illegal demonstrations, Mandela went to Addis Ababa, the capital of Ethiopia, where he spoke to a summit of African leaders. Then he and Tambo, then based in Tanzania, went to London to confer with leaders of Britain's Liberal and Labour parties. On his return to Africa, he underwent military training in newly independent Algeria. He returned through East Africa, seeking promises of help for the ANC military campaign inside South Africa.

Shortly after his return to South Africa, Mandela was arrested by police on August 2, 1962. At a subsequent trial, he was sentenced to five years of prison labor for encouraging people to strike and leaving the country illegally. Mandela was serving that sentence when, on July 12, 1963, police arrested Sisulu and others in a farm house at Rivonia, just north of Johannesburg. The farm house was the ANC's operational headquarters for the MK. During the raid, police found a copy of Mandela's plan for carrying out sabotage and new charges were brought up against him. In the 1964 trial that followed, Mandela and other Rivonia defendants admitted to carrying out sabotage against government installations, but denied engaging in guerrilla war. At the end of the trial, the only question left was whether the defendants would get death sentences.

Against advice from his lawyers, Mandela insisted on giving an opening defense statement of more than 10,000 words, explaining objectives of the ANC and indicting (accusing of crime) white supremacy. Mandela concluded his long statement:

> During my lifetime I have dedicated myself to this struggle of the African people. I have fought against white domination, and I have fought against black domination. I have cherished the ideal of a democratic and free society in which all persons live together in harmony and with equal opportunities.
>
> It is an ideal which I hope to live for and to achieve. But if needs be, it is an ideal for which I am prepared to die.

Desmond Tutu (see entry), retired Anglican archbishop of Cape Town, reacted to this speech, as quoted in Benson's biography. "When you read his testimony in court you are proud that you too are black."

On June 11, 1964, at the conclusion of the trial, Mandela, Sisulu, and six others—Govan Mbeki, Raymond Mhlaba, Elias Motsoaledi, Andrew Mlangeni, Ahmed Kathrada, and Denis Goldberg—were convicted of sabotage. They were sentenced to life imprisonment.

A "giant of a man"

Mandela was eventually sent to to prison, intially at Robben Island, the "Alcatraz" of South Africa. (He would later be moved to less harsh prison conditions.) There he was assigned tasks such as gathering seaweed and breaking rocks. He also taught himself to speak Afrikaans, and quickly became a leader and teacher among the prisoners. The middle-aged commander of a guerrilla unit who narrowly escaped the South African hangman gained an uncanny perspective on life during his 27 years in prison. But he never departed from the ideal for which he risked the gallows: a chance to live freely in a society where rules are decided by fairly elected representatives of the people.

After his sentencing, Mandela became an international symbol of resistance to the white supremacy government. Even in prison Mandela projected a natural sense of command. "He is, quite simply, a giant of a man with an enormous intellect," said Desmond Tutu. "You had no doubt when you were with him that he had what we call in our language 'shadow'—substance, presence. He was regal." At several times during his imprisonment the South African government tried to negotiate his release, but Mandela would not agree to the terms even though it meant staying in prison.

Hendrik J. Coetsee, the minister of justice, prisons, and police in South Africa's white minority government, had his first of many visits with Mandela in 1985. At the time, Mandela—sentenced to life in prison—had been in jail for 22 years and was 67 years old. He had undergone prostate surgery in a Cape Town, South Africa, hospital. Coetsee was accompanied by General Johan Willemse, the commissioner of police. From his hospital bed where he was attended by two nurses, Mandela cheerfully greeted his jailers like long-time friends. He displayed no bitterness about his lost years in prison. Allister Sparks quotes Coetsee's description of that day in *Tomorrow Is Another Country*:

> It was quite incredible. He acted as though we had known each other for years, and this was the umpteenth time we had met. He introduced General Willemse and me to the two nurses. I remember he made a little joke about this being his ward and me being his warder. He took complete command of the situation. He was like the host. He invited us to sit down, and 'General Willemse, are you comfortable and is there anything we can do for you?' I had read a lot about him—all his speeches and all these reports that came across my desk every day—and I was fascinated at what kind of man he must be to have attracted all this international attention and have all these honorary degrees and awards given to him. When I met him I immediately understood why. He came across as a man of Old World values. I have studied Latin and Roman culture, and I remember thinking that this is a man to whom I could apply it, an old Roman citizen. . . .

In mid-1984 ANC activists and others had made it virtually impossible for the white minority to govern South Africa. An upsurge in violence across the country took hundreds of lives. The government responded by declaring a state of emergency and arresting thousands. In 1988 the ANC conducted a bombing campaign against mainly civilian targets. Fearing civil war between blacks and whites, Mandela opened negotiations from his prison cell with the government of South African President P. W. Botha. A few weeks later Botha was replaced as president by F. W. de Klerk (see entry).

Freed at last

The negotiations between de Klerk and Mandela were lengthy. But on February 11, 1990, de Klerk freed Mandela from

prison with no preconditions. Following his release, 120,000 people welcomed Mandela home at a rally in a Soweto soccer stadium. When Mandela addressed the crowd, he took a moderate line. Among other things, he urged that school boycotts as a means of resisting apartheid be called off and rejected the idea that "liberation must come before education." He also called for "goodwill to our white compatriots."

Nelson Mandela and F. W. de Klerk, winners of the 1993 Nobel Peace Prize.

Mandela worked with President de Klerk for four grueling years to establish a representative government. De Klerk wanted some form of power sharing, commenting that"a party that wins 51 percent of the vote should not have 100 percent of the power." Mandela wanted a one-man, one-vote system in which the party that won a simple majority would take power. In 1992, when the talks broke down, the ANC began a series of strikes and demonstrations that eventually resulted in the deaths of 28 demonstrators. Mandela and de Klerk went back to the negotiating table.

Mandela saw his ideal become a reality on April 27, 1994. That day he was chosen in a one-person, one-vote election as the first black president of South Africa. His political party, the African National Congress, was elected as the majority in South Africa's parliament.

Mandela was married and divorced twice. He had two sons and a daughter by his first wife, Evelyn Mase, a nurse and relative of Sisulu's from the Transkei. His second marriage was to Nomzamo Winifred Madikizela, known as Winnie Mandela (see entry). She was South Africa's first black female social worker from Tambo's home area in the Transkei. They have two daughters. With Mandela in prison, Winnie Madikizela-Mandela became the beacon of the black resistance movement inside South Africa. After Nelson Mandela's release, their relationship deteriorated, ending in divorce at Mandela's initiative in 1996.

Meanwhile, Mandela developed a close relationship with Graca Machel, widow of Mozambique President Samora Machel. At times during their courtship, she filled the role of South Africa's first lady when Mandela traveled abroad or at state functions in his presidential home in Houghton, a shady residential suburb of Johannesburg where South Africa's mining barons live. Mandela married Machel on his eightieth birthday on July 18, 1998.

Further Reading

Benson, Mary, *Nelson Mandela: The Man and the Movement,* New York: Norton, 1986.

Mandela, Nelson, *Long Walk to Freedom,* Tunbridge Wells, Devon, U.K.: Abacus, 1995.

Sparks, Allister, *The Mind of South Africa,* London: Heinemann, 1990.

Sparks, Allister, *Tomorrow Is Another Country,* South Africa: Struik, 1994.

Tom Mboya

Born August 15, 1930
Kilima Mbogo, British East Africa (Kenya)
Died July 8, 1969
Nairobi, Kenya

Kenyan politician and labor leader

 frican trade unionist and nationalist Thomas Joseph Mboya played an important role in the struggle for Kenyan independence from British colonial rule. With his exceptional skills at organizing and his gift for public speaking, he attracted a large following as a labor leader and politician. While activist and future Kenyan president Jomo Kenyatta (see entry) was in prison and confined to the northern territories, Mboya laid the foundation for an active Kenya African National Union (KANU), Kenya's black-majority political party. Kenyatta assumed leadership upon his release. Mboya was outspoken and critical of government corruption. He became entangled in the ethnic and political rivalry of post-independence Kenya and was assassinated in 1969 at the age of 39.

Mboya's death brought an end to the career of one of Africa's most brilliant nationalists and to a prosperous and democratic era of Kenyan independence.

Poverty and hard work

Tom Mboya was born on August 15, 1930, on Kilima Mbogo, a sisal plantation—sisal is a strong white fiber used for making rope—located 40 miles outside of Nairobi (the present-day capital of Kenya). His family was large and impoverished. Mboya's father struggled to support his wife and eight children with the single British pound he earned each month working the land on the estate. At the time, black Africans were not allowed to own any land in this European-dominated section of British East Africa. Recalling these trying times in his 1963 autobiography *Freedom and After,* Mboya mused:

> I watched the estate workers carrying heavy burdens of sisal, dripping with water, which affected their skins. I saw them wake up for work early in the morning and come back late in the evening. My family and other workers lived in villages of mud and wattle [woven branches and poles] huts with no sanitation but the bush. We drew our water from the Athi River. The employer was brutal, sometimes to the point of beating up workers. It was a hard life.

Mboya's parents were Luos who had converted to the Catholic faith when European missionaries began spreading Christian teachings throughout eastern Africa. Young Mboya attended a local mission school for two years and then went to a primary school at Kabaa in the Ukamba district. He finished up his primary education at St. Mary's boarding school in Yala in 1945. The following year, Mboya entered Holy Ghost College High School, but his father had a hard time paying the school's fees. Although the elder Mboya's wage had increased to two pounds per month, Mboya's schooling cost eight pounds a year—four months' salary—and his father still had two younger sons about to enter primary school. Mboya took several jobs on campus to help pay for his education, but in 1947 his family's financial situation forced him to drop out of Holy Ghost.

A union post

Although he toyed with the idea of becoming a primary school teacher, Mboya ended up applying to the Jeanes School, an American-backed medical school of the Royal Sanitary Institute. The institute paid him while he trained as a sanitary inspector, so he was able to send money home to help finance his younger brothers' education. At the Jeanes School, Mboya had the opportunity to meet students from different ethnic groups throughout Kenya. He also became very involved with sports and student affairs, establishing himself as a soccer player, a leading member of the debating team, and student council president.

In 1951, when Mboya graduated from the institute, he took a job as sanitary inspector for the city of Nairobi. The Staff Association Union, the group that represented African city employees, asked him to fill the vacant post of union secretary. He was on the job for less than a year when the bloody Mau Mau revolt erupted. Mau Mau was a secret society of Kikuyu whose members had taken an oath to rid Kenya of its white settlers.

The Mau Mau revolt

Kenya was one of several British dependencies in eastern Africa referred to collectively as British East Africa. Determined to turn Kenya into a "white man's" country, the British government began urging Britons to settle in Kenya and take up farming. The grievances that led to the Mau Mau revolt had been building since the British colonial government enacted the Crown Land Ordinance of 1915. This act reserved some of the best land in East Africa for Europeans—in the region that is now Kenya, more than a quarter of the 20,000 square miles of land with good rainfall was set aside for whites. After World War I (1914-18) nearly 9,000 Europeans had settled in Kenya, and much of the highlands outside Nairobi had been set aside for whites. Close to 7 million acres of African land were taken—mostly from the Maasai and Kikuyu peoples—for European settlement. The building of a railroad connecting Mombasa—a key port off the southern coast of Kenya—with fertile Lake Victoria led to a steady stream of white immigration. Thousands of African families, especially the Kikuyu of the Central Highlands, were removed from their ancestral lands and forced into areas reserved especially for them—the so-called "native reserves." In time the reserves became overcrowded, and the soil produced fewer and fewer good harvests as it became more and more overworked.

For years the Kikuyu people campaigned to recover their land. In 1929 black rights leader Jomo Kenyatta, representing the Kikuyu, traveled to London to petition for a change in British policy. He would not return to Kenya until 1946, and the issue remained unresolved in the meantime. Resentment among the

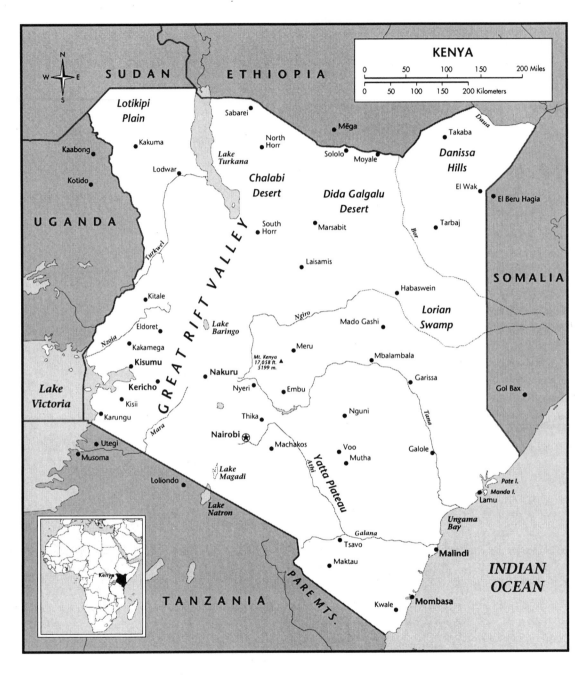

Kikuyu increased when the British government placed restrictions on how much coffee village farmers could grow. (The European growers did not want competition from the Africans.) Black Africans were also required to carry identity cards designating their reserve area. And, according to government policy, they could never be paid the same wages as whites. To fight this discrimination and to campaign for African rights, activists formed the Kenya African Union (KAU) in 1944. Two years later Kenyatta assumed leadership of the KAU, demanding political reform, African land rights, an end to racial discrimination, and real progress in the journey toward Kenyan independence.

Meanwhile, more militant Kikuyus—those more willing to fight—remained associated with the Kikuyu Central Association (KCA) and pledged to get back their land by any means necessary. By the late 1940s members of the KCA were taking secret Mau Mau oaths among the Kikuyu, pledging support for their cause. Not all Kikuyus endorsed the movement, but tens of thousands did. Around 1950 rumors of secret arms stores began circulating. By 1952 Mau Mau fighters were burning more and more white farms and intimidating Kikuyus who refused the oath. Although the British government had no evidence that Kenyatta was associated with the Mau Mau movement, he and the other leaders of the KAU were arrested and the association was banned. The mass arrest led to a violent rebellion and a grinding guerrilla war; 21,000 British troops were called in to crush the Mau Mau uprising.

Trade union speaks for African people

Mboya began organizing the Staff Association, a local interest group, into a countrywide labor union (a workers' organization dedicated to improving its members' rights, wages, and working conditions). Backed by his old classmates from the Jeanes School, the association tripled in size in just eight months. Known thereafter as the Kenya Local Government Union, the 1,300-member association had branches throughout the entire colony. Mboya's reputation as an organizer and an eloquent speaker spread quickly and caught the attention of James Patrick, a British Labour party representative sent to the colonies to encourage trade unionism. Patrick put Mboya into contact with trade unionists in Great Britain, Canada, and the United States. Mboya drew the attention of the newly formed Kenyan Federation of Labour (KFL), becoming its general secretary in 1953. The federation was the only national organization speaking for the African people. Tom Mboya, at the age of 23, was their voice.

The colonial government used extremely repressive measures to try to crush the Mau Mau rebellion. Mboya led demonstrations against the mass evacuations, detention camps, and secret trials of suspected Mau Mau supporters. In 1954, on his first trip to Britain, he made headlines for his protests against the detention camp policy. Mboya also spent time at Calcutta College in India, studying labor relations. Before returning to Kenya he published several articles that appeared in European and American publications.

Mboya successfully negotiated a settlement with the colonial authorities that ended strikes by city workers in Nairobi and by dock workers on Mombasa, an island off Kenya's southern coast. After the settlement Oxford University invited Mboya to study labor and politics there for a year. Before returning to Kenya, Mboya made a two-month speaking tour of the United States. During this time he arranged for Kenyan students to travel to the States and study in U.S. colleges.

Mboya was back in Kenya in November 1956; the Mau Mau emergency had already subsided. Due in large part to Mboya's efforts, the British government put pressure on Kenya's white authorities, forcing them to ease their grip on black rights. As a result, Africans were permitted to organize local political parties. Mboya immediately established the Nairobi-based Peoples' Convention Party (PCP) with the slogan *Uhuru Sasa*—"Freedom Now." Using his trade union connections, he gradually organized the PCP in other regions, building up his national base of support. In the first elections open to Africans in 1957, Mboya easily won in his Nairobi district, becoming one of seven black Africans to sit in the white-dominated assembly.

Chairs conference of African nationalists

In March 1957, the same month as Mboya's election, Kwame Nkrumah (see entry) had led the western African nation of Ghana to complete independence. Nkrumah called for an All-African Peoples' Conference to convene in Accra, Ghana, in December 1958. African nationalists from all over the continent gathered and discussed strategies for achieving the liberation of Africa. Among the 500 delegates attending the conference were future African presidents Patrice Lumumba (Congo; see entry), Hastings Banda (Malawi; see entry), Robert Mugabe (Zimbabwe; see entry), Félix Houphouët-Boigny (Ivory Coast; see entry), and Nnamdi Azikiwe (Nigeria; see entry). The conference elected Mboya chairman before he even arrived.

Having attracted international attention, Mboya spearheaded a movement for the release of Kenyatta, and called for real progress in the quest for independence among European-held countries in Africa. In the summer of 1959 Mboya returned to the United States to receive an honorary degree from Howard University in Washington, D.C. He also coordinated financing and sponsorships for the African-American Student Airlift Program that would send thousands of Kenyan students to American universities. While working on this program, Mboya met his future wife, Paula Odede, a sociology student. They married in 1962.

Trouble in the transition government

Mboya's next stop was Great Britain, where he served as a representative in negotiations for a multiracial transition government in his country. Kenya was preparing for independence, but the shift to black majority rule was to be gradual, with a combination European-African delegation serving in the interim. After a month of harsh and bitter debate among British officials, the white settlers, and Kenya's African population, the British agreed to lift the ban on national African political parties and to redefine who could vote. This expanded black voting rights to one million African voters. The British also agreed that Africans would have a slight majority in cabinet ministries and legislative seats.

When Mboya and the other delegates returned from their negotiating in England to organize the new political parties, internal ethnic tensions that had been brewing for years in Kenya surfaced. Most of the delegates—Mboya included—envisioned a single party that would run candidates for elections. In March 1960 these activists formed the Kenya African National Union (KANU; a reorganization of the KAU) and elected James Gichuru acting president until Kenyatta's release. Oginga Odinga served as vice-president, and Mboya was secretary.

The idea of centering control in one party—a party composed mainly of Kikuyu and Luo representatives—caused a stir in Kenya's fledgling transition government. When party officials offered Ronald Ngala and Daniel arap Moi executive positions in KANU, both men refused to join because they did not share KANU's vision of government. Most of KANU's members wanted a one-party state with a strong central government. But, fearing that the Kikuyu and Luo groups would dominate the

Mboya campaigning in Nairobi for upcoming elections as secretary general of the Kenya Africa National Union (KANU), 1961.

government, Ngala and Moi insisted that Kenya should be a confederation of regions based on ethnic groupings. They left KANU and organized an opposition party known as the Kenya African Democratic Union (KADU).

In the following elections, with Kenyatta's name and Mboya's national trade union base, KANU won eighteen of the national assembly seats, and KADU took seven. Mboya became the minister of labor and had the responsibility of formulating labor and industrial relations policies for the new nation. In 1962, he persuaded all the major unions to sign the Kenya Industrial Relations Charter, which detailed the procedures for settling labor disputes. His role in the government expanded in 1965, when he became the minister of economic planning and development. Despite interdepartmental difficulties, he forged his division into an important part of the government operations. Under Mboya's administration, Kenya enjoyed the most successful economic growth in all of Africa.

Felled by an assassin's bullet

The major opposition to Mboya's leadership in KANU came from a fellow Luo politician, Oginga Odinga. He was older than Mboya and from the same Nyanza ancestral district near Lake Victoria. Odinga, who had traveled widely in Eastern Europe and the Soviet Union, was suspicious of Mboya's close ties to the United States, particularly because many people suspected that the United States had been involved in the murder of Congolese Prime Minister Patrice Lumumba (see entry). Odinga also called for redistribution of white-owned land to the landless African farm workers and objected to Mboya's moderate land distribution policy, which paid Europeans the market price for their holdings. Odinga called for a massive redistribution of white-owned land—without payment—to the landless African peasantry. Clashes between Mboya and Odinga dominated Kenya politics until 1968, when Odinga left KANU.

Odinga's departure did not end party dissatisfaction with Mboya. Mboya was increasingly critical of the wealth and privileges accumulated by the family and friends of Kenyan president Kenyatta. As a likely successor to Kenyatta, Mboya represented a serious threat to Kikuyu power in the government. In July 1969 Mboya was shot to death by a Kikuyu who had connections to high government officials. His death brought an end to the career of one of Africa's most brilliant nationalists and to a prosperous and democratic era of Kenyan independence.

Further Reading

Forrest, Ronald. *An African Reader.* New York: Longman, 1965.

Gertzel, Cherry. *The Politics of Independent Kenya: 1963-1968.* Northwestern, 1970.

Mboya, Tom. *Freedom and After.* Boston: Little, Brown, 1963.

Meredith, Martin. *First Dance of Freedom.* New York: Harper, 1984.

Historic World Leaders. Edited by Anne Commire. Detroit: Gale, 1994.

Menelik II

Born August 17, 1845
Ankober, Shoa (Ethiopia)
Died c. December 12, 1913
Addis Ababa, Ethiopia

Emperor of Ethiopia

One key to Ethiopia's survival as a nation was Menelik's wisdom to supply his soldiers with modern weapons.

enelik II founded modern Ethiopia. His army won one of the greatest African military victories over a European aggressor by crushing an Italian force at Adowa in 1896. He was the only African leader to keep control of his country when European powers carved up the continent into colonies in the late nineteenth century. In fact, as the Europeans divided up Africa beginning in 1885, Menelik expanded Ethiopia to more than twice its original size. The new territory gave him wealth to use in his battle against a takeover of his country by colonial powers. (Colonial powers are nations that rule over other territories and countries.)

Ethiopia claims a history as a nation going back more than 3,000 years. For many years, however, the country remained cut off from the rest of the world and this isolation deprived its people of technological growth. The pioneering, diplomatic emperor Menelik II brought his nation into the dawning twentieth century with its radical new changes brought on by industrial manufacturing, scientific discoveries, expansion of world trade, and new fast-firing, long-range weapons. A key to Ethiopia's survival as a nation was Menelik's wisdom to supply his soldiers with modern weapons. He also levied (collected) a tax to pay his army. That stopped soldiers from looting, or robbing, peasants—a practice that had caused discontent among poor people who lived on farms and in villages.

The emperor's long list of accomplishments included creating Ethiopia's first national money, postage stamps, mint (place where coins are made), bank, hotel, modern school, printing press, government hospital, railroad, and modern roads and bridges. Fascinated by foreigners and their technology, especially their latest weapons, Menelik was the first emperor to send students to study in universities of other countries. He imported eucalyptus trees to help end the country's wood shortage. And he set up a central European-style government to administer the nation's affairs and unify the country.

Menelik was known for his intelligence and good humor. The emperor rode barefoot through Addis Ababa on a mule covered with a scarlet saddle cloth. A servant held each stirrup, and a boy ran beside the mule holding a golden umbrella over the emperor's head.

In 1887 Menelik established Addis Ababa around a hot springs about 8,000 feet above sea level in the Shoa region, a fertile province in Ethiopia's central highlands. (The name *Addis Ababa* means "new flower" in Amharic, the language spoken in that section of the country.) Menelik made Addis Ababa the nation's capital in 1889 after he became emperor. Since then it has grown into a city of more than 2 million people.

His early years

Menelik II was born Sahle Mariam on August 17, 1845, in Ankober, one of the capitals in the Shoa province. His grandfather, Sahle Selassie (1795-1847), crowned himself king of Shoa in 1813 and declared the province a country independent of Ethiopia. He ruled Shoa until his death in 1847. The name Menelik has its roots in the story of the mythical son of Israel's King Solomon and the Queen of Sheba, ruler of Ethiopia in the first century B.C. Ethiopian myth says the son of Solomon was named Menelik I and

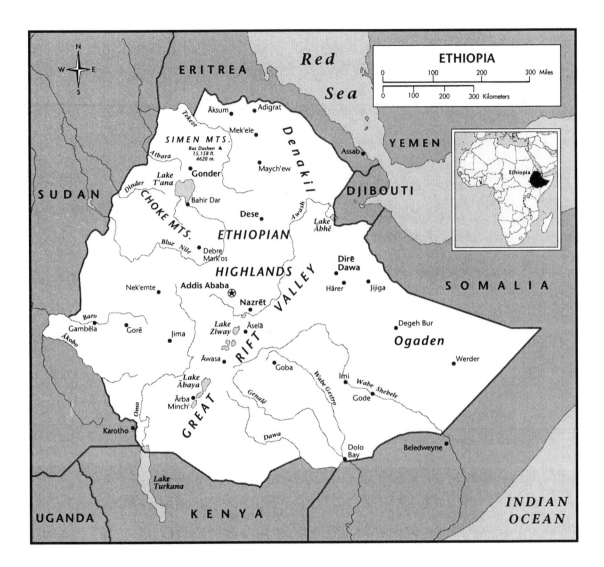

that he was the first of the Solomonic dynasty (ruling family) that had led the nation, with few interruptions, for nearly 3,000 years.

According to legend, Sahle Selassie foretold that his grandson would grow up to be a great man who would rebuild the Ethiopian empire. At Menelik's birth such a day seemed anything but likely. Ethiopia, plagued by wars and rebellions, lacked any strong, centralized authority.

Shoan independence came to an end following the brief and undistinguished reign of Menelik's father, Haile Malakot (1847-1855). Forces of Ethiopian emperor Tewodros II (1820-1868; see

Attempting to reunite the 3,000-year-old Ethiopian empire was a dangerous venture in the nineteenth century. Tewodros (1820-1868), sometimes referred to as Theodore, was the first to try it. He put reunification and modernization of Ethiopia in motion. But the ambition cost him his life.

The son of provincial governor Haylu Walda Giyorgis, Tewodros grew up near Gondar, capital of the remains of the Ethiopian empire, which had been divided among mostly independent regions. Though educated in Christian monasteries, Tewodros gained a reputation as a successful robber chieftain along Ethiopia's northwestern frontier with Islamic Sudan. He was also quite skilled in warfare and political maneuvering.

By eliminating his competitors—warlords from other provinces—he crowned himself Emperor Tewodros II on February 11, 1855, at the ancient capital of Aksum in the northern province of Tigre. Tewodros considered Christian European countries to be Ethiopia's natural ally. He dreamed of acquiring enough support from them to drive the Turks out of Jerusalem and establish Christian rule there.

At the same time, the emperor angered Coptic (a branch of the Christian church originating in Egypt) leaders by reducing church lands to finance reforms and a centralized government. In 1862 he wrote to British Queen Victoria (1837-1901) proposing an alliance between Britain and Ethiopia, perhaps with his Jerusalem crusade in mind. The queen did not answer the emperor's letter. This angered Tewodros. In 1864 he imprisoned the British consul for failing to bring back a letter from the queen. He also jailed an assortment of Christian missionaries and a special British ambassador sent to free the captives. (Tewodros II is believed to have suffered from manic depression, a mental disorder characterized by severe mood swings that range from intense excitement to very deep depression. This may have accounted for his erratic, or unpredictable, behavior.)

After four years of haggling with the emperor, the British sent a military expedition to Ethiopia to gain the prisoners' release. Thirty-two thousand British and Indian troops, accompanied by a squad of 39 Indian elephants, marched against Tewodros. Despite such overwhelming odds, the emperor refused to negotiate with the representative of Queen Victoria. "I will do nothing of the kind since he has been sent here by a woman," Tewodros declared to an aide.

Assisted by the emperor's enemies in his own country, the British cornered Tewodros in his fortress at Maqdala in central Ethiopia. Most of his army deserted him. On April 13, 1868, the British stormed Tewodros's stronghold. Although Queen Victoria refused to answer the emperor's letter, she had sent him a revolver. Tewodros used the pistol to kill himself rather than surrender to the British.

Tewodros II: Emperor of Ethiopia 1855-1868

box) defeated the Shoan army, and Menelik's father died in the fighting. Tewodros brought Shoa back into the Ethiopian empire governed from northern provinces, and he took Menelik and his mother, a woman of humble origin, to his court. Young Menelik received a clerical and military education and gained insight into the art of politics in Tewodros's court. Looked upon favorably by Tewodros, Menelik rose to *dejazmach* (a title given to provincial governors). Tewodros gave his own daughter, Aletash, to Menelik as his wife.

Proclaims himself king

In 1864 regional nobles and warlords tried to rebel against Tewodros. The emperor imprisoned those he thought threatened his throne, including Menelik. The next year Menelik escaped, returned to Shoa, defeated the province's ruler, and crowned himself king of Shoa. The young king built his power base on support from the Shoan army and conservative (traditional-minded) politicians. At the same time he permitted Muslims (followers of Islam) and believers in traditional African religions to worship freely. His kingdom's official religion was the Christian Coptic (Egyptian-based) church. Fortunately for Menelik, Shoa was relatively insulated from the civil wars that ravaged northern Ethiopia during the last years of Tewodros's reign. When Tewodros became involved in a dispute with Great Britain over the emperor imprisoning the British consul and European missionaries, Menelik remained neutral. The British sent a force that easily defeated Tewodros's army in 1868. Rather than surrender, Emperor Tewodros killed himself.

Menelik's failure to join forces with the British resulted in a major setback for the Shoan king's ambitions. With Tewodros dead, power passed to a northern rival, Kassa (1831-1889), who had assisted the British force. He received arms from the British to help him assert his claim to the title of Emperor Yohannes IV (1872-1889). Menelik also proclaimed himself emperor. But rather than fight a war with Kassa's forces armed with modern weapons, Menelik went along with Kassa becoming emperor. In exchange for not fighting for power, Menelik retained his title as king of Shoa and was assured that he would succeed Kassa upon the emperor's death.

From his encounter with Kassa, Menelik learned the value of European weaponry and technology for fortifying his own power.

Emperor Yohannes (1831-1889) was the second monarch to try to consolidate, or unify, the old Ethiopian empire in the nineteenth century. He did so while fending off attacks from the Italian and Sudanese armies. His head ended up twirling on a pole in front of the Khalifa Abdullah Muhammad, leader of Islamic forces from Sudan.

The emperor descended from a royal family in Tigre, a northern Ethiopian province. Called Kassa before being crowned, he was the son of Shum Tameben Mircha and Embeytey Silas. Kassa got his chance at the throne when the British sent an expedition in 1868 to release the British consul and Christian missionaries imprisoned by the mentally unstable Emperor Tewodros (1855-1868). Kassa assisted the British in their campaign against Tewodros. Deserted by his army and facing capture, Tewodros shot himself.

When the British departed Ethiopia, they left 12 artillery pieces and 725 rifles with Kassa, who used the weapons to install himself as Emperor Yohannes IV in January 1872 at Aksum in Tigre. He succeeded in convincing powerful Shoa king Menelik not to seek the throne himself. In exchange, Yohannes IV designated Menelik as his successor (the next in line to be crowned emperor). Yohannes tried to use the centuries of Christian ties of the Coptic (Egyptian-based Christian) church among the provinces to unify Ethiopia again as a nation.

But soon Yohannes found himself surrounded on the East by Italians who had landed at the Red Sea port of Massawa. The Italians sought to establish a colony in Ethiopia. In the West, the khalifa's Islamic warriors were wreaking havoc on the former capital at Gondar. Khalifa Abdullah Muhammad rejected Yohannes's plea to unite as African states and, together, to repel the European invaders. Yohannes attacked the Islamic army. On March 9, 1889, Yohannes was mortally wounded in battle. The Sudanese fanatics severed his head and took it to the khalifa on a pole.

Menelik—who had agreed to remain neutral in Yohannes's fight against the Italians in exchange for weapons from Italy—used the Italian arms to defeat contenders to the throne vacated at Yohannes's death.

He turned to the Italians and French for weapons as well as to other European countries for advances in Western technology. In 1878 Menelik recruited Alfred Ilg (1854-1916), a Swiss artisan to act as an engineer and to give technology-related training to Ethiopians. One of the emperor's first requests was for Ilg to make him a pair of shoes. Ilg served Menelik for 20 years as engineer, architect, adviser, and diplomat. Menelik also maintained good relations with foreign missionaries, allowing them to enter his kingdom to convert the Oromo peoples living to the south of Shoa. In addition, he sent his army on raids into the area to get ivory, which he in turn traded for profits to buy European-made rifles and artillery.

Foreign ideas and advancements

Beside importing weapons and technology from Europe, Menelik recognized the importance of establishing diplomatic ties with foreign powers. Although forced in 1872 to renounce his claim to Ethiopia's throne and pay tribute to Yohannes IV, Menelik in reality continued to act as an independent king. He cultivated the friendship of Egypt in its short-lived attempt at imperialistic expansion into the Horn of Africa, a northeast region west of the Red Sea and Indian Ocean. (Imperialism is the extension of a nation's powers beyond its own borders.) Menelik next went behind Yohannes's back and negotiated with the Mahdists, a group of Muslims who had taken power in neighboring Sudan. Moreover, Menelik had long maintained friendly relations with Victorian England and in 1883 entered into a treaty of goodwill and commerce with the Italians.

Meanwhile Menelik expanded his kingdom in order to pay taxes demanded by Yohannes IV. In addition to sending his army into the Oromo-speaking areas of the South, he sent a force to the East, where it conquered the Muslim emirate (Islamic state) of Harar. Using arms purchased from the West, these expeditions plundered the prosperous regions and gave Menelik access to important trade routes and new sources of ivory and slaves.

Expands his empire

The Shoans established fortified villages throughout the newly conquered territories to maintain control and to protect settlers and missionaries pouring in from the North. Menelik's colonization led to the spread of Shoa's Amharic culture into these new territories. This helped establish rule of Ethiopia by Amharic-speakers from 1889, when Menelik became emperor, until 1991. (In 1991 a Tigrean-led army from the North overthrew Colonel Haile Mariam Mengistu, Ethiopia's dictator who took power from Emperor Haile Selassie I [1892-1975; see box] in 1974.)

While Menelik strengthened his army and enriched his kingdom, Yohannes IV came under pressure in the northern provinces of Tigre and Eritrea. The Italians had moved in from the Red Sea port of Massawa on the east, and the Islamic Mahdists in Sudan approached on the west. In the final year of his rule, Yohannes IV fought those forces crunching him from both sides. Meanwhile, Menelik had entered into a secret pact with the Italians, agreeing not to support Yohannes IV in battle in exchange for Italian weapons. Yohannes IV died in battle against the Mahdists in March 1889.

Menelik crowned himself Ethiopia's emperor on November 2, 1889. He encountered resistance from warlords in the northern province of Tigre, but his army quickly subdued the opposition. By that time, the Italians had spread from Massawa and occupied part of Ethiopia's northern province of Eritrea. Menelik made no move to oust (remove) the Italians. Instead, he signed a treaty with Italy in May 1890. The treaty insured the Italians would recognize only Menelik's claim to the imperial title and confirmed their special relationship with Ethiopia. Menelik allowed Italy to establish a colony in Eritrea as far south as Asmara.

A prelude to battle

Within a short time relations between Italy and Ethiopia began to crumble. Differences arose about the Amharic and Italian translations of the treaty. Italy claimed its text gave Italy the right to declare a protectorate over Ethiopia. Such a status would have meant Italy would control Ethiopia as an inferior state dependent on the Italians. The Amharic version of the treaty recognized Ethiopia as a nation independent of Italy. These varying interpretations of the treaty eventually led to the fateful battle of Adowa in 1896.

In addition to the dispute over the treaty's meaning, Menelik grew suspicious of Italian ambitions in the northern Ethiopian province of Tigre, located on Eritrea's southern border. In 1893 the emperor renounced the treaty with Italy. The Italians had attempted to divide and conquer Ethiopia through an alliance with rebellious Tigre, but these efforts failed. Ultimately, Italy took more aggressive measures, sending forces into Tigre in December 1894. At that time, Italy proclaimed Ethiopia as its protectorate.

Now deprived of weapons he had been buying from Italy, Menelik turned for arms to France and Russia—two foreign countries that wanted to curb Italy's influence along the Red Sea. For its part, Italy assigned its most celebrated soldier of the time, General Oreste Baratieri, to expand Eritrea. Italy planned to send out Italian colonists to occupy the cool, lush highlands of northern Ethiopia, and so approved huge sums of money to finance Eritrea's expansion. Baratieri bragged he would bring Menelik back in a cage.

Surprise defeat of colonial power

In the latter part of 1895, Baratieri moved his troops into southern Tigre. He concentrated his forces around the towering mountain peaks overlooking the town of Adowa. Five hundred miles to the south at Addis Ababa, Menelik ordered drummers to send forth a message from village to village summoning Ethiopians to the fight. Menelik was lucky to have the loyalty of Ras Makonnen, the powerful governor of the province of Harar. (Makonnen was the father of Ras Tafari, to be crowned Emperor Haile Selassie I in 1930.) Menelik's foremost diplomat, Makonnen also headed the advance attack unit moving against General Baratieri's army.

The general was not prepared for Menelik's show of force. He found his 20,000 Italian and Askari (Eritrean soldiers trained by the Italians) fighters facing Menelik's legion of more than 100,000 Ethiopians well armed with modern European weapons. Though Baratieri—like his fellow generals—believed that one Italian soldier or Askari was worth six "savage" Africans in combat, he was inclined to retreat to Eritrea. He calculated that Menelik's huge army would soon run out of food and be forced to retreat southward. Indeed, Baratieri was right. If he had waited, Menelik would have withdrawn in humiliation. The Italians could have moved back into Tigre and taken the province without a fight.

But back in Rome, Italian Prime Minister Crispi needed a military victory for his political standing and demanded Baratieri attack, defeat Menelik, and impose an Italian protectorate. Baratieri remained reluctant, but the suggestion of retreat insulted his generals—Dabormida, commander of the Second Infantry Brigade, and Matteo Albertone, commander of the Native Brigade. So Baratieri ended up ordering an attack on the Leap Year night of February 29, 1896, against Adowa.

Luck was on Menelik's side. Brigades led by Dabormida and Albertone were supposed to stay close together in order to support each other. Instead, they wandered off in separate directions during the night. The Ethiopians cut their opposing forces to pieces. Two other brigades committed to the fight too late by Baratieri met the same fate. By noon the next day, March 1, 1896, Baratieri had to order a retreat. His remaining soldiers fell back in disarray, pursued by the fierce Ethiopians. Some leading historians describe the battle as the worst defeat ever suffered by a colonial power in Africa.

The battlefield toll included more than 4,000 Italians dead or missing with more wounded and about the same number of Askaris killed or captured. The Ethiopians paid a high price too as they charged the Italian guns: 7,000 dead and 10,000 wounded. Menelik's victory hounded General Baratieri and Prime Minister Crispi out of public life. Despite his military triumph, though, the emperor demanded from Italy only huge reparations and recognition of Ethiopia's independence. To the dismay of his followers, Menelik allowed Italy to retain its Eritrean colony. Perhaps he judged his army could not dislodge the Italians. Many Ethiopian leaders never forgave him for failing to drive the Italians into the Red Sea.

The new Ethiopia

The battle at Adowa put an end to centuries of Ethiopian isolation. Menelik had demonstrated to the world that an African kingdom could defeat a European army. Diplomats from around the world flocked to Addis Ababa.

With the threat of foreign intervention removed, Menelik spent the last active decade of his rule strengthening centralized power and modernizing Ethiopia's political system. In the provinces he replaced hereditary rulers with appointed officials and stationed troops in some of the empire's potentially rebellious districts. He also reformed the judicial system. Seeking to reduce regional differences that threatened to splinter the country, Menelik increased the power of the national government by taking a direct hand in administering affairs.

New roads, bridges, rail lines, and communications opened new markets and contributed to a stronger sense of nationhood among Ethiopians. Fascinated by Western machinery and technology, Menelik took a personal interest in photography, medicine, and mechanical devices.

Perhaps the greatest failure of Menelik's reign was his refusal to provide for a stable succession. Beginning in 1906 he suffered a series of seizures (probably small strokes, or interruptions of blood flow in the brain) and gradually began to lose his faculties. When he recognized his health was declining, Menelik created Ethiopia's first cabinet-style government (a body of advisers) in 1907. The emperor designated his grandson, Lij Iyasu (1896-1935), as heir in 1908, and created a regency (someone who ruled for him; a substitute ruler) until the 11-year-old Iyasu reached a suitable age to take on the duties of emperor himself. By October 1909 Menelik was completely paralyzed. With the emperor incapacitated, his wife, the Empress Taitu, whom he had married in 1883, ruled in all but name.

While the emperor lingered on, much of the progress he had made in creating a strong national monarchy was reversed. Menelik died December 12 or 13, 1913. The incompetence of his grandson Iyasu—who served as emperor until being deposed by a palace coup in 1916—contributed further to the breakdown of centralized authority in Ethiopia. The unfinished task of modernizing Ethiopia would be left to Haile Selassie I (reigned 1930-1974).

Further Reading

Dictionary of African Biography. Algonac, MI: Reference Publications, 1977.

Gunther, John. *Inside Africa.* North Pomfret, VT: Hamish Hamilton, 1955.

Oliver, Roland, and Anthony Atmore. *Africa since 1800.* 2nd ed. New York/UK: Cambridge University Press, 1972.

Pakenham, Thomas. *The Scramble for Africa.* Jonathan Ball, 1991.

Simpson, George L., Jr. "Menelik II." In *Historic World Leaders.* Edited by Anne Commire. Volume 1. Detroit: Gale, 1994.

Spencer, John H. *Ethiopia at Bay: A Personal Account of the Haile Selassie Years.* Algonac, MI: Reference Publications, 1984.

Mobutu Sese Seko

Born October 14, 1930
Lisala, Equateur Province, Congo (Democratic
Republic of the Congo)
Died September 7, 1997
Rabat, Morocco

*Military leader, dictator of Zaire
(now Democratic Republic of the Congo)*

mong the European powers that colonized Africa in the late nineteenth century, Belgium was notoriously the worst. And by 1900 the Belgian Congo ruled by King Leopold II (1835-1909) was well known for its violence, cruelty, and corruption. When pressures in the colonies resulted in European nations decolonizing (restoring the rule of African nations to the African people) at the end of the 1950s, the Belgians abandoned the Congo in 1960, but without preparing its people for self-government. The result was a catastrophic civil war followed by the brutal dictatorship of Mobutu Sese Seko (*mow-BOO-too SEH-see SAY-ko*; also called Joseph-Désiré Mobutu), which persisted from 1965 until 1997. Although Mobutu helped to end one of the most vicious and barbaric wars of the twentieth century, he replaced it with a government based on universal fear.

"After a time, power went to his head, like alcohol, and he thought himself as some kind of supreme being. He began to confuse the riches of the country with his own."

—Former governor of Zaire's Central Bank Albert Ndele on Mobutu

Mobutu ruled Zaire (now the Democratic Republic of the Congo) for 32 years, enriching himself and his close associates and impoverishing the citizens of one of the largest countries in Africa. Tall, imposing, never without his trademark leopard-skin hat and walking stick, he was the supreme example of an African chief. Reputed to be one of the richest heads of state in the world, Mobutu maintained his personal rule through a patronage system (a way of distributing jobs) financed from the spoils of office. He paid generously for the loyalty of 20,000 highly trained troops stationed throughout the country. The U.S. government and other western nations sustained him in power because they believed he was the only leader capable of maintaining stability in Zaire, a country rich in mineral resources and in an important place to the major powers in case of a large scale war. With the end of Cold War hostilities between Russia and the United States in the early 1990s, western nations pressured Mobutu to open up the political system to opposition parties and to end his ruthless repression of opposition leaders.

Journalism and politics

Mobutu was born in 1930 in Lisala, a member of the Bangala people, near the small village of Gbadolite, in Equatorial Province, the Belgian Congo. His parents named him Joseph-Désiré Mobutu. His father, Alberic Bemany, was a cook for Catholic missionaries and then for a Belgian magistrate in Leopoldville (now Kinshasa). His mother, Marie-Madeleine Yemo, was a maid in a hotel. His father died when Mobutu was eight years old, and his mother was forced to return to the village with the family. Mobutu went to the Leopoldville Mission School until he was 16, when he enrolled in a Catholic Mission school in Coquilhatville (Mdandaka). Mobutu did well academically, but he misbehaved; the authorities expelled him from school in 1948.

On leaving school, he was drafted into the Belgian colonial army in 1949. The army sent him to L'Ecole Centrale de Luluabourg where he learned accounting and secretarial skills. After two years, the army assigned him to military headquarters in Leopoldville, where he was promoted to sergeant-major, the highest rank an African could achieve in the Belgian colonial army. At the end of his compulsory (required) service he quit the military and went to work as a journalist on a pro-socialist newspaper in Leopoldville called

L'Avenir. Later he became chief editor of *Actualites Africaines,* another newspaper owned by the same organization.

As a journalist he met African nationalists (people who worked for self-rule in Africa) working to free the Congo from Belgian control. Among the activists at that time were Joseph Kasavubu, leader of a tribally based party, the Alliance des Ba-Kongo (ABAKO), and Patrice Lumumba (see entry), leader of the Mouvement National Congolais (MNC), which advocated a unitary state (one not divided into groups) and strong central government. Mobutu and Lumumba became friends, and Lumumba asked Mobutu to organize the MNC secretariat.

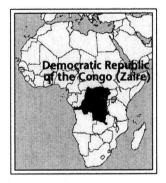

Independence

Mobutu traveled to Belgium several times on magazine assignments. In 1959 he got a grant to study in Brussels with a public relations agency of the Belgian government promoting the Congo. While Mobutu was in Brussels, he represented Lumumba's MNC at the Brussels Round Table Conference called by the Belgian government to discuss terms for an independent Congo. The Belgians agreed to hold multiparty elections in May and set June 30, 1960, as the date for independence. The Belgians feared that without such quick action a long and bloody colonial war might follow. Their hasty departure, however, made internal chaos in the country almost inevitable.

Lumumba and the MNC won more votes than any of the other parties, but failed to win a strong majority. Lumumba eventually formed a coalition government with Kasavubu, with Kasavubu becoming president and Lumumba prime minister. Lumumba appointed Mobutu first secretary of state for the President's Council. Neither man was experienced in government, and the society lacked a tradition of civil government.

Four days after independence, Congolese military units mutinied against their Belgian officers and threatened to march on the capital. Mobutu and others persuaded the mutineers to return to their barracks. In gratitude and perhaps in recognition of his skills, Lumumba reinstated the 30-year-old Mobutu in the army, promoted him to colonel and appointed him army chief of staff to replace a Belgian general. In September 1960 Lumumba appointed him Commander in Chief.

As the mutiny spread to other regions of the country, Belgium sent additional troops to protect and evacuate Belgian civilians. Chaos followed as the professional and skilled workers left the country. At Lumumba's request, the United Nations sent in 20,000 troops to prevent the situation from turning into anarchy (lawlessness). With the central government unable to govern, the copper rich province of Katanga (now Shaba) under the leadership of Moïse Tshombe (see entry) and the diamond wealthy South Kasai Province under Albert Kalonji declared themselves independent nations. Believing the United Nations was unwilling to force Katanga back into the central government, Lumumba turned to the Soviet Union and Eastern bloc communist countries for assistance.

United States backs Mobutu

The United States Central Intelligence Agency (CIA) backed Mobutu. The idea of Soviet soldiers in Zaire horrified U.S. president Dwight Eisenhower. The Cuban revolution in 1959 and the resulting rule of Fidel Castro with the Soviet Union backing him had shown Eisenhower that third world communist revolutions could happen; he wanted to avoid any repetition of that type of event. On September 13, 1960, in the name of the army, Mobutu intervened and seized control of the Congolese government. Mobutu originally appointed a group of university graduates to rule the country but the international community pressed him to return authority to Kasavubu, which he did in February 1961. Under orders from Kasavubu, army troops arrested Lumumba and, in January 1961, while in the custody of Katangan troops, he was beaten to death.

The period between 1961 and 1964 in the Congo was turbulent. Mobutu turned his attention to the military, to restructure it and bring discipline to it. Western and anti-Communist nations provided military training for the troops. The Israelis trained a unit of paratroopers, and Mobutu took the course along with his men. These Israeli-trained soldiers became Mobutu's elite bodyguard, known as the Division Speciale Presidentialle (DSP).

In 1963 United Nations troops put down the Katanga secessionist (withdrawal from the nation) movement and Katanga returned to central government control; they had put the rebellion in South Kasai down in 1962. Tshombe fled to Spain but in 1964, Kasavubu recalled him and appointed him prime minister. Parliament adopted a new constitution in August 1964, outlining a presidential system in a federal structure. The name of the country was changed to the Democratic Republic of Congo and the last of the United Nations troops withdrew. Kasavubu, however, could not hold the center without military support. In November 1965 Mobutu again seized power with the backing of the military. He also had the backing of the U.S. Central Intelligence Agency (CIA). The chief of station in Kinshasa became his confidant and kept him in contact with the U.S. White House. U.S. presidents from Richard Nixon to Ronald Reagan welcomed Mobutu.

Seizes power again

When Mobutu seized power, the population of the Congo was about 17 million people, composed of hundreds of different tribal groups, separated by custom, language, and the lack of roads and communication networks. At first the new government tried to unify a country one-fourth the size of the United States by reducing its number of provinces. The Congo started with 21 provinces, then there were 12, and later 8. Soon, Mobutu removed whatever independence the regions had kept, and took power himself. He became president, took the legislative role away from parliament, and suspended all the provincial assemblies. He seized the assets of the Belgian mining company, Union Miniére, and doubled the export tax on copper.

At the same time that he nationalized the mining concerns (put them under government control), Mobutu used financial incentives to attract foreign investors to replace the skilled workers who had left during the upheavals. Mobutu was astute enough to realize that the Congolese were not able to administer the corporations without outside assistance. By 1968 his reform measures had brought growth to the economy and provided political stability.

By the mid-1970s Western investors had come in, including the U.S.-based General Motors Corporation to set up a car assembly plant, and with them about 50,000 workers from other countries, or expatriates. By this time Mobutu was a firm ally of the U.S. government,which was providing nearly 75 percent of all the foreign aid going to the government. The U.S. military had access to Kamina air base in southern Zaire from which it supported anti-Communist forces in Angola, and the CIA had a major operation based in Zaire.

Mobutu (center) inspects a Congolese Army honor guard, 1967.

Emphasizes Africanness

At the same time that his government was courting western aid and industry, Mobutu introduced his *authenticité* campaign to turn attention away from western inroads in the economy. In 1971 he renamed the country Zaire and instructed all Congolese citizens with Christian names to adopt African names and return to African ways of life. Mobutu took the name Sese Seko Kuku Ngbendu Wazabanga, which means in English "the warrior who knows no defeat because of his endurance and inflexible will and is all powerful, leaving fire in his wake as he goes from conquest to conquest." His supporters in the Mouvement Populaire de la Révolution (MPR), the sole political party until recently, called him the Guide, the Chief, the Helmsman, the Redeemer, the Father of Revolution, and Perpetual Defender of Property and People. In a second phase of the authenticité campaign, Mobutu outlawed the collar and tie, requiring civil servants to wear an open necked outfit referred to as an "abacos." It is really a two-piece western suit minus tie and collar.

An about face

In November 1973 Mobutu did an about face on the role of foreign business and changed regulations that gave foreigners preferential treatment. Suddenly Zaire citizens appeared waving pieces of paper, claiming the right to the property of thousands of expatriates—people from other countries living throughout Zaire. Expatriates with small-scale businesses fled the country and, as local people took possession of their businesses, trade came to a stop. Locals seized some 2,000 foreign-owned plantations.

Mobutu set up an extensive patronage system to keep officials loyal to him. While the system enriched his associates, it drained the country of all the surplus that they might otherwise have reinvested in the economy and infrastructure. The deterioration in the road network is one example. According to Blaine Harden in *Africa: Dispatches from a Fragile Continent,* the number of miles of paved roads in the country in the 1980s was 10 percent of what it had been under Belgian rule. Meanwhile, Mobutu spent state funds lavishly on himself and those close to him. Officials in Kinshasa admitted privately that probably about 60 percent of the state's revenues disappeared into officials' pockets in the 1970s. The Western powers, particularly France, Belgium, and the United States, continued to fund Mobutu because he served their interests at the time.

Mobutu had amassed a fortune estimated at between $4 billion and $5 billion. Besides his palaces in Zaire, he bought villas in Belgium, France, Switzerland, Italy, Portugal, and in the Ivory Coast. He had a magnificent yacht, the *Kamanyola,* to which he retreated in times of unrest. The state spent roughly $500,000 a year educating his families' children in a boarding school in Switzerland. The Independent News Service quoted former governor of Zaire's Central Bank Albert Ndele as saying:

> It would be dishonest to say that the president has done nothing but evil. In the beginning he made a notable contribution to creating a real sense of national unity. But after a time, power went to his head, like alcohol, and he thought himself as some kind of supreme being. He began to confuse the riches of the country with his own.

The flip side to Mobuto's generosity with state funds were the harsh and repressive measures used against those who opposed him. Mobutu used the secret police, the Central National de Documentation (CND) and the Division Speciale Presidentielle (DSP) to control the country. He assured military loyalty through a complex system of divide and rule, allowing for little communication or organizing among military leaders. The command pattern required different officers to report directly through different channels. Officers did not serve in their home areas and they were shifted frequently from area to area.

Losing support

Despite his ruthless methods or because of them, Mobutu provided stability in Zaire, a volatile country bordering on nine other African countries. One of the ways he maintained the stability was with financial and political support from the West. Mobutu assured Zaire U.S. support because he provided a rear base of U.S. anti-Communist efforts in Angola. He assured the favor of Belgium and France with diamonds and copper. But with the easing of tensions between the United States and the Soviet Union in the late 1980s, and the world increasingly turning away from a reliance on copper, Mobutu's corrupt and ruthless regime became less acceptable to Western powers. International lending agencies that had loaned money to his government began to require more fiscal accountability and political openness. In 1988 several Western nations wrote off some of Zaire's $5.8 billion debt. In 1990, however, the European Community, the United States, and Canada cut off all aid to Mobutu's regime after he prevented an inquiry into the deaths of 12 University of Lubumbashi students.

In disregard of Zaire's massive debt, Mobutu spent an estimated $15 million a month on the upkeep of his presidential palace in Gbadolite and on payments to the DSP. But Mobutu did not have the money to pay the wages of the bulk of the military. In 1991 troops in Shaba Province (formerly Katanga) mutinied because they had not been paid. Because of the rampage, the expatriates working on the mines left the country, and the mines closed. In 1993 the army mutinied again when the government tried to pay them with newly printed 5 million zaire notes, which shopkeepers would not accept. The rate of inflation in Zaire was estimated anywhere between 1,000 and 6,000 percent a year. In 1989, for instance, one U.S. dollar cost 250 zaires; in 1993 one U.S. dollar cost 2.6 million zaires.

With Zaire's economy in a free fall Mobutu was forced to legalize opposition political parties. The major groups formed an umbrella group called the Sacred Union and called a national conference. The National Conference elected Etienne Tshisekedi wa Malumba, a former associate of Mobutu's turned opponent, as prime minister. They established a High Council of the Republic (HRC) to act as an interim legislative assembly and paramount political institution. Mobutu did all he could to undermine the authority of Tshisekedi and the HRC, to the extent of sending the military to lock the representatives in the parliament building for three days.

The final flight

In 1996 Mobutu began treatment for cancer of the prostate in Switzerland. While he was out of the county, the slaughter of hundreds of thousands of people occurred in Rwanda and the violence spilled over into eastern Zaire. Out of this chaos emerged rebel leader Laurent Kabila, an anti-Mobutuist for more than 30 years. His small Tutsi-based rebel force quickly filled the vacuum left by the breakdown in the Zaire military. Kabila's forces easily won support from the population as they made their way westward toward Kinshasa. Mobutu fled from Kabila's army and went to Gbadolite. Morocco finally agreed to give him sanctuary. He died in Rabat on the 7th of September 1997. Mobutu was married twice; he first married Boby Ladawa, who died before him; his second wife was Milou Moboti, the twin sister of Boby and widow of his deceased uncle. Mobutu had nine children.

Further Reading

Harden, Blaine. *Africa: Dispatches from a Fragile Continent,* New York: Norton, 1990.

Historic World Leaders, volume 1. Edited by Anne Commire. Detroit: Gale, 1994.

Stockwell, John. *In Search of Enemies: A CIA Story.* New York: Norton, 1978.

Von Rensberg, A. P. J. *Contemporary Leaders of Africa.* Haum, 1975.

Daniel arap Moi

Born September 2, 1924
Baringo District, Rift Valley, Kenya

President of Kenya

"Moi may not have studied politics at anyone's university, but he has proved himself a real 'Professor of politics' in the practical sense."

—Sunday Times (Nairobi)

Daniel arap Moi became president of Kenya in 1978 following the death of Kenya's first president, Jomo Kenyatta (see entry). Kenyatta had selected Moi as vice president because he did not pose a threat to the dominance of the Kikuyus, a large Kenyan ethnic group. Moi came from a small ethnic group and did not have a strong political base. But Kenyatta underestimated Moi's political savvy. On coming to office, Moi quickly built up a solid base of support by rewarding loyalty with access to the resources of the state. He cut off opposition politics and put down dissent through his control of the police, the courts, and local governments. Although Kenyatta had banned opposition political parties in 1969, Moi officially outlawed them and made Kenya a one-party state in 1982, following a failed attempt by air force officers to overthrow his government.

For most of his presidency Moi and the ruling party have had absolute authority over the country. Without political opposition and through strong-arm tactics to put down critics, Moi and his followers enriched themselves and their families at the expense of the nation. In response to pressure from international lending agencies in 1990 and 1991 to open up the political process and end human rights abuses, Moi held multiparty elections in 1991. Voters in that election split their votes among several opposition candidates, and although Moi did not win a majority of votes, he won more than any other candidate. Again in 1997, he only won 40 percent of the vote, but because this was more than any other candidate won, he was elected for another five-year term.

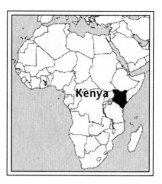

Ethnic factors influence politics

Moi is a Kalenjin from Kenya's Rift Valley. The Kalenjin are a small tribal group in the ethnically divided nation, which has more than 40 tribes belonging to four major language groups. Moi's heritage was a significant factor in his political career. Jomo Kenyatta, Kenya's first president in 1964 and a Kikuyu, selected Moi as vice president in 1967. The Kikuyu—the largest group in Kenya—were at loggerheads with the Luo, the second largest group. It was partly because Moi lacked a significant political base as a Kalenjin and was not involved in the political fight between the Luo and the Kikuyu that Kenyatta selected him as vice president.

When Kenyatta died in August 1978, Moi became president with the consent of the ruling party, the Kenyan African National Union (KANU), and the help of powerful Kikuyus like Attorney General Charles Njonjo. Moi did not face any serious contest for the presidency because he did not threaten the influential Kikuyus. He named a Kikuyu vice president, and allowed other key Kenyatta people to keep their powerful positions and parliamentary seats. Moi stressed continuation of Kenyatta's policies in his theme of *Nyayoism* or following in the "footsteps" of Kenyatta.

Education

Moi was born in Baringo District, in the Rift Valley, on September 2, 1924. He was named Daniel Toroitich arap Moi by his father, Kimoi Cheboi, and mother, Kaban. (Arap means "son of.")

Moi's father died when Moi was young, and his mother raised the family, but they were poor. Moi's paternal uncle, Senior Chief Kiplabet, arranged for his education at mission schools. Moi went to the African Inland Mission (AIM) school for four years, from 1934 to 1938. While he was at the mission schools he worked at menial jobs and during his school holidays he herded cattle. Afterward he attended a government school for Africans in Kapsabet. In addition, Moi passed his London Matriculation Examination and also got a certificate in public accounting (CPA) from London through a correspondence course.

In 1945 Moi went for teacher training at Kapsabet, and then he taught at the government African schools Tambach and Kabarnet for eight years, until 1954. Before he entered politics, his last post in teaching was as assistant principal of the government African Teachers' College.

Entering into politics

Moi's introduction to politics came in 1955 when he was selected to be an African representative to the British colonial Legislative Council, or Legco. In March 1957 Moi and seven other African members of the Legco formed a lobby group, the African Elected Members' Organisation. Others in the parliamentary pressure group included nationalists (people seeking self-rule for African nations) Tom Mboyo (see entry) and Oginga Odinga.

Preparing for independence

In 1960, as members of the Legislative Council, Moi and other nationalists participated in constitutional talks held in London in preparation for Kenya's independence from Britain. On their return, most of the participants formed a political party, the Kenya Africa National Union (KANU). Moi refused to join the party because it represented the interests of the dominant tribes, the Luo and the Kikuyu. Moi and others from minority tribal groups formed a multi-tribal coalition, the Kenyan African Democratic Union (KADU) as an alternative to KANU. Moi became head of the new party.

In the transition period to independence Moi was appointed parliamentary secretary in the Ministry of Education in 1961. In this position he represented Kenya at the United Nations Educa-

tional, Scientific, and Cultural Organization (UNESCO) Conference in Addis Ababa, Ethiopia, and he travelled to India. In the pre-independence coalition government Moi was appointed Minister for Education and later Minister for Local Government.

Moi, as vice president of Kenya, campaigns for possible succession to Jomo Kenyatta, 1970.

"A giraffe with a long neck"

In pre-independence national elections in 1963, KADU failed to present enough candidates to challenge KANU, headed by nationalist leader Jomo Kenyatta. As a result, Kenyatta became president of the new republic in 1964, and Moi lost his ministerial position. But in order to bring the opposition into his government, Kenyatta appointed Moi Minister of Home Affairs after KADU dissolved itself in November 1964. As Minister of Home Affairs, Moi was responsible for the police, the prisons, and the immigration department. The friends he made in these departments were helpful to Moi later on. His responsibility for issuing passports brought him into close touch with the Asian business community, while his job of issuing work permits brought him equally close to British business houses. It was Moi's responsibility too, as the Minister of Home Affairs, to make appointments throughout the police, prisons, and immigration services. This was to be useful in later years, when the police services were full of Moi appointees.

Kenyatta named Moi vice president in 1967. Moi presented a bland and unassuming image. But, as political rival Oginga Odinga says in his 1967 biography, *Not Yet Uhuru,* Moi was like "a giraffe with a long neck that saw from afar," meaning he was busy looking to the future and positioning himself for more power later on. Moi retained his powerful position as Minister of Home Affairs when he became vice president.

In the 1970s President Kenyatta became more remote. Moi and Attorney General Charles Njonjo were increasingly in control of the government. When Kenyatta died in 1978, Moi's assumption of the presidency went smoothly, despite some opposition from wealthy Kikuyu.

Taking over

As president, one of first things Moi did was to travel the country to rural areas, visiting every tribal group. He introduced free milk programs for school children, released all political detainees, and abolished land-buying companies that had been gouging small land holders. Popular appeal, however, was not enough to hold power, especially as he came from a small ethnic group with little power. Moi therefore began rewarding loyalty; as a consequence, the government became enormously corrupt. Officials demanded payments from bidders on major government projects; the payments, which had been between 5 and 10 percent of the value of the contract under Kenyatta, jumped to between 10 and 25 percent under Moi.

Official corruption and abuse of powers, plus a deteriorating economy, exploded in a 1982 coup (overthrow) attempt by Kenya air force officers, most of them Luos dissatisfied with being excluded as a group from power and access to the national treasury. The army remained loyal to Moi and put down the coup. The coup attempt temporarily slowed Moi's plans for consolidating power in the hands of his supporters and Kalenjin loyalists. He focused for a while on putting down possible opposition in the military and shoring up his supporters even more. He detained (arrested) most of the 2,100 person air force and created a totally new force. Then he eliminated Kikuyu and Luo officers from the military and put in Kalenjin and non-ethnic challengers; for instance the Army Chief of General Staff was General Mahmoud Mohammed, an ethnic Somali. Military officers were awarded bonuses. Officers above the rank of major got free farms as gifts of the government. Moi gave the military plentiful reasons to remain loyal to him.

On the grassroots level, the KANU youth wing conducted a massive membership recruitment drive, reported to have attracted four million new members and raised millions of dollars for the party. The party was so strong even at the market level that buyers and sellers could not trade without a party card. The General Services Unit, a paramilitary wing of the police force with a reputation for brutality, squashed pro-democracy activities and demonstrations.

As part of his effort to rid the inner circles of government of Kikuyus, Moi arranged the spectacular fall from power of his backer Charles Njonjo in mid-1983. Njonjo was branded a traitor to the nation, thus forcing him to resign from the cabinet and parliament. "You know a balloon is a very small thing," Moi said to Blaine Harden in explaining his control over political cronies. "But I can pump it up to such an extent that it will be big and look very important. All you need to make it small again is to prick it with a needle."

Pressures for change

Internally, pressure for political change had been repressed by a police state that used detentions, torture, and killings as well as a tight control of the media and the courts to keep opposition at bay. International demands for a more just society only came in the 1990s, when Western countries that had given financial aid to Kenya became alarmed by misappropriation of aid money and human rights abuses. They began exerting pressure on the Kenyan government to legalize opposition parties and hold multiparty elections. U.S. State Department officials estimated that as president Moi had accumulated a personal fortune equal to that of Zairean president Mobutu Sese Seko (see entry) who was reported to have $4 billion outside the country.

In July 1991 Africa Watch, a human rights organization with offices in New York and London, published a scathing attack on the Moi government, accusing it of committing torture and gross human rights violations. Africa Watch documented incidents of torture and deaths of political detainees and pro-democracy advocates by the security forces.

Pressures for change were building from other quarters as well. In 1990 Minister of Foreign Affairs Robert Ouko was brutally murdered shortly after returning from a trip with Moi for meetings with U.S. State Department officials in Washington, D.C. Moi's head of internal security Hezekiah Oyugi and Minister of Energy Nicholas Biwott were prime suspects in the murder. Moi stopped investigations into the murder, leaving widespread belief among Kenyans that he covered up the crime by his two top associates. As much as anything else, that provoked an outpouring of domestic and international demands for an end to Moi's one-party autocracy (rule of one person with unlimited power) and the establishment of multiparty elections.

As demands for elections increased, the government stepped up its repression; opposition leaders and university students were detained and tortured, their families beaten, their homes burned; publications were removed from the newsstands; an outspoken cleric died in suspicious circumstances. On July 7, 1990, security forces brutally put down a political rally. Police charged 1,000 people with "riot-related offenses." Officials said 20 people died.

In November 1991 the international lending agencies suspended payment of $350 million in aid to the Kenyan government. With the economy in poor condition, tourism declining, and low export prices for Kenya's goods, Moi and the ruling party bowed to the pressure. He ordered Parliament to amend Kenya's constitution to allow the establishment of political parties other than KANU and to permit multiparty elections.

Multiparty elections and intimidation

On December 29, 1992, in the first multiparty elections in Kenya in 26 years, Moi was elected president by a minority of voters. He took just over 34 percent of the popular vote. The three opposition candidates split nearly 64 percent of the vote. KANU, the ruling national party, won 100 parliamentary seats and the opposition party won 88.

The elections that returned President Moi and KANU to power were marked by violence and intimidation. Shortly before the elections, tribal fighting occurred in the Rift Valley between the Kalenjin (Moi's people) and the Kikuyu (Kenya's largest tribal group), leaving approximately 700 people dead and 10,000 homeless. In 16 of these constituencies, no opposition candidates for Parliament ran against the ruling party. KANU supporters physically prevented either the candidates or their agents from submitting their registration papers. The deaths and registration intimidation support claims made by the opposition that Moi and KANU employed violence and threats to win the elections.

International election monitors brought in at the request of the opposition parties refused to certify the elections as free and fair. In their report on the elections, the Commonwealth Observer Group criticized KANU for not curbing the "worst excesses of their supporters," as well as for creating obstacles to free election, including bribery, intimidation, and violence. Despite all these reservations, the Commonwealth observers said the election "results in many instances directly reflect, however imperfectly, the expression of the will of the people."

Divided opposition

If the opposition parties had united behind a single candidate, they could have defeated Moi, even in rigged elections. But the opposition parties, legalized only in December 1991, were divided amongst themselves. The divisions tended to break down along tribal lines. For instance, former vice president Jaramogi Oginga Odinga (in his eighties) headed the Forum for the Restoration of Democracy (FORD Kenya). Odinga is a Luo, the second largest tribal group in the country. Mwai Kibaki, another former vice president and a Kikuyu, lead the Democratic Party. Wealthy Kikuyu businessman Charles Matiba was the presidential candidate for FORD Asili (Original), a spin-off from FORD Kenya. Thus, the opposition was split between the two largest language groups, and the largest of these groups, the Kikuyu, was further divided. The egoism of the opposition leaders played neatly in Moi's favor.

A professor of politics

In the 1997 elections Moi and his ruling party won a small majority of seats in the national Parliament. As in the 1991 election, the opposition was badly divided and Moi received the most votes, although only 40 percent of the total votes cast. Moi's "country boy cunning" and craftiness in exploiting tribal divisions should not be forgotten. As Kenya's pro-government *Sunday Times* said: "Moi may not have studied politics at anyone's university, but he has proved himself a real 'Professor of politics' in the practical sense."

Further Reading

Africa Confidential. June 1, 1990; December 6,1991.

Africa Watch. *Kenya: Taking Liberties.* 1991.

Days, Drew S., et al. *Justice Enjoined: The State of the Judiciary in Kenya.* Robert F. Kennedy Memorial Center for Human Rights, 1992

Harden, Blaine. *Africa: Dispatches from a Fragile Continent.* New York: HarperCollins, 1990.

Odinga, Oginga. *Not Yet Uhuru: An Autobiography.* Heineman, 1967.

The Standard (Nairobi). January 5, 1993.

Sunday Times (Nairobi). December 27, 1992.

Eduardo Mondlane

Born 1920
Gaza Province, Mozambique
Died February 3, 1969
Dar es Salaam, Tanzania

Political activist and nationalist

 t the end of World War II (1939–45), when many young African soldiers came home from serving in colonial armies overseas, they began to ask for the same rights for themselves and their countries that they had fought for in Europe. As a student from Portuguese-controlled Mozambique who was studying in South Africa in the late 1940s, Eduardo Chivambo Mondlane was caught up in this spirit of change. He was part of the first wave of African nationalists after the war who believed their people should be independent and free of colonial control. Mondlane was an intellectual and the driving force behind the first nationwide opposition group to Portuguese rule in Mozambique. Mondlane never lived to see the independence of Mozambique, however. He was killed by a letter bomb in his office in Dar es Salaam in Tanzania in 1969. Mondlane was 49 years old when he died.

Mondlane worked to create a truly united opposition to Portuguese colonialism in Mozambique.

Mondlane was born in Manjacase, a small village in southern Mozambique. His father was Nwadjahane Mussengane Mondlane, a chief of the Tsonga people. His mother was Makungu Muzamusse Bembele, her husband's third wife. Eduardo was the last born, and his father died before Eduardo was two years old. After his father's death, his mother stayed in the village. She did not remarry and so had no one to support her. Until Eduardo was 11, he looked after the sheep, goats, and cattle in the fields. But his mother talked to him about how important it was to get an education. He also saw what happened to his brothers who did not get an education.

The value of education

Mondlane had three brothers, and each of them ran away to South Africa. They left Mozambique to avoid being forced into the work gangs set up by the colonial government for the benefit of Portuguese farmers and plantation owners. In South Africa one brother died when his chest was crushed in an accident on the docks. Another died of a lung disease that he got from working in the mines. A third brother died of tuberculosis.

Mondlane started school when he was 11 years old at a government school that was a two-hour walk from his village. Two years later he transferred to a mission school nearer to home. His mother died that year, and one of his sisters helped with his education. He finished his elementary education in 1936, when he was 16 years old. Following that he went to Laurenço Marques (Maputo) to take the exams for his diploma. To pay his way, he got work at the Swiss Calvinist Mission Hospital washing dirty linen and bloody bandages. A nurse at the hospital helped him take classes at the mission school in the morning and work for the headmaster in the afternoons.

Too late Mondlane learned that the government had changed the rules and would only accept students from Catholic but not Protestant missions in the secondary schools. A Swiss missionary, Andre Clerc, realized the potential of the young Mondlane and helped him enroll in the American Methodist Episcopal Mission at Khambane, where he took a two-year course in dry land farming methods. When he finished, he traveled to the rural areas and taught peasant farmers in the Manjacase region.

Experiences racism

In 1944 Mondlane's mission sponsors arranged for him to study at the Douglas Laing Smit Secondary School at Lemana in the northern province of Transvaal in South Africa. And so in 1945 Mondlane left Mozambique. He completed the equivalent of his high school education at Smit and in 1948 enrolled in the Jan Hofmeyr School of Social Work in Johannesburg. At the end of his year at Hofmeyr he got a scholarship to study at the University of Witwatersrand for a degree in social sciences.

Of the 5,000 students at Witwatersrand, only 300 were black. Even as a minority student, Mondlane was popular, and his fellow students elected him as the representative of the Social Science Department to the Student Representative Council and the National Student Council. Unfortunately, his high profile caused him trouble with the authorities. In the past, the South African government had renewed Mondlane's study permit every year. By 1949, however, the apartheid Nationalist government had won the elections in South Africa. (Apartheid is an Afrikaans word meaning apartness or separateness. It is a system of segregation based on race that favors whites and restricts blacks to labor reserves.) One of the new government's early targets were the even slightly multiracial universities. Despite appeals from high-level officials, the government refused to renew Mondlane's permit, and in 1949 the authorities withdrew his permission to study. Mondlane left South Africa. In his autobiography he said of that time: "The desire to fight the white man and liberate my people was intensified after I was expelled from South Africa in 1949."

While he had been in South Africa, Mondlane experienced firsthand the power of political organizing. He applied what he had learned when he got back to Mozambique and organized Mozambican students into a national union, UNEMO. The Portuguese police wasted no time, however; in October 1949 they arrested him. The police worried that Mondlane might have too much influence over the Africans in Mozambique and further that he might be a communist. Without any evidence to keep him in jail, and wanting to be rid of him, they strongly suggested he study in Portugal, where he would not be any threat.

Studies overseas

Mondlane entered the University of Lisbon in Portugal. There, the Portuguese police kept a close watch on him, searching his rooms nearly every week for political materials. After the first year Mondlane, wanting to be free of the Portuguese authorities, accepted a scholarship to study in the United States. At the age of 32 he entered Oberlin College as an undergraduate. Besides his studies, he was active in the Christian church. He met his future wife Janet Rae Johnson at a Christian summer camp in 1951.

Janet Johnson was a young white woman from Indianapolis, Indiana, whose conservative family strongly opposed her relationship with Mondlane. Nevertheless, the young couple prevailed and married in 1956. After receiving his bachelor's degree at Oberlin College, Mondlane went to Northwestern University where he completed his Ph.D. He did a year of research at Harvard University.

When he finished his studies, Mondlane took a job with the United Nations in New York City where he worked as a research officer in the Trusteeship Department. While he worked at the United Nations, he met and became friends with African nationalist Julius Nyerere (see entry) of Tanganyika. Nyerere promised him a base of support in Tanganyika, soon to become independent Tanzania, for a Mozambican independence movement. At this time, for the first time in 10 years, Mondlane returned to Africa on a United Nations-sponsored trip. A subsequent trip to Mozambique convinced him that he should return to Africa to work for his country's independence.

Organizes a united opposition

Mondlane left his job with the United Nations and took a teaching job with Syracuse University in New York. In June 1962, during his summer break, Mondlane went to a meeting in Dar es Salaam, Tanzania, with representatives of the three major Mozambican nationalist groups operating outside the country. These three groups agreed to form one political party, FRELIMO (the Front for the Liberation of Mozambique). Mondlane was elected president. Although he returned to Syracuse at the beginning of the term, he found he was unable to do both jobs. He left the United States and returned to Africa. He and his family settled in Dar es Salaam in Tanzania.

For the next two years, Mondlane worked to create a truly united opposition to Portuguese colonialism in Mozambique. This was a difficult task because the members of FRELIMO were from different parts of the country and came from many different cultures, educational levels, social classes, and political beliefs. The Portuguese security police from Mozambique worked in secret to heighten the conflicts caused by these differences; they wanted them to get bigger so that FRELIMO would not be effective.

FRELIMO in Mozambique

In Mozambique, the government had outlawed FRELIMO and so it was forced to work secretly to build up its support in the country. The Mozambican people were receptive to the idea of getting organized to defeat the Portuguese. In the past they had protested against Portuguese rule, but they had little strength left after years of severe repression. In 1960 in Cabo Delgado

FRELIMO soldiers.

province, for instance, when workers complained about wages, the governor of the province invited the people to come to a meeting. When everyone had gathered, the police began arresting people. When the crowd got angry, the provincial governor ordered the police to shoot into the crowd. They killed nearly 600 people.

In 1964 FRELIMO's leaders realized they had to do more than organize local farmers. They decided to take up arms to win independence. When the attacks began, FRELIMO quite quickly freed two northern provinces, except for their military bases. These provinces were the farthest away from the capital and difficult for the Portuguese to supply. They were also on the border with Tanzania and easily accessible to FRELIMO.

FRELIMO's victory in Cabo Delgado province led to a serious break in the party. When the Portuguese offered independence to Cabo Delgado before the rest of Mozambique was liberated, Lazaro Kavandame, a Makonde from that region and an early organizer of cooperatives, argued for Cabo Delgado's independence. When Mondlane refused, Kavandame joined forces with the Portuguese. In 1968 Kavandame was directly implicated in the

Samora Machel

Samora Moises Machel was commander of the nationalist army in Mozambique's struggle for independence from Portugal, and he was the first president of independent Mozambique. Born in 1933, Machel came from a farming family in Gaza Province, the home of the Shangaans. He joined FRELIMO, the nationalist party, in 1962 and he went to Algeria for military training. Later, he became commander-in-chief of FRELIMO's army. After Eduardo Mondlane's death in 1969, Machel became leader of the party. He took part in the peace talks in Portugal in 1974 and in 1975 he became the first president of independent Mozambique.

As president, Machel adopted socialist economic policies: the state took over all property owned by individuals and companies—houses, businesses, hotels. The Portuguese then left Mozambique, taking their professional skills with them. The economy collapsed because the Africans did not have the training or the experience to run the country.

When Machel gave sanctuary to the nationalists struggling for independence in Rhodesia, the white Rhodesian government closed its border with Mozambique, cutting the country off from its normal trade links. The Rhodesians also set up a rebel group to try to take control away from the Machel government. At the same time, the South Africans put economic and military pressure on Mozambique because Machel gave sanctuary to the African National Congress (ANC).

In 1984 Mozambique told the ANC to leave and South African businesses began to invest money in Mozambique. The Portuguese also started to come back and invest. On October 19, 1986, Samora Machel died when his plane crashed along the border of Mozambique and South Africa. Joaquim Chissano became the next president.

assassination of a FRELIMO military commander and in the following year in Mondlane's death.

Divisions grow

Within FRELIMO conflicts grew as different groups formed around different ideas. Some members wanted to develop the already freed northern provinces first, before reaching out to free the ones to the south. Other groups argued that they should kick out the Portuguese and take over everything, but rule in a traditional manner, while others wanted to change everything. As more peasant farmers joined the movement, FRELIMO became more radical and called for major changes in the way things would be run in Mozambique.

As the Portuguese secret police learned of the divisions in FRELIMO, they began to communicate with some of its conservative groups in an effort to persuade them to help get rid of, or even to assassinate, Mondlane. On February 3, 1969, Mondlane went to his office and opened a package addressed to him. The package exploded and killed him. Mondlane left his wife and three children. Samora Machel, the commander in chief of FRELIMO's army, became the new chair of the party. In 1975, 11 years after the armed struggle began and six years after Mondlane's death, Mozambique became the People's Republic of Mozambique. The transitional government appointed Machel the first president and Joaquim Chissano (see entry) the prime minister.

Further Reading

Mondlane, Eduardo. *The Struggle for Mozambique.* Zed Press, 1983.

The Struggle for Africa. Edited by Mai Palmberg. Zed Press, 1983.

Moshoeshoe I

Born c. 1786
Menkwaneng, southern Africa (Orange Free State,
South Africa)
Died March 11, 1870
Basutoland (now Lesotho)

Sotho chief

The early 1800s was a time of turmoil and mass migration in the region of southern Africa that runs along the Indian Ocean Coast. Fighting among several major power groups had resulted in the expansion of the Zulu kingdom under the leadership of the famed chief Shaka (see entry) and his highly disciplined warriors. In the process, however, millions of people had been displaced from their homeland. As people fled their villages, they spread out individually or in roving bands across the hills in search of safety and food. Out of this terrible mayhem, Moshoeshoe, the chief of a small Sotho clan, laid the foundation for the current-day nation-state of Lesotho. (Moshoeshoe's name is sometimes spelled "Mshweshwe"; pronounced *mesh-WASH-way*.)

The violent power struggle in Zululand spread outward, changing the face of southern and central Africa. By the time it

> "Peace is like the rain which makes the grass grow, war is like the wind which dries it up."
>
> **—Moshoeshoe I, speaking to a British high commissioner in 1852**

was over people as far north as the Great Lakes region of central Africa had been affected. The area inhabited by Moshoeshoe—west of the Drakensberg Mountains and north of the Orange River—bore the brunt of the upheavals.

Moshoeshoe and a small band of his Sotho followers left the fertile lands of the plains and took refuge in the Drakensberg Mountains. Once established and out of danger, they welcomed fleeing refugees and in this way increased their numbers. In the late 1830s, however, white Afrikaans-speaking farmers (known as Afrikaners or Boers) moved north from the British colony at Africa's Cape and settled on land claimed by Moshoeshoe. Unable to stop the threats to Sotho land, Moshoeshoe placed his people under the protection of the British government. Like Shaka, Moshoeshoe earned a reputation as a shrewd leader and a military genius. Unlike his ruthless contemporary, though, Moshoeshoe created an enduring state through diplomacy, wisdom, and compassion.

Goes to the mountain

Moshoeshoe was in his thirties when his people felt the shock waves of the warring migrations. By this time he had left his father, who was a village headman of the Mokoteli clan, and established his own following. He originally settled in a valley south of the upper Caledon River.

Between 1820 and 1821 Moshoeshoe resettled his people in a village on the slopes of Butha-Buthe Mountain. Recognizing that war was not necessarily the best way for the Sotho to protect themselves, Moshoeshoe developed his skills of bartering, diplomacy, and negotiation. When the Hlubi threatened to attack, Moshoeshoe offered them cattle. When the Ngwane sent raiding parties, Moshoeshoe and his followers retreated into the mountains. When the Tlokwa attacked, Moshoeshoe again retreated. In retreat, however, he formed alliances with groups fleeing from the Ngwane. The next time the Tlokwa attacked, Moshoeshoe beat them off.

By 1824 Moshoeshoe realized he needed a better defensive position than the one he had established on the mountain slope. He moved his people farther up into the mountains to Thaba Bosiu, an ideal mountain fortress. A spacious, well-watered summit, it was surrounded by sheer cliffs and had only six narrow paths giving access to the fortress. The only drawback to Thaba Bosiu was that it was close to Chief Matiwane of the Ngwane. Moshoeshoe tried to be agreeable and get along with his neighbor, but in 1827 the Sotho became vulnerable to an attack by Matiwane. Zulu warriors had crossed the mountains and entered Ngwane territory, stealing their cattle. Matiwane's people needed to replace the stolen cattle, so they in turn went after the Sotho people's cattle. Moshoeshoe repelled the attack and took control of territory belonging to the Ngwane. Shortly afterward, the Cape colonial army crushed Matiwane. The ever-generous Moshoeshoe allowed the defeated Ngwane to settle in his area and live under his protection.

Welds a nation together

Although the local disputes and cattle raiding continued, Moshoeshoe was building and consolidating (unifying) his kingdom. He encouraged everyone to stay who was willing to accept his authority; he created alliances with other tribes; and he married into other chiefly families. Newcomers gravitated to him, for by now his reputation as an able military leader had spread. Moshoeshoe earned the good will of the new communities by lending them cattle if they did not have their own and by establishing a system of loose supervision over them. He shrewdly settled the newcomers on the perimeter (outer edges) of the kingdom to act as a protective buffer against invaders.

Between 1824 and 1848 the number of people under Moshoeshoe's rule had increased to about 40,000, and by 1865 it numbered about 150,000. The remarkable aspect of the Sotho kingdom was that it incorporated diverse groups in a time of great unrest and upheaval. To ensure stability, Moshoeshoe delegated power to chiefs in outlying areas. Despite this system of shared power, Moshoeshoe remained the ultimate authority in the kingdom.

Moshoeshoe also allowed foreign missionaries into the territory. In 1833 three priests from the Paris Evangelical Society led by Eugene Casalis settled in the kingdom. According to Noël Mostert in *Frontiers: The Epic of South Africa's Creation and the Tragedy of the Xhosa People,* one priest described Moshoeshoe as a man of striking looks and demeanor: "The chief bent upon me a look at once majestic and benevolent. . . . I felt . . . that I had to do with a superior man, trained to think, to command others, and above all himself."

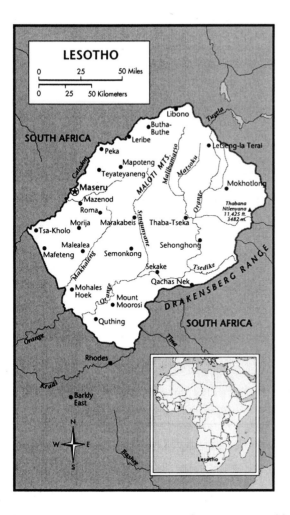

The French missionaries and others that followed established schools and taught literacy in the Sotho kingdom. They also exposed the kingdom to manufactured goods from Europe. Moshoeshoe acquired a taste for imported goods such as clothing, horses, saddles, and eating utensils. To please the missionaries he did away with some traditional rites, but he steadfastly refused to outlaw polygyny, the practice of men taking more than one wife. Moshoeshoe used marriage as a way to hold the state together. He consolidated his hold on the territory by marrying women from many different chiefly families. By 1833 he had already taken 30 wives; by 1864 he had about 150, some of whom were daughters of his chiefs.

White farmers grab land

Throughout the 1830s three main power groups—besides Moshoeshoe's people—developed on the plateau, a large and elevated piece of level land around Thaba Bosiu. Of these peoples, the Tlokwa led by Sikonyela posed the greatest threat to Moshoeshoe's kingdom. Around the same time a new threat began approaching from the south: Afrikaner farmers from the Cape Colony headed north toward the plateau in search of land and freedom. Afrikaners were people of Dutch, German, or French descent speaking the Afrikaans language. They greatly resented the British laws imposed on them in the Cape, particularly the law prohibiting slavery. In 1834 they began what is called the "Great Trek" in search of new lands. For this reason, they are often called Trekkers or Trek Boers.

When the whites arrived, the fertile grazing lands between the Caledon River and the Orange River were unoccupied, so they claimed them for themselves. Various tribes and communities had fled the land for safety while turmoil brewed on the plateau. Because the land was unoccupied, the Afrikaner farmers were able to justify their claims to it.

At first, Moshoeshoe dealt diplomatically and cautiously with these better-armed newcomers. For their part the early farmers respected the African chiefs. At one point, when Ndebele warriors had attacked Afrikaner leader Hendrik Potgieter and taken all his cattle, a group of Tswana in Moshoeshoe's kingdom gave them help. Under the direction of their chief, Moroka, they sent the Afrikaners cows and milk until they could fend for themselves. Other white farmers who came through the territory received permission to graze their cattle until they moved on. The trouble started when these farmers decided *not* to move—they stayed and claimed the land as their own. As more Afrikaners arrived, the situation worsened. They began regarding the land as their own. Inevitably, conflicts followed. By the middle of 1837 nearly 5,000 Boers had ventured across the Orange River. In the mid-1840s the number hadreached 14,000—about 20 percent of the white population of South Africa.

Unable to reach agreement

By 1834 Moshoeshoe realized he could not stop the Afrikaners from settling on his land. He asked Cape governor Sir George Napier to sign a treaty of friendship that would protect him and his people from the Boers. Napier drew up a treaty defining the bounds of Moshoeshoe's territory, which would be called Basutoland. The treaty failed to settle the land disputes with the Boers, and in 1844 all land exchange between the Boers and the Sotho people were canceled. The next year Great Britain sent an agent to settle the disputes. The British resident commissioner, Major Warden, believed Moshoeshoe was responsible for all the border violations. He set out to make an example of Moshoeshoe and sent troops in after him. Moshoeshoe's forces soundly defeated Warden on June 30, 1851.

The next year British high commissioner George Cathcart tried to force Moshoeshoe to accept British authority. Cathcart demanded that Moshoeshoe offer up 10,000 head of cattle to make amends for Warden's defeat. When Moshoeshoe offered only a few thousand, Cathcart paid him a visit. When he told Moshoeshoe that he hoped to meet in peace, Moshoeshoe answered: "I hope so, for peace is like the rain which makes the grass grow, war is like the wind which dries it up." In reply to Cathcart's demand for more cattle, Moshoeshoe is said to have answered: "Do not talk of war, for however anxious I may be to avoid it, you know that a dog when beaten will show his teeth." And show his teeth he did. When Cathcart went after the cattle, Moshoeshoe's forces retaliated. Cathcart barely managed to escape.

Boers at war with the Sotho people

Britain decided to withdraw from this tumultuous area of southern Africa. In the early 1850s the Boers formed two independent republics: the Transvaal and the Orange Free State. British withdrawal from the region left the Sotho unprotected and the boundary on the western side of Basutoland unresolved. Not surprisingly, Boer-Sotho tensions increased.

In 1857 the Orange Free State went to war against Moshoeshoe to take his lands and drive his people out. The Free Staters, however, could not deal with Moshoeshoe's forces or get him out of his mountain fortress. The war ended shortly and at the Treaty of Aliwal North the two parties agreed to split the disputed territory. In 1865, however, the Free State again went to war against the Sotho over boundary issues. Boer fighters were more successful this time; they destroyed Sotho villages and captured vast amounts of cattle. By April 1866 Moshoeshoe was forced to accept unfavorable peace terms. With the kingdom in a desperate state, the chief appealed to the British for protection. Great Britain agreed to annex or add Basutoland to its holdings in 1868, thereby saving the region from the hands of the Free Staters.

Moshoeshoe's legacy

In his old age Moshoeshoe's powers weakened, and rivalry among his four eldest sons and his brothers made his kingdom more vulnerable to a takeover. Britain tried to establish a colonial administration in Basutoland, but after Moshoeshoe died in 1870 the land was given to the Cape Colony. Because the Cape administration was unable to sustain satisfactory relations with the Basuto people, Britain agreed to take the kingdom back as a protectorate, or dependent political unit, in 1884. As a British holding, Basutoland escaped becoming part of the Union of South Africa, a country known for its racist apartheid government's discriminatory policies.

Moshoeshoe was a remarkable military leader who led his people through a time of turbulence and war and then created the foundation for a nation-state. In 1966, nearly 100 years after his death, his kingdom achieved independence as Lesotho.

Further Reading

Marquard, Leo. *The Peoples and Pc̄ ̄ies of South Africa.* 4th ed. New York/UK: Oxford University Press, 1969.

Maylam, Paul. *A History of the African People of South Africa: From the Early Iron Age to the 1970s.* New York: St. Martin's, 1986.

Mostert, Noël. *Frontiers: The Epic of South Africa's Creation and the Tragedy of the Xhosa People.* North Pomfret, VT: J. Cape, 1992.

M'Siri

Born c. 1830
Nyamwezi, Central Africa (Tanzania)
Died December 12, 1891
Shaba province, Katanga (then called Congo Free State; now the
Democratic Republic of the Congo)

Leader of Katanga kingdom

M'Siri's power rested in his army. His wealth came from the monopoly the kingdom had over all trade in copper, ivory, and slaves.

'Siri (*UM-sir-ee*; or Mushidi) Ngelengwa and his followers, who became known as Bayeke, were originally traders from the Nyamwezi area to the east of Lake Tanganyika. They went to the Katanga region of southeastern Congo (called Zaire, 1971-97; renamed Democratic Republic of the Congo, May 17, 1997) in the 1830s and overwhelmed the local people with their guns and fierce fighting style. The Katanga region (today known as Shaba province) was especially rich because it held large deposits of copper. It also held a key location in equatorial Africa, situated so that it was equally accessible to traders from the continent's Atlantic and Indian ocean coasts. M'Siri (his name means "the Mosquito") expanded his territory methodically, taking captives and trading them—along with ivory and copper—for more guns and powder, which he used to take more slaves. His kingdom grew rich on the sweat of these slaves. At the height of his reign M'Siri controlled a territory larger than the state of California. In the late 1800s the wealth of M'Siri's empire drew the attention of of two formidable Europeans: King Leopold II (1835-1909) of Belgium and British industrialist Cecil John Rhodes (1853-1902). When these two powerful forces competed with each other to lay claim to M'Siri's kingdom, it joined the many other African territories that had fallen victim to the greedy determination of expanding European interests.

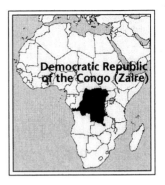

Running a trade caravan

M'Siri came from Nyamwezi, Tanzania, an area renowned for its skilled traders. His mother was named Manena Lyabanza, and his father, Kalasa Mazuri, was the chief of Usumba province and leader of a trading caravan (group of travelers). Kalasa Mazuri worked his way up to this prestigious position, beginning as a porter or bearer for Swahili merchants. The Swahili came from the East Coast of Africa, establishing trade routes in the interior of the country as they searched for ivory and slaves. They required a small army of strong men to carry their purchases back to the coast for sale to Arab and Indian merchants.

The Nyamwezi traveled far into the interior of Africa for slaves as the demand for them increased. The fields of clove plantations on the Indian Ocean islands of Zanzibar and Pemba required many workers. The Nyamwezi were particularly good slavers because they had a large supply of guns and a brutal fighting technique.

M'Siri's father took over a caravan route lying to the south, between Itabwa and the Lunda kingdom. In 1830, around the year M'Siri was born, his father and cousin led a caravan south to Katanga to purchase copper ingots (metal casts). The traders were well received by the chiefs, and they made agreements to protect some against others. Over the years the traders bought copper, ivory, and probably slaves and established a good relationship with the Lunda people.

M'Siri took over his father's trading network and continued the caravan routes. In 1856 M'Siri received permission from the Kazembe, the ruler of the Lunda kingdom, to travel farther south. M'Siri eventually arrived at the court of an old chief named

Katanga. The chief welcomed him as the son of an old friend and gave M'Siri some land and two of his daughters in marriage. M'Siri settled in; soon other Nyamwezi joined him. Having gained a reputation as a powerful man, M'Siri helped settle disputes between local chiefs. Gradually he became known as an enforcer. He took slaves and traded them with the caravans from the West (from present-day Angola). M'Siri traded without the permission or the knowledge of his overlord, the Kazembe.

Expanding his empire

When his patron, Katanga, died around 1860, M'Siri killed Katanga's son and heir and took over the chiefdom for himself. He began to expand his empire through his military strength, conquering other chiefs and taking control over them. M'Siri made his capital at Bunkeya. About 20,000 people lived there. A palisade—a fence made of large pointed stakes stuck in the ground—surrounded M'Siri's palace. Placed on the top points of the palisade were the skulls of M'Siri's enemies. M'Siri reinforced the loyalty of his sub-chiefs by marrying their wives and daughters. He had more than 600 wives. (Polygyny was practiced in many African societies. A chief or king might take several hundred wives, the daughters or wives of other chiefs, in order to strengthen his hold on his territory.)

M'Siri's power rested in his army. A Swahili, Said bin Ali, commanded the army, which had 10,000 warriors, 3,000 of which were armed with rifles. M'Siri's wealth came from the monopoly (exclusive control) the kingdom had over all trade in copper, ivory, and slaves. By the 1880s Bunkeya had become one of the largest trading centers in central Africa. African traders came from Tanganyika (now Tanzania) to buy iron for hoes; Arab traders came from Uganda to buy copper and salt; traders from Africa's West Coast came to buy slaves and ivory in exchange for guns and powder.

Brother Fred Arnot, a British missionary who lived in M'Siri's kingdom in the 1880s, described the ruler as "a thorough gentleman." Arnot said he found M'Siri perplexing; although he treated his subjects brutally, he befriended the missionaries and showed an "uncommonly kind heart." In *The Scramble for Africa,* the author describes him as looking "the part of a venerable chief: white-bearded, six foot and fourteen stone [196 pounds], wearing two yards of dirty calico, day in, day out."

As guns and ammunition became available to other chiefs, M'Siri's hold on his kingdom weakened. One group after another staged revolts and broke away from his control. Slave traders encouraged the rebellions, often providing the guns, because warfare meant captives and that contributed to the traders' business.

By 1890, with so many people armed and so many groups disloyal to M'Siri, he could not safely go outside his capital. As his power weakened he lost some of his mental facilities, becoming confused and even more repressive toward those subjects unlucky enough to remain under his control. Historians tell us that he seemed to enjoy seeing people suffer. Women were thrown into pits full of starving dogs. One Belgian who reached the capital described the scene he saw to author Smith Hempstone:

> Human hearts, still beating, were thrown into mugs of pombe (native beer), which were then enjoyed by the entire court. Men were tied to trees, and when they groaned in hunger, were given their own ears, nose and arms to eat, and . . . perished after devouring themselves.

Outside powers intrude

Ever since Scottish explorer and missionary David Livingstone's time (1813-1873), stories of Katanga's wealth have been told and retold. Explorers related tales of people smelting (melting and separating) the metal into bars of solid copper—as heavy as one man could lift—and of huge solid copper crosses being used as money. Because of the potential wealth of the Katanga hills, agents for Rhodes and Leopold II were both anxious to win territorial concessions (rights to the land) from M'Siri. According to the terms of the 1895 Conference of Berlin, the Congo River basin—including Katanga—was Leopold's preserve (meaning it was a region reserved for him). But the boundaries of the preserve had not been specified. Under the rules established in Berlin, effective occupation was the standard that European countries used to stake their claim in Africa. This meant that the occupier had to establish border posts and military camps on the land; to do this, the Belgians needed M'Siri's permission.

Several Belgian agents of Leopold II set off for Bunkeya, attempting to persuade M'Siri to join Katanga to Leopold's Congo Free State. Rhodes also sent agents to try to talk M'Siri into annexing Katanga to Northern Rhodesia (now Zambia). In 1891, by intercepting a message to Rhodes, Leopold's agents sought to establish their claim to Bunkeya before the British. M'Siri was very difficult to deal with, though, and in a fit of fury a Belgian agent shot him dead when he refused to sign the treaty. M'Siri's guards then killed the agent. At M'Siri's death, his son became the chief; he signed the agreement annexing Katanga to the Congo Free State of Leopold.

Further Reading

Dictionary of African Biography. Volume 2. Algonac, MI: Reference Publications, 1976.

Hempstone, Smith. *Katanga Report.* Winchester, MA: Faber, 1962.

Pakenham, Thomas. *The Scramble for Africa.* Jonathan Ball, 1991.

Wilson, Derek. *A History of South and Central Africa.* New York/UK: Cambridge University Press, 1975.

Robert Mugabe

Born February 21, 1924
Kutama Mission, Southern Rhodesia (Zimbabwe)

*Nationalist leader and first prime minister
and president of Zimbabwe*

R hodesia was the last of the British colonies in Africa to become independent. The nationalist struggle there was made more complicated by the stubbornness of the white settlers in the face of inevitable black rule. Robert Gabriel Mugabe *(MOO-gah-bay)* was one of the most important nationalist leaders in that fight for independence—a nationalist leader for 20 years, a political prisoner for 10 years, and leader of his party's military wing for 5 years. In the newly independent Zimbabwe—as Rhodesia was renamed— Mugabe was the first black to be elected head of state. He presided over the transition from a nation with a white minority government to that of one with black majority rule. Under his leadership the government at first proclaimed itself a socialist state. With the change of governments in East Europe moving from communism to capitalism in the late 1980s, however, the Mugabe government

From the outset Mugabe addressed the nation's need for national reconciliation.

reluctantly relaxed controls over the economy. Nevertheless, Mugabe is an authoritarian leader—one who keeps power to himself and often makes one-sided decisions without consulting parliament or his cabinet. Opposition political parties exist in Zimbabwe, but they are denied fair treatment by the state-controlled media and other government institutions.

"A very clever lad"

Mugabe was born in Kutama Mission in Southern Rhodesia on February 21, 1924. His mother was a schoolteacher and his father a carpenter in a Jesuit mission. When Mugabe was young his father left the family to go to work in South Africa, and he never returned. Mugabe's mother raised the four children on her own. Like other African boys his age, Mugabe looked after his family's cattle and helped earn money whenever he could. He went to school at the mission, where his teachers singled him out as a "very clever lad." He went on to take the teacher training course and graduated in 1945. After several years of teaching, he left Rhodesia for South Africa where he enrolled at Fort Hare University, an an all-black university in Cape Province.

In the years immediately after World War II (1939-1944), Fort Hare was fertile ground for African nationalism, the movement for independence and self-rule in African nations. Mugabe met many of South Africa's future nationalists who were also studying there, men like Nelson Mandela (see entry) and Oliver Tambo. "My hatred and revulsion for the [colonial] system had started at Fort Hare, and now it grew," Mugabe once said. "I decided I would fight to overthrow it. . . ."

Activism in the nationalist movement

The politics of reform in Rhodesia were divided. In 1955 Mugabe's childhood friend, James Chikerema, founded the Southern Rhodesia African National Congress, an organization aimed at removing whites from power. At the other end of the spectrum was Joshua Nkomo, who advocated sharing power with whites and was already involved in negotiating with the white minority government for more rights for blacks.

Mugabe was initially not very interested in the two black movements. After he received his university degree, he taught in

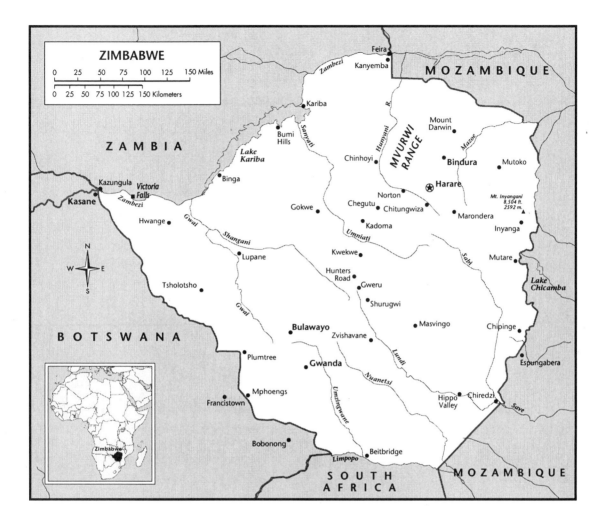

several schools in Southern and Northern Rhodesia (Zambia) and then in Ghana, where he began to change his mind about the political struggle at home. Mugabe was teaching in Ghana in 1951, when Ghana was in transition from a British colony to an independent state. There, for the first time in his life, he experienced being an African in a country free of European domination.

In 1960 he returned to Southern Rhodesia to introduce Sally Heyfron, his Ghanaian wife-to-be, to his family. He had planned on returning to Ghana, but when he realized the strength of the nationalist movement in his own country, he decided to stay. In Southern Rhodesia in the late 1950s the liberal government had been voted out of office by conservative whites who did not like its policies toward blacks. The new government banned black political organizations as it became more and more repressive. In 1959 the government outlawed the African National Congress (ANC). Within days political activists formed a new party, the National Democratic Party (NDP), with the goal of attaining black majority rule in Southern Rhodesia without sharing power. Mugabe joined the NDP and became its publicity secretary.

In November 1960, the British foreign minister held a conference in the capital, Salisbury (now Harare), to work out a new constitution. The Southern Rhodesian whites agreed to set aside 15 seats for blacks in the proposed 65-seat parliament and allow Britain to veto laws it felt were racist. To the surprise of many black nationalists, NDP leader Joshua Nkomo (see entry) agreed to the proposals. The NDP's executive committee, however, rejected the deal outright. On other occasions over the next 20 years, Nkomo's willingness to settle would divide the nationalist movement.

As the government became more repressive, unrest spread nationwide. Mugabe traveled around the country, telling people about the situation and asking for their support. In 1961 the government banned the NDP. Ten days later the Zimbabwe African People's Union (ZAPU) replaced it. Mugabe again worked as publicity secretary for the president, Nkomo, in the new party. The following year the government banned ZAPU and the police picked Mugabe up and held him in custody for three months.

Leaders take sides

In December 1962 the government passed legislation calling for the death penalty for saboteurs (people who carried out deliberately destructive acts against the government or its forces). Mugabe, Nkomo, and others in the party leadership fled to Tanzania where the party had established its operational headquarters. Mugabe had been led to believe that Tanzania President Julius Nyerere (see entry) had requested the party leadership to come there. Nyerere, however, was furious that the leaders had left Rhodesia. He ordered them to go home immediately. Some of the leadership—Mugabe among them—believed that Nkomo had deceived them and that he should no longer be leader of the party. But when Nkomo learned of their feelings, he moved before they could do anything. He called a press conference to announce the suspension of four members of the executive. Mugabe and fellow nationalist Ndabaningi Sithole were among the four. Eventually ZAPU executives split and formed their own party, the Zimbabwe African National Union (ZANU), with Sithole as their leader. The bad feelings created by this episode were to have long-lasting repercussions in the relationship between Mugabe and Nkomo.

Struggle for power among the nationalists

In preparation for his return to Rhodesia in December 1963, Mugabe had sent his wife, Sally, and their three-month old son back to Ghana, fearing that the government might hurt his family. As he expected, he was arrested on his arrival in the country. Within a few months of his arrest, nearly 150 ZAPU and ZANU leaders were detained. The government had effectively crushed the nationalist movement by putting its leaders in prison. In August 1964, the government outlawed both parties. During the 10 years that Mugabe spent in prison, he earned two advanced degrees through correspondence courses. He also tutored his fellow prisoners.

With their leaders in prison and with the Rhodesian army standing in their way, the nationalists turned on themselves. Groups of supporters from ZAPU and ZANU fought openly; they burned houses and often killed those who had hidden inside. Mob rule had taken over. The Southern Rhodesian government sat back and watched the violence as its opposition tore itself apart.

With most of its leaders in prison, ZANU operated outside the country. Herbert Chitepo, the first black man to qualify as a lawyer in Southern Rhodesia, ran the external wing of ZANU from Lusaka, Zambia. ZANU fighters infiltrated Rhodesia from Zambia and made some attacks against whites. The attacks were more symbolic than effective, and they resulted in the Rhodesian army getting involved. The presence of the Rhodesian army, combined with a power struggle among the nationalists, weakened the liberation movement.

The power struggle in ZANU came to a climax in 1969 when ZANU president Sithole, on trial for plotting to assassinate Ian Smith (see entry), publicly denied any guerrilla activity. Betrayed by Sithole, ZANU leaders secretly elected Mugabe to head the party, even though he was still in prison.

Ian Smith's Unilateral Declaration of Independence

The Federation of Rhodesia and Nyasaland was a self-governing union of Southern Rhodesia (now Zimbabwe), Northern Rhodesia (now Zambia), and Nyasaland (now Malawi). It existed from 1953 to 1963. The English-speaking whites in the three territories thought federation would allow them to develop the region. They wanted to take the profits from the rich copper deposits in Zambia to build dams and highways in the three countries. They also wanted to become a large enough political unit that they could become a white-controlled independent state. During Federation, major improvements for the region were made: the Kariba Dam and electric power station were built, a railway line connecting Southern Rhodesia with Mozambique was constructed, and a government-supported university was opened in Salisbury (Harare). Federation gave the whites an unfair advantage over the majority of the people. In the legislature, 35 seats were for whites and 6 for Africans.

Rather than face a black majority government in Rhodesia, as Great Britain was demanding with the end of Federation, in 1965 the government under Ian Smith declared Rhodesia an independent nation. His declaration of independence (known as UDI or unilateral declaration of independence) was not recognized by Great Britain or by most of the rest of the world. Malawi and South Africa were among the few countries that continued to have diplomatic relations with Rhodesia.

A series of negotiations

The struggle for independence in Rhodesia continued at a slow pace. The next significant guerrilla attack did not occur until 1972, six years after the first. The turning point for the nationalists was the military coup (overthrow) in Portugal in 1974. The new Portuguese government withdrew its troops from Angola and Mozambique, and when the army left, the white settlers left. A Marxist government (a form of socialist government in which the state controls property and jobs) took over in Mozambique and offered support to Mugabe and his ZANU forces.

Hoping that with the change in Mozambique the whites might be more willing to negotiate, the nationalists called a conference in Lusaka in 1974. Mugabe and Nkomo were released from prison so they could attend as the leaders of the nationalist movement. For the purposes of negotiating, the nationalists created an umbrella group (one that covers a broad range of interests) called the United African Nationalist Congress (UANC). Ian Smith, the prime minister of the unrecognized white-minority government of Rhodesia, was not willing to settle and the

negotiators came away empty-handed. This would be the first of several attempts to negotiate a settlement.

Shortly after the 1974 Lusaka conference, ZANU's representative in Lusaka, Herbert Chitepo, was assassinated. Mugabe and Edgar Tekere, a loyal supporter, afraid that they would also be hit, fled to Mozambique. While in Mozambique, Mugabe solidified his role as party leader by taking command of ZANU's army. In 1976, with assistance from the Chinese, ZANU sent large numbers of fighters into Rhodesia from Mozambique and the guerrilla warfare intensified. ZANU forces destroyed bridges, blew up mills and water-pumping stations, and terrorized white mines and farms. The Mugabe-led warfare forced thousands of whites to abandon their property.

On the domestic political front, Smith had made an alliance with some of the moderate nationalist leaders still in the country. He had persuaded them to take part in elections as the leaders of the nationalist movement. With the true nationalist leaders out of the country, Bishop Abel Muzorewa was elected prime minister of Zimbabwe-Rhodesia. Neither Britain, nor any other western

Mugabe arrives in Geneva, Switzerland, to attend the Conference on Rhodesia, 1976.

nation, recognized his government. Most viewed it as a puppet government with whites still retaining political power. Mugabe and his army continued to attack.

The nation of Zimbabwe is born

When it became clear that Muzorewa's election would not end the fighting, Britain called for another conference. For this meeting at Lancaster House in London in late 1979, the nationalist groups formed another umbrella group, the Patriotic Front. Mugabe was persuaded to agree to supervised elections. He says that this was the "most painful signature I've ever had to put on paper." In the supervised elections Mugabe's party, ZANU-PF, won 57 out of 80 seats in the parliament. After 20 years of struggle, the nation of Zimbabwe was born. Mugabe was sworn in as prime minister on April 18, 1980.

Problems at independence

At independence, the new government faced the difficult task of uniting a badly divided country. The war years meant that whites were divided among themselves; suspicion between whites and blacks was high; and blacks were divided along tribal lines. The Shona were the majority ethnic group and in power; the Ndebele had made a great contribution to the war and they were on the sidelines. At the highest level, Mugabe and Nkomo held one another in mutual suspicion and dislike.

From the outset Mugabe addressed the nation's need for national reconciliation. Realizing that the removal of all white structures would bring economic disaster to the new nation, he did not establish a socialist government in Zimbabwe, although he was himself a socialist at the time. Mugabe achieved a remarkable degree of support from the white community as their fears of retribution and nationalization (government takeover of businesses) eased. The three armies—Rhodesian, ZANU and ZAPU—were successfully integrated, although the divisions among the two main political groups ZANU and ZAPU took nearly 10 years to resolve.

Political improvements in Zimbabwe

Despite the divisions in the nation, Mugabe was able to make strides in providing blacks with health services and education. During the early years he served as president, the Zimbabwe government built hundreds of rural health centers and primary schools and improved the road access to rural areas. Laws introduced by the ZANU government gave women rights equal to those of men.

The constitution worked out at the Lancaster House conference restricted the new government by guaranteeing whites 20 seats in the 100-seat parliament for the first seven years of independence. In December 1987, the parliament approved a new constitution making Mugabe executive vice president. The new constitution received the required two-thirds vote partly as a result of an accord reached between Mugabe and Nkomo. The two parties agreed to merge and work toward creating a one-party state. In return for ZAPU's support, Mugabe appointed Nkomo senior minister in the president's office. With the only potential source of opposition brought into the fold, Mugabe's control became nearly absolute. The poor economic situation in the country, however, forced Mugabe to abandon his idea for a one-party state, to restrict state spending on social programs, and remove the government from the business sector.

Mugabe is a rather austere man, regarded as extremely intelligent and a pragmatic politician. In 1995 he married his former secretary, Grace Marufa. They have three children, two of whom were born before his first wife died in 1992. Mugabe and his government officials have become increasingly shut off from the concerns and worries of the average Zimbabwean. In the nearly 20 years ZANU has been in control, arrogance, corruption and inefficiency have become the hallmarks of the government.

Further Reading

Smith, David, and Colin Simpson. *Mugabe*. Salisbury: Pioneer Head, 1981

Verrier, Anthony. *The Road to Zimbabwe: 1890-1980*. London: Jonathan Cape, 1986.

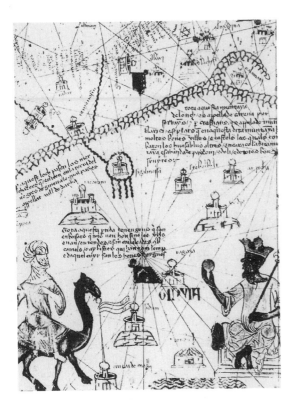

Mansa Musa

Born 1312
Mali kingdom (Mali)
Died 1337
Mali kingdom (Mali)

Emperor of Mali kingdom

Musa's image adorned world atlases prepared by European mapmakers. Pictured above, a detail from the Catalan atlas of 1375; Musa on throne at lower right.

Mansa Musa ruled a fabulously wealthy fourteenth-century empire in the central part of western Africa. He provided the financing and inspiration to transform the small nomadic village of Timbuktu (Tombouctou) into an intellectual and economic center deep inside the continent. European explorers would not set foot there for another 500 years. Mansa Musa spearheaded the spread of Islamic law and civilization in the region. (Islam is the religion of those who worship Allah). His leadership and the achievements of the old Mali kingdom contradict all claims that little was achieved in black Africa until whites arrived.

Few outsiders other than Muslim traders from northern Africa and the East knew of Musa's legendary country until 1324, when the flamboyant king made an extravagant pilgrimage to Mecca, the holiest city of Islam (located in today's Saudi Arabia). By the end of his

The Mali Kingdom encompassed a vast area, including parts of Senegal, Mauritania, and Guinea as well as present-day Mali.

pilgrimage, he had attracted the world's attention. Soon Musa's image adorned world atlases prepared by European mapmakers who knew little of the geography of the unexplored continent below Africa's northern rim. These early atlases cited Musa as evidence that riches and "Negro" royalty existed in central and western Africa.

Expands his empire

On Musa's way through Cairo, the lavish spending and distribution of alms (goods given to help the poor) by his massive

The Origin of the Mali Kingdom

Sundiata Keita, or Sunjaata (c. 1190s-c. 1255), was the legendary founder of the medieval Mali kingdom. Sundiata is credited with freeing his small Mandé-speaking community from its oppressive overlords and laying the foundation for one of the wealthiest, most powerful kingdoms of Africa. His father, Nare Fa Maghan, ruled a small kingdom called Kangaba, located between the headwaters of the Niger and Senegal rivers around the border of modern Mali and Guinea. The first Keita ruler of Kangaba was Barmandana, who converted to Islam around A.D. 1050.

To protect themselves from their more powerful neighbors who raided for slaves, the Keita family united previously scattered family-based communities, villages, and clans under their leadership. The Kangaba were not strong enough, however, to defend themselves against the Soso, who raided their kingdom and killed 11 of Nare Fa Maghan's sons. The Soso did not bother executing Sundiata because he was crippled and they did not think he was a threat.

Another of Sundiata's brothers, Dankaran-Tuma, made a bargain to become king of the Kangaba under the domination of the Soso. Meanwhile, Sundiata, who miraculously recovered the use of his limbs, devoted himself to hunting and gained fame and favor with his people. The king became passionately jealous of his brother's popularity and forced him to flee the kingdom. Sundiata took refuge in the court of

group of followers flooded the city with gold. The Egyptian financial market, then one of the world's most important, plunged. It required more than 10 years for the price of gold to recover. With his gold Musa also persuaded the leading Islamic scholars and builders living in Cairo to follow him back home across the vast Sahara Desert to Timbuktu on the crucial bend of the fertile Niger River.

These scholars and architects built Timbuktu into one of the world's foremost Islamic academic and financial centers. Trade in gold, salt, slaves, and kola nuts made Timbuktu the Wall Street of Africa. By the fifteenth century Timbuktu rivaled the leading European cities of Venice, Paris, and Milan in population and economic and intellectual activity. Since then, however, the golden age of the old Mali kingdom has faded into obscurity. Today's Mali is a landlocked African country, one of the world's poorest.

Musa's fourteenth-century empire spread eastward from the Atlantic coasts of today's Senegal and Gambia along the agriculturally rich Niger River delta to beyond Timbuktu. The hot, dry Sahara Desert extending into today's Mauritania formed the

the king of Mema. When the Kangaba rose up spontaneously against the taxation and harsh conditions imposed on them by the Soso, Dankaran-Tuma ran away, abandoning his people.

Informed of the situation in Kangaba, Sundiata raised a large cavalry force (soldiers on horseback) and joined together with other discontented states that were being controlled by the Soso. This army stormed Kangaba and took power in 1234. Sundiata challenged the Soso; each side mobilized for battle. Legend has it that in 1235 the opposing columns fought a terrible battle, so vicious that "blood poured out of a thousand wounds," according to an eyewitness. Sundiata won the battle and ended Soso control over the Kangaba.

Sundiata then built a new capital at Niani. Niani attracted Muslim traders and scholars from North Africa and became not only a political capital but a thriving commercial center. Encouraged by his military victory, Sundiata grew ambitious. He conquered territories "in all directions": the gold-bearing fields to the South, the eastern territories extending to the Upper Niger, the western state up to the Atlantic Ocean, and the northern lands well into the Sahara Desert. He transformed the small kingdom of Kangaba into the vast and formidable empire of Mali, which reached its peak of power in the fourteenth century under Mansa Musa.

empire's northern border. To the south lay tropical jungle stretching down to the steaming Guinea coast.

According to oral tradition, Musa's predecessor, known as Muhammad, expanded his power over territories that included or had access to the plentiful gold deposits of western Africa. Rulers of the Mali kingdom were extremely ambitious. Unverifiable reports indicate that Muhammad may have sent fleets of ships numbering in the thousands to explore the other side of the Atlantic Ocean nearly 200 years before Christopher Columbus discovered the New World.

Region's resources are important

The Niger River was key to the success of the Mali kingdom. The 2,600-mile river rises in southwest Guinea and follows a circuitous, eastward course through West Africa down into Nigeria before emptying into the Atlantic Ocean. Much like the Nile that gave birth to Egypt's early civilization, the Niger floods each year, leaving behind deep layers of fertile soil along its banks. Centuries before the Christian era, major cities rose along the Niger delta (the deposit at the river's mouth).

Good economic prospects and the domestication of camels opened the way for Muslim traders from northern Africa, Arabia, and the Orient. These traders transported goods across the broad Sahara Desert to trade with people along the Niger River. Musa and other Malian leaders denied non-Muslims access to the Niger River markets. Christian "infidels" (or nonbelievers in Islam) gained access to the region only in the nineteenth century.

Timbuktu became a natural trading crossroad. Camels stopped at the northern bank of the river because blood-sucking tsetse flies carrying fatal diseases made the southern bank dangerous. From the central bend in the river where Timbuktu was located, goods were moved by boats east and west along the Niger. A natural exchange of goods between the North and South developed. Trade boomed. From the tropical South came gold, slaves, and kola nuts. The gold paid for trade along the Silk Road to the Far East and financed much of the European Renaissance (a rebirth of art and literature that began in fourteenth-century Italy). Slaves provided labor to dig salt out of the northern Sahara Desert mines. Slaves also became servants for Arabian and European households. Nuts from the kola tree supplied relief from thirst in the desert.

From the North came salt, high-grade textiles, and metal instruments. So important was salt in the tropical South that at one time it traded equally with gold on Timbuktu markets—an ounce of salt for an ounce of gold. Manufactured clothing from the North was of higher quality than the handmade clothes of the South. And a boom in weapons and ammunition occurred in the tropics as Africans began using guns to defend themselves and capture slaves.

Returns from pilgrimage with an architect

Reveling in all his kingdom's glory and surplus gold, Musa set off in 1324 on one of the five essential Muslim duties: to make a pilgrimage to Mecca (the Holy Land). Reports vary according to scholars and others about the extent of the expedition through Sudan, Egypt, and across the Red Sea to Mecca. Some sources say Musa's entourage (attendants and associates) numbered as many as 80,000, including 500 slaves bearing golden staffs and 100

El Saheli grew up in Andalusia, a region in southern Spain. Almost certainly the Grand Mosque in the Andalusian city of Cordova influenced his architectural training. The mosque, the most magnificent Islamic structure in the Western world, was built between the eight and ninth centuries by the Moors (North African Muslims who ruled part of Spain from A.D. 711 to 1492).

The interior of Timbuktu's Djinguereber mosque bears a striking similarity to that of the Grand Mosque of Cordova. The Timbuktu mosque has nine rows of square pillars, 95 in all, providing prayer space for 2,000. Cordova's mosque is supported by rows of pillars supporting graceful Moorish arches. But El Saheli had less building material to work with than the plentiful stone at Cordova. In fact, all he really had available to him was mud, so the Djinguereber mosque's exterior resembles the Islamic architectural style common in the Sahara Desert and Niger River valley. Musa was apparently pleased with the mosque: he gave the architect 132 pounds of gold upon the building's completion.

camels each transporting 300 pounds of gold—an incredible total of 30,000 pounds.

During his trip Musa encountered a brilliant Spanish architect living in Cairo, Egypt. The emperor lured the architect, El Saheli, to Timbuktu, where he built five exquisite mosques (a building used for public worship by Muslims) and became a rich man. One of the five—Djinguereber mosque, completed in 1327—remains the religious center of Timbuktu and is regarded as its greatest treasure. Muslims continue to use the mosque for daily prayers. Timbuktu's *imam*, the city's main religious leader, still conducts special Friday prayers from the mosque.

Kingdom emerges as multicultural commercial center

While much of Europe fell victim to wars and plagues, Timbuktu emerged under Musa's guidance as an urban center of commerce and learning with the second largest imperial court in the world. According to Arabic geographers and historians, Musa claimed that his own rise to power stemmed from the actions of Muhammad, his predecessor, who sailed into the Atlantic Ocean to explore the water's limits. Arabic author Shihab al-Din Ibn Fadi al-'Umari quoted a version of Musa's story as told by a man named Abu'l Hasan Ali ibn Amir Hajib. Muhammad is said to have equipped 200 ships and filled them with men. He filled another 200 with enough gold, water, food, and other supplies to last the men for years. He instructed the ships' commanders to return only after they had explored the other side of the sea or had run out of food and water. Years later, as the story goes, a single ship returned. The commander told Muhammad that the other ships had disappeared in a violent, mid-ocean current. Muhammad then set out to survey the situation himself, taking 2,000 vessels along on the journey. He he left Musa in charge of the kingdom and set out with his companions. "This was the last time that I saw him and the others," Musa said, "and I remained absolute master of the empire."

In recent years, the report by al-'Umari has formed the basis of controversial claims by some U.S. Africanists—claims that Africans arrived in the New World long before the Europeans and therefore played a key role in the development of the Americas. But other scholars caution against believing any of Musa's grandiose claims. Musa was well known for his tall tales, and his story about Muhammad may well have been fabricated. (After all, he often boasted that he owned a gold plant—a plant that grew the precious metal in the ground just like a carrot.) Whatever the circumstances of Musa's ascent to power—whether true, false, or just slightly exaggerated—there is no denying that under his leadership Timbuktu became a multicultural trading hub and a center of learning in western Africa.

Further Reading

al-'Umari, Shihab al-Din Ibn Fadi and el Amsar. *Masalik el Absar fi Mamalik.* Traduit par Gaudefroy-Demombynes, Librarie Orientaliste Paul Geuthner, 1927.

Boahen, Adu. *Topics in West African History.* New York: Longman, 1966.

Curtin, Philip, and others, eds. *African History: From Earliest Times to Independence.* 2nd ed. New York: Longman, 1995.

Davidson, Basil. *The Growth of African Civilisation: History of West Africa, 1000-1800.* New York: Longman, 1965.

Harris, Joseph E. *Africans and Their History.* New Jersey: New American Library, 1972.

Izuakor, Levi Ifeanyi. "Sundiata Keita." In *Historic World Leaders.* Edited by Anne Commire. Volume 1. Detroit: Gale, 1994.

Levtzion, Nehemia. *Muslims and Chiefs in West Africa.* New York/UK: Oxford University Press, 1968.

Murphy, E. Jefferson. *History of African Civilization.* New York: Dell, 1972.

Niane, D. T. *General History of Africa.* Volume 4. UNESCO, 1984.

Niane, D. T. *Sundiata: An Epic in African History.* New York: Longman, 1965.

Trimingham, J. Spencer. *A History of Islam in West Africa.* New York/UK: Oxford University Press, 1974.

Yoweri Museveni

Born c. 1944
Ntungamo, Ankole, Uganda

President of Uganda

s president of Uganda since 1986, Yoweri Museveni has faced the staggering task of restoring peace and prosperity to a country devastated by 15 years of civil war. Museveni became president on January 29, 1986, after his forces stormed the capital city of Kampala and overthrew the existing government. Since then he has tried to reverse two decades of army brutality, government corruption, and economic decline in Uganda, formerly one of Africa's most prosperous countries. "I've got a mission—to transform Uganda from a backward country to an advanced country," " he told *Time* magazine.

A history of fragmentation

Uganda is a landlocked country in East Africa, approximately the size of England. Although it has no ocean coastline, it shares massive Lake Victoria with neighboring Kenya and Tanzania, and its rivers are plentiful. Once known as the "pearl of Africa," its game reserves formed the backdrop for the filming of American director John Huston's 1951 movie *The African Queen*. Unlike some other African nations, Uganda is favored with good rains and fertile soils.

British explorers and missionaries arrived in Uganda in the mid-1800s. At that time the region consisted of a series of small kingdoms and chiefdoms, each with its own leadership, army, and ethnic identity. Uganda consists of about 40 different tribes, divided into two major language groups: the Bantu and the Nilotic. Much of the divisiveness (conflicts among groups) in the country can be traced to ethnic rivalries.

Toward the end of the century, as various European powers were grabbing land in Africa, Britain declared Uganda a protectorate (or dependent political unit) in an effort to block German territorial advances. Britain did not encourage the formation of a white settler community in Uganda. After a major railway was completed in the region—it stretched from Mombasa, Kenya, through Nairobi, to Uganda—many indentured laborers from India settled in Uganda. They came to dominate the area's trading activity. The arrival of Catholic and Protestant missionaries added more religious rivalries to an already tense ethnic situation.

"He of the Seven"

Yoweri Kaguta Museveni was born in a village in the Ankole province of southwestern Uganda sometime around 1944. (Even he is not exactly sure of the year of his birth.) His parents were Tutsis—Nilotic people who had settled in the region centuries earlier. Museveni's father, Amosi Kaguta, was a member of the Banyankole tribe; his mother, Eteri Kokundeka, was a member of the Banyarwanda tribe. The couple gained considerable wealth as landowners and cattle ranchers. During World War II (1939-45) Museveni's father had been a member of the British army in the King's African Rifles brigade. He named his son "Museveni" (meaning "He of the Seven") after the 7th battalion, or military unit, in which the Ugandans served.

Museveni's parents insisted that he get a good education. When he was nine years old, they sent him away to study at a missionary boarding school. After that, he completed his high school and college-prep classes at Ntare School in Mbarara, the district capital. Museveni was a teenager when Britain granted Uganda its independence in 1962. Uganda's first president was Milton Obote.

Exiled freedom fighter

Later in the 1960s Museveni left Uganda to study political science and economics at University College in Dar es Salaam, the capital of Tanzania. After earning a bachelor's degree in economics in 1970, he returned to Uganda and went to work for the government as a research assistant. Within a year, however, Uganda was thrown into political turmoil. In January 1971 Obote's top-ranking army officer, Idi Amin Dada (see entry), overthrew the government. Amin's regime was brutal and violent. Hundreds of thousands of Ugandans—academics, professionals, and business-people—went into exile (meaning they fled from Uganda to another country). Many thousands more went to their graves. Amin allowed his armed forces to run rampant over the country-side. They looted and robbed, pillaged and raped. Uganda's economy collapsed as the army destroyed the crops and stole the cattle. The military government forced the Indians in Uganda to leave their homes and businesses; inexperienced and illiterate soldiers then tried to run the Indians' once-thriving companies.

Museveni went into exile in Tanzania, where he taught economics while forming the Front for National Salvation (FRONASA), an opposition group dedicated to getting rid of Amin. Museveni and his soldiers trained in Mozambique with a guerrilla group called FRELIMO (an acronym for an independent fighting unit known as the Front for the Liberation of Mozambique.) While in Tanzania, he formed firm opinions about various economic philosophies. Under the presidency of Julius Nyerere (see entry) from 1962 to 1985, Tanzania had experimented with socialism—the government had taken over all businesses and corporations in the country. Museveni told *Time* magazine that he had gained important economic insights by observing Tanzania's model: "Communal property was nobody's property. So nobody worked. The problem was motivation. None of these fellows had a stake. You have to base your production strategy on the selfish individual, not the altruistic [selfless] minority."

Museveni and his fighters prepared to invade Uganda at the first sign of Amin's weakness. In 1979 FRONASA united with a larger rebel band loyal to Obote and got support from Tanzania's military. A hastily assembled confederation known as the Uganda National Liberation Front (UNLF) marched on Kampala and chased Amin from the country in March 1979. The eight years of Amin's rule of terror had devastated Uganda.

Independence

The job of rebuilding was enormous, and a power struggle within the UNLF—Uganda's coalition government—made it more difficult. The new government was something of a union of distinctive political elements; these elements had formed a temporary alliance for joint action. At first the government was headed by former university president Yusufu Lule. Lule appointed Museveni minister of defense in charge of the army. But only 68 days into Lule's term in office, another civilian (nonmilitary) leader, Godfrey Binaisa, became Uganda's head of state.

Museveni's responsibility was to clear the country of Amin's soldiers and to recruit new soldiers for the army. He used his FRONASA troops and other fighters recruited from his Banyankole tribe. Soon other government officials began to worry about the young commander's growing strength. Museveni formed a political party, the Uganda Patriotic Movement, to run in the December 1980 elections. Although Museveni was a popular figure, Obote's Uganda People's Congress soundly defeated him, winning the presidency by a large margin.

Back to the bush

Claiming that Obote had rigged the election, Museveni left Kampala and returned to the bush with 30 men and 27 rifles on February 6, 1981. From that small cluster of supporters he forged the National Resistance Army (NRA), one of four rebel groups seeking to undermine the Obote regime. Based in Luwero, north of Kampala, Museveni groomed a force of highly disciplined soldiers.

Under Obote's leadership, Uganda fell into political, economic, and social chaos. The army ravaged the country, just as Amin's men had done, and Obote did not attempt to stop them. Museveni's small disciplined army stood in contrast to this turmoil, and it gained supporters as the atrocities (horrifying and bru-

tal acts) increased. Then in 1985 army officers from the Acholi
tribe in northern Uganda overthrew the Obote government. Still,
the violence continued.

Museveni agreed to negotiate with the new military government of Tito Okello, but he refused to disband his army. Even as
peace talks went on in Nairobi, Kenya, the horror persisted in
Uganda. Both sides agreed to a cease-fire, but it lasted only a few
weeks. In January 1986, the NRA marched on Kampala. Okello
fled into exile, where he died in 1990. Museveni was sworn in as
Uganda's new president on January 29, 1986.

Trying to hold back the tide

In his acceptance speech Museveni declared that his government would strive for "a fundamental change in the politics of our
country." Initially, he pulled together Uganda's fragmented society by appointing a diverse range of civilian and military people to
his cabinet (a body of advisers). He also restored the thrones to

several traditional monarchies (African peoples such as the Buganda, Banner, and Toro, who had been ruled by a royal family prior to Amin's takeover.) Museveni postponed any movement toward developing a multiparty democracy, making the National Resistance Movement the only legal party in the country. In 1996, for the first time since his rise to power, the government held presidential elections. The candidates, however, ran on an individual basis, not as representatives of their parties. Museveni called this a "no-party" state. Museveni's argument for a "no-party" state was based on Uganda's economic past. He claimed that the country was not yet developed enough to have a middle class. Without a well-educated middle class in Uganda, Museveni believed the voters would form political groups along tribal lines. Tribal divisions were at the root of the most serious problems in Uganda's troubled history. For this reason, Museveni viewed multiparty elections as a low priority in the 1990s. With all the resources of the government behind his party, the National Resistance Movement not surprisingly won 74 percent of the vote in 1996.

Economic growth in Uganda is slow but steady. Museveni adopted some policies proposed by the International Bank for Reconstruction and Development, commonly known as the World Bank, an agency of the United Nations that lends money to member nations. Uganda has received substantial amounts of foreign aid. Although various cutbacks have caused hardship for many of his people, the measures hold out some hope for the future. Corruption, however, remains a major problem and is undermining economic development. Political observers note that the corrupt practices of his officials are having a detrimental effect on the country. Museveni is also facing several resistance movements in the North and the West of the country. Back in 1988 the government put down a mutiny, or rebellion, by dissatisfied soldiers, detaining some 700 army officers in connection with the incident.

A regional powerbroker

Museveni believes that African governments should help one another, and he has long been involved in the situation in the Great Lakes region of eastern Africa (including Uganda, Congo, Tanzania, Rwanda, and Burundi). Like dominos, events in one country influence events in another. The background to the regional turmoil began in Rwanda in 1958. Until then, the minority Tutsis had been the overlords of the majority Hutus in Rwanda. With Rwanda's nearing independence from Belgium, the Hutus staged a revolt against the Tutsis, killing hundreds of thousands and forcing the survivors to flee to Uganda, Tanzania, and Burundi. In Uganda the exiles learned to speak English and served in the military. Some joined Museveni's guerrilla army to fight against Ugandan president Obote.

Despite many efforts to persuade Rwandan authorities to allow the Tutsis back in the country, the Hutu government refused. In the late 1980s the Tutsis formed a guerrilla army, the Rwandese Patriotic Front, RPF, whose goal was to overthrow the Hutu government in Rwanda. The Tutsis invaded Rwanda in 1990 and by 1994 they had forces close to the capital, Kigali. In the mayhem that followed the death of the Rwandan president in 1994, the Tutsi rebel army established a Tutsi-dominated government. Paul Kagame, a long-time friend of Museveni's, became the leader of Rwanda.

Museveni feels that a new type of leadership is on the rise in Africa—leaders who share "common aims," not just personal connections. Museveni has been assisting John Garang, an old university classmate, in his 14-year struggle to gain independence for southern Sudan. In addition, he and Rwanda's Kagame gave military support to rebel leader Laurent Kabila and his forces as they fought their way to Kinshasa, forcing former Zairean leader Mobutu Seso Seko (see entry) out of the country in 1997. Kagame and Museveni continue to act as advisers in the region.

Further Reading

Africa Report, January/February 1988; July/August 1991.

Berkeley, Bill. "Paying for Past Crimes: Uganda's Murderous Lessons." In *The Alicia Patterson Foundation Reporter.* Volume 16, number 3, 1994.

Contemporary Black Biography. Volume 4. Detroit: Gale, 1993.

Gertzel, Cherry. "Uganda's Continuing Search for Peace." In *Current History,* May 1990.

Hallett, Robin. *Africa since 1875.* Ann Arbor: University of Michigan Press, 1974.

Oloka-Onyango, J. "Uganda's 'Benevolent' Dictatorship." In *Current History,* May 1997.

Time, February 10, 1986; November 23, 1987; November 6, 1989; September 1, 1997.

Washington Post, March 3, 1992.

Wole Soyinka.

Bibliography

Books

Adam, H., and K. Moodley. *The Negotiated Revolution.* Jonathan Ball, 1993.

Adamolekun, Ladipo. *Sékou Touré's Guinea: An Experiment in Nation Building.* New York: Methuen, 1976.

Africa Watch staff. *Conspicuous Destruction: War, Famine, and the Reform Process in Mozambique.* New York: Africa Watch/Human Rights Watch, 1992.

Africa Watch staff. *Kenya: Taking Liberties.* New York: Africa Watch/Human Rights Watch, 1991.

al-'Umari, Shihab al-Din Ibn Fadi and el Amsar. *Masalik el Absar fi Mamalik.* Traduit par Gaudefroy-Demombynes, Librarie Orientaliste Paul Geuthner, 1927.

Anglin, Douglas G., and Timothy M. Shaw. *Zambia's Foreign Policy: Studies in Diplomacy and Dependence.* Boulder, CO: Westview Press, 1979.

Arhin, Kwame. *Traditional Rule in Ghana, Past and Present.* Sedco Publishing Ltd., 1985.

Arnold, Millard. *Steve Biko: Black Consciousness in South Africa.* New York: Random House, 1978.

Ayittey, George B. *Africa Betrayed.* New York: St. Martin's Press, 1992.

Azikiwe, Nnamdi. *My Odyssey.* Hurst, 1970.

Beach, D. N. *The Shona and Zimbabwe: 900-1850.* Mambo Press, 1980.

Beach, D. N. *Zimbabwe before 1900.* Mambo Press, 1984.

Bender, Gerald J. *Angola under the Portuguese: The Myth and the Reality.* Berkeley: University of California Press, 1978.

Benson, Mary. *African Patriots: The Story of the African National Congress.* 1963.

Benson, M. *Chief Albert Luthuli of South Africa.* 1963.

Benson, M. *South Africa: The Struggle for a Birthright, International Defence, and Aid Fund for Southern Africa.* 1966.

Bermann, Richard A. *The Mahdi of Allah.* 1931.

Biko, Steve. *I Write What I Like: A Selection of His Writings.* South Africa: Ravan Press, 1996.

Binsbergen, W. M. J. van. "Religious Innovation and Political Conflict in Zambia: A Contribution to the Interpretation of the Lumpa Rising." In *African Perspectives: Religious Innovation in Modern African Society.* Volume 2. Leiden: Afrika-Studiecentrum, 1976.

Black Literature Criticism. Detroit: Gale, 1992.

Black Writers. Detroit: Gale, 1989.

Blake, Robert. *A History of Rhodesia.* Eyre Methuen, 1977.

Blakely, Thomas D., Walter E. A. van Beek, and Dennis L. Thomson. *Religion in Africa.* Provo, UT: David M. Kennedy Center, 1994.

Boahen, Adu. *Topics in West African History.* New York: Longman, 1966.

Bond, George C. "A Prophecy That Failed: The Lumpa Church of Uyombe, Zambia." In *African Christianity: Patterns of Religious Continuity.* Academic Press, 1979.

Botman, H. R., and Robin M. Petersen, eds. *To Remember and to Heal: Theological and Psychological Reflections on Truth and Reconciliation.* Human & Rousseau, 1996.

Bourdillon, Michael, *The Shona Peoples,* revised edition. Mambo Press, 1982.

Bouscaren, A. E. *Tshombe.* 1967.

Bradt, Hilary. *Guide to Madagascar.* Bradt Publications, 1988.

Bretton, Henry. *The Rise and Fall of Kwame Nkrumah.* New York: Praeger, 1966.

The Cambridge History of Africa. Vol. 8. Edited by Michael Crowder. New York/UK: Cambridge University Press, 1984.

Cary, Robert, and Diana Mitchell. *African Nationalist Leaders in Rhodesia: Who's Who 1980.* Books of Rhodesia, 1980.

Cary, Robert. *A Time to Die.* 1969.

Churchill, Lord Randolph. *Men, Mines, and Animals in South Africa.* Originally published in 1892. Reprinted. Books of Rhodesia, 1975.

Contemporary Authors. Detroit: Gale, 1990.

Contemporary Black Biography. Detroit: Gale, 1994.

Contemporary Literary Criticism. Detroit: Gale, 1983.

Contemporary Musicians. Detroit: Gale, 1992.

Contemporary Newsmakers. Detroit: Gale, 1989.

Contemporary Novelists. Detroit: St. James Press, 1991.

Cooper-Chadwick, J. *Three Years with Lobengula.* Books of Rhodesia, 1975.

Cromwell, Adelaide M. *An African Victorian Feminist: The Life and Times of Adelaide Smith Casely Hayford, 1868-1960.* Washington, DC: Howard University Press, 1992.

Crosby, Cynthia. *Historical Dictionary of Malawi.* Metuchen, NJ: Scarecrow Press, 1980.

Crowder, Michael. "History of French West Africa until Independence." In *Africa South of the Sahara: 1982-83.* London: Europa Publications, 1982.

Crowder, Michael. *The Story of Nigeria.* Winchester, MA: Faber, 1978.

Curtin, Philip, ed. *Africa Remembered: Narratives by West Africans from the Era of the Slave Trade.* Madison: University of Wisconsin Press, 1967.

Curtin, Philip, and others, eds. *African History: From Earliest Times to Independence.* 2nd ed. New York: Longman, 1995.

Dantzig, Albert van. *Forts and Castles of Ghana.* Sedco Publishing Ltd., 1980.

Davenport, T. R. H. *South Africa: A Modern History.* Toronto, Ontario, Canada: University of Toronto Press, 1987.

Davidson, Basil. *Africa in History.* New York: Macmillan, 1974.

Davidson, Basil. *Africa History, Themes and Outlines.* New rev. ed. New York: Collier Books, 1974.

Davidson, Basil, *The Black Man's Burden: Africa and the Curse of the Nation-State.* James Curry, 1992.

Davidson, Basil. *The Growth of African Civilisation: History of West Africa, 1000-1800.* New York: Longman, 1965.

Davis, Dorothy K. *Race Relations in Rhodesia.* Rex Collings, 1975.

Days, Drew S., et al. *Justice Enjoined: The State of the Judiciary in Kenya.* Robert F. Kennedy Memorial Center for Human Rights, 1992

Decalo, Samuel. *Psychoses of Power: African Personal Dictatorships.* Boulder, CO: Westview Press.

DeKlerk, W. A. *The Puritans in Africa.* Rex Collings, 1975.

De Klerk, Willem. *The Man in His Time: F. W. De Klerk.* Jonathan Ball, 1991.

Delf, George. *Jomo Kenyatta: Towards Truth about "The Light of Kenya."* New York: Doubleday, 1961.

Depelchin, H., and C. Croonenberghs. *Letters of Journey to Gubuluwayo.* Books of Rhodesia, 1979.

Dickie, John, and Alan Rake. *Who's Who in Africa.* Africa Buyer and Trader, 1973.

Dictionary of African Biography. Algonac, MI: Reference Publications, 1977.

Drechsler, Horst. *Let Us Die Fighting.* Akademie-Verlag, 1966.

Du Boulay, Shirley. *Tutu: Voice of the Voiceless.* North Pomfret, VT: Hodder & Stoughton, 1988.

Duerden, Dennis, and Cosmo Pieterse, eds. *African Writers Talking: A Collection of Radio Interviews.* Africana Publishing, 1972.

Duggan, William Redman, and John R. Civille. *Tanzania and Nyerere: A Study of Ujamaa and Nationhood.* London: Orbis Books, 1976.

Eilersen, Gillian Stead. *Bessie Head: Thunder Behind Her Ears.* North Pomfret, VT: Heinemann, 1996.

Ellert H. *Rivers of Gold.* Mambo Press, 1993.

Ellert, H. *The Rhodesian Front War.* Mambo, 1989.

Encyclopaedia Africana, Dictionary of African Biography. Vol. 2. Sierra Leone-Zaire: Reference Publications, 1977.

Equiano's Travels: His Autobiography: The Interesting Narrative of the Life of Olaudah Equiano or Gustavus Vassa the African Life. Paul Edwards, editor. London: Heinemann, 1967.

Farrant, Leda. *Tippu Tip and the East African Slave Trade.* London: Hamish Hamilton, 1975

Farwell, Byron. *Prisoners of the Mahdi: The Story of the Mahdist Revolt Which Frustrated Queen Victoria's Designs on the Sudan.* New York: Norton, 1989.

Fisher, John. *The Afrikaners.* Cassell, 1969.

Forbath, Peter. *The River Congo.* New York: Harper & Row, 1977.

Forrest, Ronald. *An African Reader.* New York: Longman, 1965.

Forster, E. M. *Alexandria: A History and a Guide.* Bath Press, 1922.

Froehlich, Manuel. "The Old and the New UN Secretary-General." In *Aussen Politik,* 48:3, 1997, pp. 301-9.

Gérard-Libois, J. *Sécession au Katanga.* 1963

Gertzel, Cherry. *The Politics of Independent Kenya: 1963-1968.* Northwestern, 1970.

Gertzel, Cherry. "Uganda's Continuing Search for Peace." In *Current History,* May 1990.

Gibbs, James, ed. *Critical Perspectives on Wole Soyinka.* Washington, DC: Three Continents, 1980.

Gossler, Horst. *Portfolio Lalibela.* Africa Environment and Wildlife, 1996.

Graham, Shirley. *Julius K. Nyerere: Teacher of Africa.* New York: Messner, 1975.

Gray, Stephen. *Southern African Literature: An Introduction.* 1979.

Greschat, Hans-Jurgen. "Legends? Frauds? Reality? Alice Lenshina's Prophetic Experience." In *Africana Marburgensia.* Edited by Hans-Jurgen Greschat and Hermann Jungraithmayr. Volume 1. 1968.

Gunther, John. *Inside Africa.* North Pomfret, VT: Hamish Hamilton, 1955.

Guy, Jeff. *The Destruction of the Zulu Kingdom: The Civil War in Zululand, 1879-1884.* University of Natal Press, 1994.

Hallet, Robin. *Africa since 1895.* Ann Arbor: University of Michigan Press, 1974.

Halpern, Jack. "Botswana: Recent History." In *Africa South of the Sahara, 1981-1982.* London: Europa, 1981.

Harden, Blaine. *Africa: Dispatches from a Fragile Continent.* New York: HarperCollins, 1990.

Harris, Joseph E. *Africans and Their History.* New York: New American Library, 1974.

Hatch, John. *Tanzania: A Profile.* New York: Praeger, 1972.

Hatch, John. *Two African Statesmen.* Regnery, 1975.

Helbig, Ludwig, and Werner Hillebrecht. *The Witbooi.* Longman Namibia, 1992.

Hempstone, Smith. *Katanga Report.* Winchester, MA: Faber, 1962.

Hibbert, Christopher. *Africa Explored: Europeans in the Dark Continent, 1769-1889.* New York: Norton, 1982.

Hiskett, Mervyn. *The Sword of Truth: The Life and Times of the Shehu Usuman dan Fodio.* New York/UK: Oxford University Press, 1973.

Historic World Leaders. Edited by Anne Commire. Detroit: Gale, 1994.

Hoile, David. *Mozambique: A Nation in Crisis.* Claridge Press, 1989.

Holt, P. M. *The Mahdist State in the Sudan: 1881-1898.* 1958.

Holt, P. M. *A Modern History of the Sudan.* 1966.

Hymans, Jacques Louis. *Léopold Sédar Senghor: An Intellectual Biography.* Edinburgh University Press, 1971.

James, Lawrence. *The Rise and Fall of the British Empire.* Boston: Little, Brown, 1994.

Jenny, Hans. *South West Africa: Land of Extremes.* Southwest Africa Scientific Society, 1976.

Johnson-Odin, Cheryl. *For Women and the Nation: Funmilayo Ransome-Kuti of Nigeria.* University of Illinois Press, 1997.

Jones, Eldred. *Wole Soyinka.* New York: Twayne, 1973.

Jones, G.I. "Olaudah Equiano of the Niger Ibo," *Africa Remembered: Narratives by West Africans from the Era of the Slave Trade.* Philip D.Curtin, ed. Madison: University of Wisconsin Press, 1977.

Kaplan, Irving, Howard Blutstein, Peter Just, and others. *Area Handbook for Mozambique.* American University Press, 1977.

Katrak, Ketu. *Wole Soyinka and Modern Tragedy: A Study of Dramatic Theory and Practice.* Westport, CT: Greenwood Press, 1986.

Kaunda, Kenneth D. *The Riddle of Violence.* New York: Harper, 1980.

Kaunda, Kenneth D. *Zambia Shall Be Free: An Autobiography.* New York: Praeger, 1963.

Kenney, Henry. *Power, Pride & Prejudice.* Jonathan Ball, 1991.

Kenyatta, Jomo. *Facing Mount Kenya.* North Pomfret, VT: Secker & Warburg, 1938.

Kenyatta, Jomo. *Harambee! The Prime Minister of Kenya's Speeches, 1963-1964.* New York/UK: Oxford University Press, 1964.

Kenyatta, Jomo. *Kenya: The Land of Conflict.* International African Service Bureau, 1945.

Killam, G. D. *The Novels of Chinua Achebe.* Africana Publishing, 1969.

King, Bruce. *Introduction to Nigerian Literature.* Africana Publishing, 1972.

Kuper, Hilda. *Sobhuza II: Ngwenyama and King of Swaziland.* London: Duckworth, 1978.

Lamb, David. *The Africans.* New York: Random House, 1984.

Landeg, White, and Tim Couzens, eds. *Literature and Society in South Africa.* 1984.

Larson, Charles R. *The Emergence of African Fiction.* Bloomington: Indiana University Press, 1972.

Lau, Brigitte. *Namibia in Jonker Afrikaner's Time.* Namibia Archives, 1987.

Laurence, Margaret. *Long Drums and Cannons: Nigerian Dramatists and Novelists.* New York: Praeger, 1968.

Leakey, Louis. *White African: An Early Autobiography.* Originally published in 1937. Reprinted. New York: Ballantine Books, 1973.

Leakey, Louis. *By the Evidence: Memoirs, 1932-1951.* Orlando, FL: Harcourt, 1974.

Leakey, Mary. *Disclosing the Past.* New York: Doubleday, 1984.

Leakey, Richard. *One Life: An Autobiography.* Salem House, 1984.

LeMay, G. H. L. *Black and White in South Africa: The Politics of Survival.* American Heritage Press, 1971.

Levtzion, Nehemia. *Muslims and Chiefs in West Africa.* New York/UK: Oxford University Press, 1968.

Lipschutz, Mark, and R. Kent Rasmussen. *Dictionary of African Historical Biography.* Aldine Publishing, 1978.

Lodge, Tom. *Black Politics in South Africa since 1945.* Ravan Press, 1990.

Lunn, John, and Christopher Saunders. "Recent History of Namibia." In *Africa South of the Sahara: 1994.* 23rd ed. London: Europa, 1994.

Luthuli, Albert. *Let My People Go.* Collins, 1962.

Mack, John. *Madagascar: Island of the Ancestors.* British Museums Publications, 1986.

MacPherson, Fergus. *Kenneth Kaunda of Zambia: The Times and the Man.* New York/UK: Oxford University Press, 1974.

Maier, Karl. *Into the House of the Ancestors.* Chichester, W. Sussex, U.K.: John Wiley, 1998.

Major Twentieth-Century Writers. Detroit: Gale, 1991.

Makeba, Miriam, and James Hall. *Makeba: My Story*. New York: New American Library, 1987.

Makers of Modern Africa: Profiles in History. 3rd. ed. Africa Books, 1996.

Mandela, Nelson. *Long Walk to Freedom*. Boston: Little, Brown, 1994.

Mandela, Winnie. *Part of My Soul Went with Him*. Edited by Anne Benjamin. New York: Norton, 1985.

Marquard, Leo. *The Peoples and Policies of South Africa*. 4th ed. New York/UK: Oxford University Press, 1969.

Maylam, Paul. *A History of the African People of South Africa: From the Early Iron Age to the 1970s*. New York: St. Martin's, 1986.

Mboya, Tom. *Freedom and After*. Boston: Little, Brown, 1963.

McLynn, Frank. *Hearts of Darkness: The European Explorations of Africa*. Pimlico, 1992.

Meintjes, Johannes. *President Paul Kruger*. Cassell, 1974.

Meltzer, Milton. *Winnie Mandela: The Soul of South Africa*. New York: Viking Kestrel, 1986.

Meredith, Martin. *First Dance of Freedom*. New York: Harper, 1984.

Meredith, Martin. *The Past Is Another Country: Rhodesia UDI to Zimbabwe*. London: Pan Books, 1980.

Modern Twentieth-Century Writers. Detroit: Gale, 1991.

Mondlane, Eduardo. *The Struggle for Mozambique*. Zed Press, 1969.

Moore, Gerald. *Wole Soyinka*. New York: Africana Publishing, 1971.

Moorehead, Alan. *The White Nile*. New York: Harper, 1971.

Morell, Virginia. *Ancestral Passions: The Leakey Family and the Quest for Humankind's Beginnings*. New York: Simon & Schuster, 1995.

Morris, Donald R. *The Washing of the Spears: The Rise and Fall of the Great Zulu Nation*. Abacus, 1992.

Mosely, Nicholas. *African Switchback*. Travel Book Club, 1958

Mosley, Leonard. *Haile Selassie I: The Conquering Lion*. Englewood Cliffs, NJ: Prentice Hall, 1965.

Mostert, Noël. *Frontiers: The Epic of South Africa's Creation and the Tragedy of the Xhosa People*. North Pomfret, VT: J. Cape, 1992.

Mudenge, S. I. G. *A Political History of Munhumutapa: c. 1400-1902*. Zimbabwe Publishing House, 1988.

Murray-Brown, Jeremy. *Kenyatta*. Allen & Unwin, 1979.

Murphy, E. Jefferson. *History of African Civilization*. New York: Dell, 1972.

Murphy, E. Jefferson. *The Bantu Civilization of Southern Africa*. New York: Thomas Crowell, 1974.

Niane, D.T. *General History of Africa*. Volume 4. UNESCO, 1984.

Niane, D.T. *Sundiata: An Epic in African History*. New York: Longman, 1965.

Nichols, Lee, ed. *Conversations with African Writers*. Washington, DC: Voice of America, 1981.

Nkomo, Joshua. *Nkomo: The Story of My Life*. New York: Methuen, 1984.

Nkrumah, Kwame. *Autobiography*. Sunbury-on-Thames, Middx., U.K.: Thomas Nelson, 1957.

Nyagumbo, Maurice. *With the People*. Akron, OH: Graham Publishing, 1980.

Nyerere, Julius K. *Freedom and Development*. New York/UK: Oxford University Press, 1974.

Obeng, Ernest E. *Ancient Ashanti Chieftaincy*. Ghana Publishing Corporation, 1988.

Odinga, Oginga. *Not Yet Uhuru: An Autobiography*. Heineman, 1967.

Oliver, Roland. *The African Experience*. Pimlico, 1994.

Oliver, Roland, and Atmore, Anthony. *Africa since 1800*. 2nd ed. New York/UK: Cambridge University Press, 1972.

Oloka-Onyango, J. "Uganda's 'Benevolent' Dictatorship." In *Current History,* May 1997.

Omara-Otunnu, Amii. *Politics and the Military in Uganda: 1890-1985*. New York: St. Martin's, 1987.

Omari, T. Peter. *Kwame Nkrumah: An Anatomy of African Dictatorship*. Accra, 1970.

O'Meara, Dan. *Forty Lost Years: The Apartheid State and the Politics of the National Party, 1948-1994*. Athens: Ohio University Press, 1996.

Ousby, Ian. *The Cambridge Guide to Literature in English*. New York/UK: Cambridge University Press, 1993.

Pakenham, Thomas. *The Boer War*. Macdonald, 1982.

Pakenham, Thomas. *The Scramble for Africa: 1876-1912*. Jonathan Ball Publishers, 1991.

Parker, Kenneth, ed. *The South African Novel in English*. 1978.

Paton, Alan. *Towards the Mountain: An Autobiography*. David Philip, 1980.

Paton, Anne. *Some Sort of a Job: My Life with Alan Paton*. New York: Viking, 1992.

Peck, Richard. "Nadine Gordimer: A Bibliography of Primary and Secondary Sources 1938-1992." In *Research in African Literatures*, March 1, 1995.

Pedler, F.J. *West Africa*. New York: Methuen, 1951.

Perham, Margery, and J. Simmons. *African Discovery: An Anthology of Exploration.* The Travel Book Club, 1943.

Petersen, Kirsten Holst, and Anna Rutherford, eds. *Chinua Achebe: A Celebration*. North Pomfret, VT: Heinemann, 1991.

Phillips, Claude S. *The African Political Dictionary*. Santa Barbara, CA: ABC-CLIO, 1984.

Pieterse, Cosmo, and Dennis Dueren, eds. *African Writers Talking: A Collection of Radio Interviews*. New York: Africana Publishing, 1972.

Nwangwu, Chido. "USAfrica: The Newspaper." USAfrica ONLINE. www.usafricaonline.com, August 4, 1997.

"Revolutionary Worker Online." www.msc.net.rwor, #920, August 17, 1997.

UXL Biographies CD. Detroit: Gale, 1995.

WUSB 90.1 FM (Stony Brook, NY) radio broadcast featuring Lister Hewan-Lowe, June 21, 1986.

Index

Italic type indicates volume numbers.
Boldface type indicates entries and their page numbers.
(Iill.) indicates illustrations.

Wangari Maathai

El Saheli 2: 393
Elizabeth II (queen of England) 1: 44
England 1: 19, 53, 68, 110, 141-143;
    2: 204, 295, 316, 326, 334, 372;
    3: 467, 486, 549, 563, 584
Epps, Maeve 2: 236
Equiano, Olaudah (Gustavus
    Vassa the African) 1: 119-124,
    119 (ill.)
Eritrea 1: 143, 145, 146, 148; 2: 337
Erosion 2: 272
Ethiopia 1: 138-148; 2: 220, 330,
    332 (map)
Ezana (emperor) 2: 222

F

Farewell, Francis 3: 517-518,
    518 (ill.)
Federal Theological Seminary 3: 585
Federation of Rhodesia and
    Nyasaland 1: 53, 166, 170;
    2: 384; 3: 522, 523-525
Federation of Workers' Unions of
    Guinea 3: 555
Firestone, Harvey Samuel 3: 574
Firestone Rubber Company 3: 574
Forbes, Frederick 1: 134
Fordham University 1: 170
Fort Hare College 1: 188, 190
Fort Hare University 2: 380
Fourah Bay College 1: 98
France 1: 122, 133, 137, 143, 157,
    160; 2: 207, 257, 335, 347;
    3: 483, 487, 550, 558, 560
Franco, Francisco 1: 144
Francois, Curt von 2: 295
FRELIMO (the Front for the
    Liberation of Mozambique)
    1: 90 (ill.), 91; 2: 363, 364 (ill.),
    365, 398
French West Africa 1: 161
Frere, Bartle 1: 76, 77
Front for National Salvation
    (FRONASA) 2: 398
Frumentius 2: 222
Fulani-Hausa 1: 4, 35, 40, 41, 45,
    104, 105, 107, 109; 3: 542
Fynn, Henry 3: 517-518

G

Gabon 1: 13
Gama, Vasco da 2: 224
Gandhi, Mohandas 1: 169
Garang, John 2: 402
Garfield, James A. 1: 37
Garvey, Marcus 1: 36, 71, 73
Gelele 1: 134, 136
General Motors 2: 345
George V 3: 533
George VI 3: 533
Germany 1: 68, 84, 137, 142, 143,
    188; 2: 207, 250-251, 294-303,
    397; 3: 449, 474, 550
Ghana 1: 28, 29, 35, 36, 38, 46, 52,
    72, 145, 161; 2: 217, 257-258,
    381; 3: 426-436, 428 (map),
    478, 480, 482, 498, 542, 554,
    556, 598
Gichuru, James 2: 327
Girls' Vocational and Industrial
    Training School 1: 72
Giyorgis, Haylu Walda 2: 333
Gobir Kingdom 1: 105
Goering, Heinrich 2: 295
Goering, Hermann 2: 295
Gold Coast. See Ghana
Gold and gold mines 1: 52, 127;
    2: 207, 248, 250-251, 295,
    390-391, 394; 3: 479, 483,
    499, 523, 531, 562
Goldberg, Denis 2: 317
Goldie, George 1: 103
Gordimer, Nadine 1: 125-131,
    125 (ill.), 130 (ill.)
Gordon, Charles George 2: 286, 289,
    291, 292 (ill.)
Gowon, Yakubu 2: 217
Great Britain 1: 4, 19, 50, 68, 110,
    120; 2: 204, 295, 316, 326, 334,
    372; 3: 487, 499, 521, 550, 564
Green Belt Movement 2: 271,
    273, 275
Guezo 1: 132-137
Guinea 2: 390; 3: 554-561, 557 (map)
Guinea-Bissau 3: 558
Gulf War 1: 30
Gustavus Vassa the African (Olaudah
    Equiano) 1: 119

H

Haile Malakot 2: 332

Haile Mariam Mengistu 1: 147 (ill.),
148; 2: 336

Haile Selassie I 1: **138-148**
138 (ill.), 143 (ill.); 2: 336, 338

Haiti 3: 572

Hamed Bin Muhammmed el Murjebi
3: 547

Hammarskjöld, Dag 3: 568

Harba 2: 221-222

Harris, Rutherford 2: 251

Harvard University 2: 362

Hausa-Fulani 1: 4, 35, 40, 41, 45,
104, 105, 107, 109; 3: 542

Head, Bessie 1: **149-156** 149 (ill.)

Head, Harold 1: 152

Henrique 1: 8, 12, 16

Henry the Navigator 1: 10; 2: 224

Herero 2: 294-303

Hereroland 2: 299

Hertzo, J. B. 3: 474

Heyfron, Sally 2: 381

Hicks, William 2: 291

Hitler, Adolf 1: 138, 142-144;
3: 474, 591

Hodgson, Frederick 3: 601

Hofmeyr, Jan 3: 476

Homo habilis 2: *231, 237*

Homo erectus 2: *234*

Homo sapiens 2: *231*

Houphouët-Boigny, Félix 1: **157-
165**, 157 (ill.), 162 (ill.); 2: 326;
3: 509, 555, 558

Howard University 2: 327

Huddleston, Trevor 3: 583

Huggins, Godfrey 3: 523

Hughes, Langston 3: 507

Hussein, Saddam 1: 31

I

Ibo people 1: 1, 2, 4, 5, 34-36,
40-42, 46, 48, 49, 119;
3: 444, 447, 552

Ibo Union 1: 40

Ileo, Joseph 3: 570

Ilg, Alfred 2: 335

Impis 3: 514

India 1: 8, 12

Indian (Asian) traders in Uganda
1: 24

Institut Universitaire Des Hautes
Études Internationales 1: 29

International Monetary Fund 1: 173

Iran 3: 549

Isaacs, Nathaniel 3: 517

Isandlwana 1: 73, 77

Islam 1: 25, 104-111, 106, 108, 142;
2: 220, 285-293, 388, 390

Ismail 2: 286, 289

Israel 1: 20; 2: 344

Italy 1: 141-143, 146; 2: 330, 335

Ivory 1: 91; 2: 255, 374; 3: 547, 550

Ivory Coast *See Côte D'Ivoire*

Iyasu, Lej 1: 142; 2: 340

J

Jamaica 1: 138, 142

Jameson, Leander Starr 2: 248,
251-252

Jan Hofmeyr School of Social Work
2: 279, 361; 3: 420

Jehovah's Witnesses 1: 83

Jerusalem 1: 139; 2: 221

Jobe 3: 514

Johanson, Donald 2: 235

John II (king of Portugal) 1: 9

John III (king of Portugal) 1: 15

Johnson, Harry 3: 574

Johnson, Janet 2: 362

Joubert, Piet 2: 206

K

Kabila, Laurent 2: 349, 402

Kakari, Kofi 3: 481-482

Kalahari Desert 2: 295

Kalonji, Albert 2: 258-259, 261, 344

Kamaherero 2: 296-297

Kamwana, Eliot 1: 83

Kango River 1: 9

Kapwepwe, Simon 1: 168

Kasavubu, Joseph 2: 258, 259, 261
(ill.), 343, 344; 3: 566

Kasonga 3: 549

Kassa 2: 334

P

Q

R

S

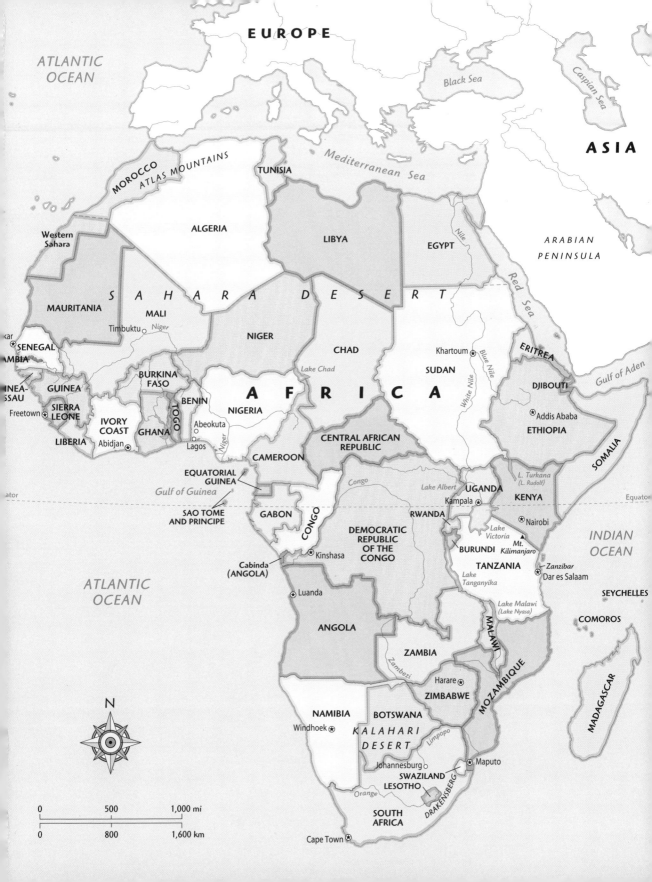